EIGHTH EDITION

Writing with a Thesis

A Rhetoric and Reader

EIGHTH EDITION

WRITING WITH A THESIS
A Rhetoric and Reader

David Skwire

Sarah E. Skwire
College of DuPage

HARCOURT COLLEGE PUBLISHERS

Fort Worth   Philadelphia   San Diego   New York   Orlando   Austin   San Antonio
Toronto   Montreal   London   Sydney   Tokyo

Publisher:	Earl McPeck
Marketing Strategist:	John Meyers
Project Manager:	Andrea Archer

ISBN 0-15-506855-5

Library of Congress Catalog Card Number: 00-102062

Address for Domestic Orders
Harcourt College Publishers, 6277 Sea Harbor Drive, Orlando, FL 32887-6777
800-782-4479

Address for International Orders
International Customer Service
Harcourt College Publishers, 6277 Sea Harbor Drive, Orlando, FL 32887-6777
407-345-3800
(fax) 407-345-4060
(e-mail) hbintl@harcourtbrace.com

Address for Editorial Correspondence
Harcourt College Publishers, 301 Commerce Street, Suite 3700, Fort Worth, TX 76102

Web Site Address
:http://www.harcourtcollege.com

Printed in the United States of America

0 1 2 3 4 5 6 7 8 9   039   9 8 7 6 5 4 3 2 1

To the Instructor

I love the young dogs of this age: they have more wit and humor and knowledge of life than we had; but then the dogs are not so good scholars. Sir, in my early years I read very hard.

Samuel Johnson

In many respects, *Writing with a Thesis* tries to do a traditional job in a traditional way. Its readings are arranged according to traditional rhetorical patterns, one pattern per chapter. Each group of readings is preceded by a detailed discussion of the writing techniques appropriate to that pattern. Headnotes, explanatory footnotes, and questions on content and style accompany each reading. The book wholeheartedly accepts such traditional ideas about teaching composition as the value of omnivorous reading, the utility of close analysis of individual works, and the salutary influence of models.

In some other respects, *Writing with a Thesis* is less traditional, though its commitment to the job of improving writing skills remains constant.

First, the traditional reader or rhetoric-reader tends to approach each rhetorical pattern as a separate entity requiring the development of a new set of writing skills. Chapter 1 of this book presents what it calls *the persuasive principle:* the development and support of a thesis. It goes on to demonstrate how the persuasive principle underlies almost all good writing, and subsequent chapters show how the persuasive principle functions within each of the rhetorical patterns. A major unifying theme thus runs through the entire book, each pattern being viewed not as a separate entity but as the application of a permanent writing principle to varying subject matter, insights, and purposes. The concept of the persuasive principle has long been stressed in some of the most popular handbooks and rhetorics. It has not ordinarily been the animating force behind a general reader.

Second, in addition to the standard apparatus, the book includes after each selection brief comments titled "What About *Your* Writing?" These comments, directly related to the selection just studied, offer pointers and tips, quick practical lessons that students can apply to their own work. The stress generally is on style because major issues of organization are dealt with in the opening sections of each chapter, but the coverage is wide and by no means confined to style. Topics range all the way from common high school superstitions—"Can I begin a sentence with *and?*"—to such broader issues of invention as finding new slants on old subjects.

"What About *Your* Writing?" tries to duplicate in some fashion one of the important ways by which people improve their writing: they read, and they pick things up. What can best be taught systematically must be so taught, of course, but not everything can be. Every instructor knows the benefits that can come when a student raises a hand and says, "This doesn't have anything to do with the subject exactly, but I was just wondering . . ." As an instructor structures a lesson and a course but builds into the structure an atmosphere that welcomes the sudden, just-wondering question, *Writing with a Thesis* uses "What About *Your* Writing?" to complement the rigorously structured elements of the rest of the book.

On pages xv–xvi, a guide to "What About *Your* Writing?" provides a convenient listing of all topics.

Finally, one of the traditional problems with many traditional textbooks is that they bore and scare too many students. Instructors write them for other instructors, and the students suffer. *Writing with a Thesis*, with all its traditional philosophy, is written in an informal, simple, and, we hope, engaging style. The reading selections themselves, although a few are deliberately long and challenging, are generally short and easy to read. Class time can be devoted primarily to showing not what the readings mean, but what they mean for the student's writing.

To the Student

Buying textbooks is more than the dreariness of waiting in line at the bookstore. It probably also marks the only time in your life when you pay good money for books you know nothing about.

The process isn't quite as outrageous as it might seem. Your instructors already know what your courses are designed to teach and are in a solid position to decide which books will be most helpful. You can safely assume that they've spent a long time wading through piles of texts in order to make their final selections and that you wouldn't have enjoyed taking that drudgery on yourself. Still, in many ways your purchase of this book is an act of faith, and before committing yourself much further, you have a right to some information.

This book is designed to help you in several ways to become a better writer.

First, each section begins with a detailed, practical discussion of how to handle the writing assignments you are likely to get: comparison and contrast, classification, cause and effect, and so on. These assignments are based on highly artificial writing patterns. The patterns often overlap and are rarely encountered in their pure form. A paper devoted primarily to classification, for example, could easily spend a good deal of time comparing and contrasting each class. Most instructors find it valuable, however, to discuss and assign the patterns separately. Nobody ever played a set of tennis using only a forehand drive, but serious players may devote hours at a time to practicing that one shot. Similarly, a substantial piece of writing is likely to demand a combination of patterns, but each pattern is best practiced and mastered by being treated at the start as an independent unit.

Second, each section of the book contains one outlined student essay and a group of readings by professional writers designed to show effective use of the pattern under consideration. These writers had to put ideas together in the same pattern that will be required of you, and they went about their task in such and such a way. Studying the techniques by which they achieved their success can stimulate any writer faced with similar problems—but nobody wants you to write a barren imitation of someone else's work. A tennis player can profit from studying Pete Sampras's serve without attempting to duplicate it. The writer, as well as the athlete, uses models to discover the basic principles for shaping individual strengths into an effective force, not to follow blindly some particular conception of good form.

Third, questions on each reading selection are designed to help you look closely at the means by which each writer worked. A vague impression that an essay was competently written will be of little practical benefit to your own efforts.

Fourth, in order to add to the practical emphasis of this book, each reading selection is followed by a brief comment called "What About *Your* Writing?" These comments tend to get away from the presentation of broad principles and deal instead with specific pointers and suggestions, ranging all the way from avoiding overused words like very to tips on how to find a subject when your mind seems to be a complete blank.

Fifth, all the readings are designed to drive home a special approach to writing that runs through this book: if writing is thought of, wherever possible, as an attempt to persuade the reader of the validity of a particular point, many common problems virtually disappear or solve themselves. We call this approach *the persuasive principle.* Chapter 1 presents this principle in detail; the following chapters show how it can be applied to particular writing assignments.

That's the theory. You and your instructor are the only authorities on whether the theory works for you. If it does, the book was worth the money.

Acknowledgments

Special thanks go to Fritz Logan, Coordinator of the University of Maryland's English/Speech program in Asia. His many kind words and tough-minded strictures have been both helpful and inspiring.

We also want to acknowledge with gratitude the valuable reviews of Rita Keogh, College of Dupage; and Albert W. Lum, Chaminade University of Honolulu.

A Note on the Eighth Edition

Readers familiar with previous editions will note significant revisions from the first chapter on. Chapter 1, for example, has added two examples of personal ads to its much-praised emphasis on writing in everyday life as well as in the classroom. The longstanding business letters have been updated to reflect e-mail as well as traditional form. Each of the remaining chapters has at least one new professional model, fourteen new selections in all. Four of eleven student essays are also new. Finally, we call your attention to Chapter 10½, a strong reminder to students that school and life go on even after passing English 101 or its equivalent. In a real sense, they have not yet begun to write—and the lessons they have learned should continue to serve them well.

We can also happily report that there is much that has not changed. "The Persuasive Principle" remains as central to our thinking as ever. The readings continue to be short, accessible, and lively. The discipline of success and the nearly unanimous message of user surveys not to mess with what works have made it easy to resist indulging in massive overhauls for their own sake.

Contents

10   Argumentation   275

10½ What About the *Rest* of Your Writing?   313

Credits   315

Index   317

Guide to "What About *Your* Writing?"

As noted in "To the Instructor" (pp. v–vi), "What About *Your* Writing?" entries offer comments and pointers on matters of practical concern to the student writer, as such matters turn up in the readings. For general perspectives and quick references, the following guide is appended.

The Persuasive Principle

This book offers you one central piece of advice: *Whenever possible, think of your writing as a form of persuasion.*

Persuasion is traditionally considered a separate branch of writing. When you write what's usually called a persuasion paper, you pick a controversial issue, tell your readers what side you're on, and try to persuade them that you're correct: the defense budget needs to be decreased, handguns should be outlawed, doctors must be protected against frivolous malpractice suits, required freshman English courses should be abolished. Persuasion is supposed to be based on different principles from those of other kinds of writing—description, narration, exposition, and so forth.

It isn't.

A description of a relative, an account of what you went through to get your first job, a comparison of two brands of dishwashers—if you can approach such assignments as an effort to persuade your reader of the validity of a particular opinion or major point, you're in business as a writer. Your paper's opinion or major point is called its *thesis.* Your thesis may be that your relative is the most boring person you have ever met, that getting your first job was easier than you thought it would be, that a General Electric dishwasher is likely to last longer than a Whirlpool. If you have a thesis and if you select and organize your material so that it supports the thesis, a number of basic writing problems begin to solve themselves. You have built-in purpose. You have built-in organization. You have the potential for built-in interest. Aside from a few obvious exceptions like newspaper reports, encyclopedia articles, instruction manuals, recipes, and certain types of stories, poems, and plays, *all writing can benefit from a commitment to the persuasive principle: Develop a thesis, and then back it up.*

There is no better way to demonstrate the effectiveness of the persuasive principle than to take a close look at what goes on, or ought to go on, as a paper is being planned.

General Subject

"Write something worth reading about . . ." In essence, all writing assignments—for students, business executives, Nobel Prize winners, and everyone else—begin this way, though ordinarily the directions aren't that frank.

Let's start from scratch and assume that your instructor has left the choice of subject mostly up to you. You may be entirely on your own or you may have a list of general subjects from which you must make your selection. Imagine that you have to write something worth reading about one of the following: education, sports, prejudice, politics, or television.

You make your choice, if you're like the majority of people, by deciding what you're most interested in and informed about or what will go over best with your audience. Let's say you pick education. You now have a subject, and your troubles have now begun.

You have to write 500 words or so on a subject to which tens of thousands of books have been devoted. Where do you begin? Where do you stop? Will it ever be possible to stop? What's important? What's not important? Until you *limit your subject*, you have no way of answering any of these questions. You are at the mercy of every miscellaneous thought and scrap of information that drifts into your mind.

Limited Subject

Narrow down your subject. Then narrow it down some more. Narrow it down until you have a subject that can be treated effectively in the assigned length. In many respects, the narrower your subject, the better off you are, as long as you still have something to say about it. With a properly limited subject, you explore only a small part of your general subject, but you explore it thoroughly:

General Subject	Limited Subject
Education	Professor X
Prejudice	Interracial marriages
Politics	People who don't vote

General Subject	Limited Subject
Television	Commercials
Sports	Baseball salaries

A paper of 500 words on education is doomed to be superficial at best. It might be possible, however, to write 500 words worth reading on one of your teachers, essay versus objective examinations, reasons for attending college (narrowed down to just one reason if you have enough to say), registration procedures, fraternities, physical education requirements, and so on.

With a sensibly limited subject, you have a chance of producing a good paper. You are no longer doomed to superficiality. If you write a description of one of your teachers, for example, you possess immensely more knowledge of your subject than do fellow students who have not taken a course from that teacher. Certainly, you are no longer at the mercy of every thought about education that you have ever had.

Your troubles are not over, though. You've limited your subject, and you've done it well, but what now? Look at the most limited of the subjects in the preceding table. You're writing a description of a teacher—Professor X. Do you tell your reader about the teacher's height, weight, age, marital status, clothing, ethnic background, religious background, educational background? Publications? Grading policy? Attendance policy? Lecture techniques? Sense of humor? Handling of difficult classroom situations? Attitude toward audio-visual aids? Knowledge of field? How, in short, do you determine what belongs in your paper and what doesn't?

The truth is that you're still at the mercy of every thought that occurs to you. This time it's every thought about Professor X, not every thought about education in general. But until you find a *thesis*, you still have trouble.

Thesis

Your thesis is the basic stand you take, the opinion you express, the point you make about your limited subject. It's your controlling idea, tying together and giving direction to all of the separate elements in your paper. *Your primary purpose is to persuade the reader that your thesis is a valid one.*

You may, and probably should, have secondary purposes; you may want to amuse or alarm or inform or issue a call to action, for instance—but unless the primary purpose is achieved, no secondary purpose stands a chance. If you want to amuse your readers by making fun of inconsistent dress codes at your old high school, there's no way to do it successfully without first convincing them of the validity of your thesis that the dress codes *were* inconsistent and thus *do* deserve to be laughed at.

A thesis is only a vibration in the brain until it is turned into words. The first step in creating a workable thesis is to write a one-sentence version of the thesis, which is called a *thesis statement*, for example:

Professor X is an incompetent teacher.

Professor X is a classic absentminded professor.

Professor X's sarcasm antagonizes many students.

Professor X's colorful personality has become a campus legend.

Professor X is better at lecturing than at leading discussions.

Professor X's youthful good looks have created awkward problems in class.

If you need more than one relatively uncomplicated sentence, chances are either that the thesis isn't as unified as it ought to be or that it's too ambitious for a short paper.

Limited Subject	Thesis Statement
Professor X	Professor X is an incompetent teacher.
Interracial marriages	Hostility to interracial marriages is the prejudice least likely to die.
People who don't vote	Not voting may sometimes be a responsible decision.
Commercials	Television commercials can be great entertainment.
Baseball salaries	Many baseball players are paid far more than their abilities can justify.

Writing with a thesis gives a paper a sense of purpose and eliminates the problem of aimless drift. Your purpose is to back up the thesis. As a result, writing with a thesis also helps significantly in organizing the paper. You use only what enables you to accomplish your purpose. Weight problems and religion have nothing to do with Professor X's abilities as a teacher, so you don't bother with them. Most of all, writing with a thesis gives a paper an intrinsic dramatic interest. You commit yourself. You have something at stake: "This is what I believe, and this is why I'm right." You say, "Professor X is incompetent." Your reader says, "Tell me why you think so." You say, "I'll be glad to." Your reader says, "I'm listening." And you're ready to roll.

So far, then, we've established that a thesis is the main idea that all elements in the paper should support and that you should be able to express it in a single sentence. We've established that a thesis has several important practical benefits. That's the bird's-eye view, but the concept is important enough to demand a closer look.

What a Thesis Isn't

A Thesis Is Not a Title

A title can often give the reader some notion of what the thesis is going to be, but it is not the thesis itself. The thesis itself, as presented in the thesis statement, does not suggest the main idea—it *is* the main idea. Remember, too, that a thesis statement will always be a complete sentence; there's no other way to make a statement.

Title: Not a Thesis	Thesis Statement
Homes and Schools	Parents ought to participate more in the education of their children.
James Cagney: Hollywood Great	James Cagney was one of the greatest actors ever to appear in movies.
Social Security and Old Age	Continuing changes in the Social Security System make it almost impossible to plan intelligently for one's retirement.
A Shattering Experience	My first visit to the zoo was a shattering experience.
The Fad of Divorce	Too many people get divorced for trivial reasons.

A Thesis Is Not an Announcement of the Subject

A thesis takes a stand. It expresses an attitude toward the subject. It is not the subject itself.

Announcement: Not a Thesis	Thesis Statement
My subject is the incompetence of Professor X.	Professor X is an incompetent teacher.

Announcement: Not a Thesis	Thesis Statement
I want to share some thoughts with you about our space program.	Our space program is a waste of money.
The many unforeseen problems I encountered when I went camping are the topic of this theme.	I encountered many unforeseen problems when I went camping.
This paper will attempt to tell you something about the emotions I felt on viewing the Grand Canyon.	The Grand Canyon was even more magnificent than I had imagined.
The thesis of this paper is the difficulty of solving our environmental problems.	Solving our environmental problems is more difficult than many environmentalists believe.

A Thesis Is Not a Statement of Absolute Fact

A thesis makes a judgment or interpretation. There's no way to spend a whole paper supporting a statement that needs no support.

Fact: Not a Thesis
Jane Austen is the author of *Pride and Prejudice.*
The capital of California is Sacramento.
Suicide is the deliberate taking of one's own life.
President Lincoln's first name was Abraham.
The planet closest to the Sun is Mercury.

A Thesis Is Not the Whole Essay

A thesis is your main idea, often expressed in a single sentence. Be careful not to confuse the term as it is used in this text with the book-length thesis or dissertation required of candidates for advanced degrees in graduate schools.

What a Good Thesis Is

It's possible to have a one-sentence statement of an idea and still not have a thesis that can be supported effectively. What characterizes a good thesis?

A Good Thesis Is Restricted

Devising a thesis statement as you plan your paper can be a way in itself of limiting, or restricting, your subject even further. A paper supporting the thesis that Professor X is incompetent, besides taking a stand on its subject, has far less territory to cover than a paper on Professor X in general. Thesis statements themselves, however, may not always be sufficiently narrow. A good thesis deals with restricted, bite-size issues rather than issues that would require a lifetime to discuss intelligently. The more restricted the thesis, the better the chances are for supporting it fully.

Poor	Better
The world is in a terrible mess.	The United Nations should be given more peace-keeping powers.
People are too selfish.	Human selfishness is seen at its worst during rush hour.
The American steel industry has many problems.	The worst problem of the American steel industry is unfair competition from foreign countries.
Crime must be stopped.	Our courts should hand out tougher sentences to habitual criminals.

A Good Thesis Is Unified

The thesis expresses *one major idea* about its subject. The tight structure of your paper depends on its working to support that one idea. A good thesis may sometimes include a secondary idea if it is strictly subordinated to the major one, but without that subordination the writer will have too many important ideas to handle, and the structure of the paper will suffer.

Poor	Better
Detective stories are not a high form of literature, but people have always been fascinated by them, and many fine writers have experimented with them.	Detective stories appeal to the basic human desire for thrills.
The new health program is excellent, but it has several drawbacks, and it should be run	The new health program should be run only on an experimental basis for two or three years.

Poor	Better
only on an experimental basis for two or three years.	*Or* Despite its general excellence, the new health program should be run only on an experimental basis for two or three years.
The Columbus Cavaliers have trouble at the defensive end and linebacker positions, and front-office tensions don't help, but the team should be able to make the play-offs.	The Columbus Cavaliers should be able to make the play-offs. *Or* Even granting a few troubles, the Columbus Cavaliers should be able to make the play-offs.

A Good Thesis Is Specific

A satisfactorily restricted and unified thesis may be useless if the idea it commits you to is vague. "The new corporate headquarters is impressive," for example, could mean anything from impressively beautiful to impressively ugly. With a thesis statement like "James Joyce's *Ulysses* is very good," you would probably have to spend more words defining "good" than discussing *Ulysses*. Even when there's no likelihood of confusion, vague ideas normally come through as so familiar or dull or universally accepted that the reader sees no point in paying attention to them.

Poor	Better
James Joyce's *Ulysses* is very good.	James Joyce's *Ulysses* helped create a new way for writers to deal with the unconscious.
Drug addiction is a big problem.	Drug addiction has caused a huge increase in violent crimes.
Our vacation was a tremendous experience.	Our vacation enabled us to learn the true meaning of sharing.
My parents are wonderful people.	Everything my parents do is based on their loving concern for the welfare of the family.

You may also extend your thesis statement to include the major points you will discuss in the body of the paper. The previously cited thesis statements could be extended as follows:

Specific	Extended Specific
James Joyce's *Ulysses* helped create a new way for writers to deal with the unconscious.	James Joyce's *Ulysses* helped create a new way for writers to deal with the unconscious by utilizing the findings of Freudian psychology and introducing the techniques of literary stream-of-consciousness.
Drug addiction has caused a huge increase in violent crimes.	Drug addiction has caused a huge increase in violent crimes in the home, at school, and on the streets.
Our vacation enabled us to learn the true meaning of sharing.	Our vacation enabled us to learn the true meaning of sharing our time, space, and possessions.
Everything my parents do is based on their loving concern for the welfare of the family.	Everything my parents do is based on their loving concern for maintaining the welfare of the family by keeping us in touch with our past, helping us to cope with our present, and inspiring us to build for our future.

These extended thesis statements have certain virtues, but they have their drawbacks, too. They can be considered summaries or mini-outlines, in some respects, and therefore they can be useful because they force you to think through the entire essay beforehand. They may be especially helpful if you are uneasy about your organizing abilities. In short essays, on the other hand, extended thesis statements frequently may not be necessary or desirable. They may, for example, tell readers more than you want them to know and tell it to them too soon. After all, a summary usually belongs at the end of an essay, not at the beginning. Be sure you know if your instructor has any preference. Remember the main point, though: It is essential that the thesis be specific.

Exercises for Review

A. Write *T* next to each thesis statement below. Write *NT* if there is no thesis statement.

_____ 1. My sister is a terrible cook because she seldom follows essential recipe instructions, forgets the time variable in meal preparation, and knows absolutely nothing about foods that clash.

_____ 2. I want to tell you about the many defects in the administration's proposals for decreasing the budget deficit.

_____ 3. Al Capone, the Chicago gangster, was nicknamed Scarface.

_____ 4. Justice delayed is justice denied.

_____ 5. My thesis asks whether affirmative action programs are just a new form of racism.

_____ 6. It's not only poor people who get government handouts.

_____ 7. How to Grow Prize-Winning Roses.

_____ 8. This paper will examine recent efforts to ease the parking problem on campus by pointing out new regulations, identifying schedule possibilities outside prime-time parking hours, and suggesting alternative transportation.

_____ 9. Christmas shopping shows that the law of the jungle is still with us.

_____ 10. My husband cooks all the meals for our family, his hunting club, and the patrons at Al's Shrimp O'Rama where he works.

B. Write G next to each good thesis statement. Write NG next to each statement that is not sufficiently restricted, unified, or specific, and be prepared to suggest revisions.

_____ 1. The history of the United States is dominated by lust for money.

_____ 2. Common sense is sometimes the enemy of genius.

_____ 3. British and American poets through the centuries have vastly overrated the glories of romantic love.

_____ 4. Thirst is harder to endure than hunger.

_____ 5. Exercise is a worthwhile activity.

_____ 6. Jogging can add years to one's life by improving cardiovascular function, strengthening muscles, and enriching emotional health.

_____ 7. Teaching tricks to a dog is easier than most people think.

_____ 8. Men's mustaches can reveal something about their characters.

_____ 9. Natural beauty must be preserved, but government agencies often make foolish decisions on this matter, and jobs must also be preserved.

_____ 10. In _Moby-Dick_, Melville does a very good job.

The Thesis at Work in the Paper

The thesis statement is a tool, not an end in itself. It has two outstanding values. First, it serves as a test of whether your main idea meets the requirements we have just discussed: whether it is a firm concept that can actually be put into words or only a fuzzy notion that is not yet ready for development. Second, the thesis statement is a constant, compact reminder of the point your paper must make, and it is therefore an indispensable means of determining the relevancy or irrelevancy, the logic or lack of logic, of all the material that goes into the paper.

In itself, however, the thesis statement is a deliberately barebones presentation of your idea. In your paper, you will attempt to deal with the idea in a far more interesting way. The thesis statement, for example, may never appear word for word in your final paper. There's no special rule that in the final paper you must declare the thesis in a single sentence. In some rare cases, the thesis may only be hinted at rather than stated openly. The proper places for the barebones thesis statement are in your mind with every word you write, on any piece of scratch paper on which you jot down the possible ingredients of your essay, and at the beginning of a formal outline. (If you are ever required to construct such an outline, all of the student papers in Chapters 2–10 begin with formal topic outlines that you can use as examples. Your instructor will give you further guidance.)

In most short papers, the thesis is presented in the first paragraph, the *introduction*. Again, no absolute rule states that this must always be the case—just as no rule demands that an introduction must always be just one paragraph (the last "Sample Introduction" below is three paragraphs)—but in practice, most papers do begin that way. It's what seems to work for most people most of the time. As a general guideline, it's helpful to think of the first paragraph's job as presenting the thesis in an interesting way.

The word *interesting* is important. The introduction should not ordinarily be a one-sentence paragraph consisting solely of the unadorned thesis statement. The introduction certainly should indicate clearly what the thesis is, but it also should arouse curiosity or stress the importance of the subject or establish a particular tone of humor, anger, solemnity, and so forth.

Thesis Statement	**Sample Introduction**
Professor X is an incompetent teacher.	Any school the size of State is probably going to get its share of incompetent teachers. I'm told that last year an elderly history professor came to class to give a final exam and then realized he'd forgotten to make

(continued)

Thesis Statement	**Sample Introduction**
	one up. Professor Z tells jokes nobody understands and keeps chuckling to himself about them through the whole class period. Professor Y doesn't return term papers until the last day of class; so her students never know how they're doing until it's too late. As far as I'm concerned, though, the biggest dud of all is Professor X.
Hostility to interracial marriages is the prejudice least likely to die.	Progress in relations between the races often seems grotesquely slow. Looking at bundles of years instead of days, however, one can see that there has been real progress in jobs, education, and even housing. The most depressing area, the area in which there has been no progress, in which no progress is even likely, in which progress is not even seriously discussed, is the area of interracial marriages.
Not voting may sometimes be a responsible decision.	Public service ads tell us to be good citizens and make sure to vote. On election eves, the candidates tell us to exercise our sacred rights and hustle down to the polling booth, even if we're not going to cast our ballots for them. Network philosophers tell us that the country is going downhill because so few people vote for President. But my neighbor Joe is totally indifferent to politics; he knows little and cares less. My neighbor Jennifer thinks both candidates are equally foul. I believe that Joe, Jennifer, and thousands like them are making intelligent, responsible decisions when they stay home on Election Day, and I admire

Thesis Statement

Sample Introduction

them for not letting themselves be bullied.

Television commercials can be great entertainment.

I like television commercials. It's a terrible confession. I know I'm supposed to sneer and brood and write letters to people who want to protect me, but I like commercials. They can be great entertainment, and it's time somebody said so.

Many baseball players are paid far more than their abilities can justify.

An essay in *Forbes Magazine* by sports commentator Dick Schaap tells a story about the great Baseball Hall of Famer and Detroit Tiger of the 1930s and 1940s, Hank Greenberg, the first player to make $100,000 a year. Greenberg's son Steve, now an important baseball official, was once an agent negotiating contracts. He told his father about a player he was representing whose batting average was .238. "What should I ask for?" Steve inquired.

"Ask for a uniform," Hank replied.

Today, unfortunately, any agent would also ask for a million dollars—and would probably get it. Baseball players' salaries have become ridiculously high and have little or nothing to do with actual athletic abilities.

The function of subsequent paragraphs—paragraphs generally referred to as the *body*—is to support the thesis. All sorts of paragraph arrangements are possible. The important consideration is that the body paragraphs, individually and as a whole, must persuade your reader that your thesis makes sense.

One of the most common paragraph arrangements is worth studying at this time since it's the easiest to follow and since our concern here is with the essential connection between body paragraphs and thesis, not with fine points. This arrangement gives a separate paragraph to each supporting point and the specific evidence necessary to substantiate it. In sketchy outline form, the progression of paragraphs might look something like this:

¶ 1—Presentation of thesis: There are at least three good reasons for abolishing capital punishment.

Start of ¶ 2—First, statistics show that capital punishment is not really a deterrent . . .

Start of ¶ 3—Second, when capital punishment is used it is forever impossible to correct a mistaken conviction . . .

Start of ¶ 4—Third, capital punishment has traditionally been used in a discriminatory fashion against poor people and African-Americans . . .

Using the same form of one paragraph for each supporting idea, but abandoning the neatness of numbered points, we might find the following:

¶ 1—Presentation of thesis: Dieting can be dangerous.

Start of ¶ 2—Some diets can raise cholesterol levels alarmingly . . .

Start of ¶ 3—In other cases, over an extended period, some diets can lead to serious vitamin deficiencies . . .

Start of ¶ 4—One further danger is that already existing medical problems such as high blood pressure can be drastically aggravated . . .

Most papers also have a distinct *conclusion*, a last paragraph that provides a needed finishing touch. The conclusion can be a quick summary of your thesis and main supporting points. It can emphasize or reemphasize the importance of your thesis. It can relate a seemingly remote thesis to people's everyday lives. It can make a prediction. It can issue a call for action. In one way or another, the conclusion reinforces or develops the thesis; it should never introduce a totally unrelated, brand-new idea. The conclusion should bring your paper to a smooth stop. Just as the introduction steers clear of direct announcements, the conclusion should avoid the blatant "Well, that's about it" ending. There are dozens of possible conclusions, but almost all papers benefit from having one. (For specific examples of different kinds of conclusions, see pages 170–172.)

The group of readings that follows shows the persuasive principle in action by offering contrasting examples of good and not-so-good writing. From short thank-you notes to freshman English compositions, the results of writing with and without a thesis can be explored in detail. Later chapters will comment on and provide examples of the techniques appropriate for particular patterns of writing: classification, description, and so on. Patterns change depending on subjects and approaches. Principles do not change. The basic nature of good writing, as discussed in this chapter, remains constant.

Two Ads on the Community Bulletin Board

A.   Babysitter

Experienced high school student available, weekdays to midnight, weekends to 2 A.M. Reasonable rates. Call Sandy, 335-0000.

B.   Babysitter

A HIGH SCHOOL STUDENT WHO KNOWS *THE THREE R'S*
Ready—any weekday to midnight, weekends to 2 A.M.
Reliable—four years' experience, references available.
Reasonable—$4.00 per hour, flat fee for more than five hours.
Call Sandy, 335-0000

Discussion and Questions

Even a short "position wanted" ad can use the persuasive principle to its advantage. A dozen high school students pin a dozen different typed or handwritten index cards to the bulletin board at the local library or supermarket. Most of the cards convey lifeless facts. One or two cards make the same facts come alive by using them to support an idea. Those are the cards that get a second look—and get their writers a phone call.

1. Which ad has a thesis?
2. Does the ad support its thesis?
3. Which ad uses more specific facts?

Two "Personals"

A.

Clark Kent seeks Lois Lane. I know I'm no Superman, but I'm a good guy. I'm not faster than a speeding bullet, but I love to bike and take long walks. I'm not more powerful than a locomotive, but I am in upper management at my company. I can't leap tall buildings in a single bound, but I do love to travel and just returned from a rock climbing trip in the Southwest. Where can I find an intrepid "girl reporter" with lots of moxie who won't mind that I can't fly and that I don't wear a cape? Could you be the one?

B.

Single male, professional in an upper management position is looking for a woman for bike rides and long walks. I also like to travel and have done a lot of it. Call if interested.

Discussion and Questions

Much like an advertisement for a baby-sitting business, an advertisement for yourself is most effective when in addition to being informative, it is lively and stands out from the competition in some way. The same person describes himself in both of the previous ads, but we think that one ad is much more likely to attract interest.

1. Which ad has a thesis?
2. Which ad makes an effort to attract the reader's interest?
3. Which ad uses more specific facts?

Two Sets of Directions

A.

How to Get from Town to Camp Wilderness

Take Freeway west to Millersville Road exit. Go north on Millersville Road to Route 256. West on 256 to Laurel Lane. North on Laurel Lane until you see our sign. Turn right, and you're there.

B.

How to Get from Town to Camp Wilderness

You'll have an easy trip if you avoid three trouble spots.

1. You have to take the MILLERSVILLE ROAD Exit as you go west on the Freeway, and it's a *left-hand* exit. Start bearing left as soon as you see the "Millersville 5 miles" sign.
2. After turning north (right) on Millersville Road, don't panic when you see Route 526. You want ROUTE 256 and that's 8 more miles.
3. Go west (left) on Route 256 to LAUREL LANE. The street signs are almost impossible to read, but Laurel Lane is the second road on the right after the Mobil station.

   Once on Laurel Lane, you're all set. Go 2 miles until you see our sign. Turn right, and you're there.

Discussion and Questions

Writing competent directions is a difficult task. When you are explaining something you know well, it's hard to put yourself in the place of a total novice. You may be excessively casual about some step or even forget to mention it. Directions can also be hard to read: For novices they can seem to be a series of one disconnected step after another. Writing with a thesis helps the steps come together in the readers' minds and gives them a comforting sense of security.

1. Which set of directions has a thesis?
2. Which tries to anticipate difficulties?
3. Explain the unconventional capitalization in B.

Two Thank-You Notes

A.

July 23, 2000

Dear Aunt Molly,
"Thanks for everything" is an old, old phrase, but I've never meant it more. Thanks for your generous, great big check. Thanks for coming to the graduation ceremonies. Thanks for years of hugs and funny comments and good advice. Thanks for caring so much for me, and thanks for being Aunt Molly.

Much love,

Alice

B.

July 23, 2000

Dear Aunt Molly,
Thank you so much for your generous check. I was really happy that you could come to my graduation, and I hope you had a good time. Thank you so much again.

Much love,

Alice

Discussion and Questions

Back in the days before long-distance phone calls became routine, people wrote many more personal letters than they do now. For a good number of people today, the thank-you note is probably the only personal letter writing they do, other than a cheerful "Hi, there!" on postcards or Christmas cards. Graduates, newlyweds, new parents, and grieving widows and widowers all need to write thank-you notes. There's not much choice of subject, of course, and even most of the ideas are predetermined. How can the writer make a thank-you note sound like a sincere expression of emotion, not just good manners? The persuasive principle is a valuable aid.

Two Letters of Complaint

(in traditional and e-mail form)

13 Pier St
New York, NY 10016
July 23, 2000

Customer Complaints
Maybach Company
123 Fifth Avenue
New York, NY 10001

Subject: Defective Coffee Table

I have tried calling three different times and have not received any satisfaction, so now I am going to try writing.

I have absolutely no intention of paying any $749.60. I returned my coffee table more than a month ago. One of the legs was wobbly and the top had a bad scratch. Two times the pickup men did not come on the day they said they would. I returned the first bill for the table, and now you just sent me another one, and all I get from people when I call the store is "We'll look into it."

Also the price was $174.96, not $749.60. I await your reply.

Yours very truly,

Augusta Briggs

Augusta Briggs

B.

Subject: Defective Coffee Table
Date: Fri, 23 July 2000 16:14:30–0500 (CDT)
From: abriggs@somedomain.com (Augusta Briggs)
To: customerservice@Maybach.com

When you folks make mistakes, you don't kid around. You make big ones. Phone calls haven't done me much good, so I'm hoping that this letter can clear things up.

Early last month—probably June 9 or 10—I returned a defective coffee table. Since you had no more in stock, I canceled the order.

When the bill came for the table, I returned it with a note of explanation. Exactly one week ago, July 16, I received a second bill. To add to the fun, this second bill was for $749.60 instead of the original $174.96.

When I called the store, I was told I'd be called back by the next day at the latest. I'm still waiting.

I'm sure you agree that these are too many mistakes, and that they are big enough to be extremely annoying. Shall we get this matter settled once and for all?

Thank you for your attention.

Yours very truly,

Augusta Briggs
13 Pier St
New York, NY 10016

Discussion and Questions

The letter to a friend may not be as common as it once was, but business writing—and business plays a role in our private lives as well as in our jobs—is as important as ever. Indeed, the advent of e-mail may have made business writing even more common. When the clear and methodical statement of ideas and facts is essential, putting it into writing, on paper or electronically, becomes inevitable.

The writer of a letter of complaint has two special difficulties, both of which must be resolved if the letter is to be effective. On the one hand, the writer must communicate the gravity of the complaint, or the complaint may be treated casually, perhaps even ignored. On the other hand, the writer must simultaneously come through as a rational human being calmly presenting a grievance. It's essential that the writer not be dismissed as a crackpot or crank. Letters from crackpots and cranks get shown around the office, everyone has a good laugh, and then the letter goes to the bottom of the fattest pile of unanswered correspondence.

Business correspondence is increasingly done by e-mail these days. It is important to remember that although e-mail allows you to communicate with your correspondent more quickly than traditional mail, it should not be treated with any less care. It's easy, when sending e-mail, to ignore conventions of organization, grammar, spelling, and so on. It's easy to fall into bad habits that are unique to e-mail as well: "emoticons" and long and self-consciously cute signature files, for example. Don't. A sloppy piece of business e-mail is as much of an embarrassment as a sloppy piece of traditional mail. Neither one is likely to generate the response you're hoping for.

1. Which letter has a thesis?
2. Does the letter support the thesis with specific evidence?
3. Does the letter have a conclusion to reinforce or develop the thesis?
4. Why does the writer of letter B say nothing specific about what was wrong with the coffee table?
5. What is the purpose of the informal phrasing ("you folks," "kid around") and humorous touches in letter B?
6. Are there elements in letter A that might allow the reader to dismiss the writer as a crank?
7. Why do business-letter paragraphs tend to be so short?

Two Replies to the Second Letter of Complaint

(in traditional and e-mail form)

A.

Maybach Company
123 Fifth Avenue
New York, NY 10001
(212) 333-3333

Customer Relations   July 26, 2000

Ms. Augusta Briggs
13 Pier Street
New York, NY 10016

Dear Ms. Briggs:

We apologize. We made a lot of mistakes, and we are truly sorry.

We tried to phone you with our apology as soon as we got your letter of July 23, but you weren't at home. Therefore, we're taking this opportunity to apologize in writing. We also want to tell you that your bill for the coffee table has been canceled once and for all, and you won't be bothered again. If something should go wrong, please call me directly at extension 4550.

Good service makes happy customers, and happy customers are the heart of our business. We appreciate your letting us know when our service isn't so good, and we want to assure you that we've taken steps to see that these mistakes don't recur.

Again, please accept our sincere regrets. Do we dare call your attention to the storewide furniture sale all of next month, including an excellent stock of coffee tables?

Yours very truly,

Rose Alonso

Rose Alonso

B.

Subject: Defective Coffee Table
Date: Sat, 26 July 2000 11:12:38–0500 (CDT)
From: customerservice@Maybach.com
To: abriggs@somedomain.com (Augusta Briggs)

Dear Ms. Briggs:

Persuant to your letter of July 23, please be advised that your bill for the returned coffee table has been canceled.

This department attempted to phone you immediately upon receipt of your letter, but no answer was received.

We apologize for any inconvenience you may have experienced, and we hope that we may continue to deserve your patronage in the future. There is a storewide furniture sale all of next month in which you may have a special interest.

Yours very truly,
Rose Alonso
Manager

Discussion and Questions

1. Which letter develops a thesis? Which is a collection of separate sentences?
2. Which letter makes the phone call seem an indication of the company's concern? Which makes the call seem as if the company had been inconvenienced?
3. Which letter is superior in convincing the customer that her problems are finally over?
4. Both letters express hope for the customer's continued trade. Why is letter A far better in this respect?

Two "How I Spent My Summer Vacation" Essays

(In-Class Assignment)

A.

I couldn't find a job this summer, and it's hard to write much about my summer vacation.

Every morning I would get up between 8:30 and 9:00. My breakfast would usually be juice, toast, and coffee, though sometimes I would have eggs, too.

For a couple of weeks, after breakfast I would mow some neighbors' lawns, but after a while I got bored with that, and mostly I just hung around. Usually I read the paper and then straightened up my room.

For lunch I had a sandwich and a glass of milk. I remember once my mother and I had a real argument because there wasn't anything for a sandwich.

After lunch, if my mother didn't need the car, I'd usually drive over to the big shopping center with some of my friends. We'd walk around to see what was happening, and sometimes we'd try to pick up some girls. Mostly, we'd just look at the girls. Sometimes, instead of going to the shopping center, we'd go swimming.

After supper, it was usually television or a movie. Television is mostly reruns in the summer, and it was a bad scene. Some of the movies were okay, but nothing sensational.

In the middle of the summer, my older sister and her family came to visit from out of town. That was fun because I like my two little nephews a lot, and we fooled around in the backyard. My brother-in-law kept asking what I was doing with my time, and my mother said at least I was staying out of trouble.

B.

I couldn't find a job this summer, and most people would probably say that I spent my summer doing nothing. In fact, I spent most of my summer practicing very hard to be a pest.

To start with, I developed hanging around the house into an art. It drove my mother crazy. After breakfast, I'd read the paper, spreading it out over the entire living room, and then take my midmorning nap. Refreshed by my rest, I'd then ask my mother what was available for lunch. Once when there was no Italian salami left and the bread was a little stale, I looked at her sadly and sighed a lot and kept opening and closing the refrigerator. She didn't take my suffering too well. As I recall, the expression she used was "no good bum" or something of that order. In the evenings, I'd sigh a lot over having to watch television reruns. When my mother asked me why I watched if I didn't enjoy myself, I sighed some more.

The other main center for my activities as a pest was at the big shopping center a short drive from home. My friends and I—we figured we needed protection—would stand in people's way on the mall and make them walk around us. We'd try on clothes we had no intention of buying and complain about the price. We'd make eyes, and gestures, and offensive remarks at any pretty girls. We'd practice swaggering and strutting and any other means of looking obnoxious that occurred to us.

Miscellaneous other activities during the summer included splashing people at the beach, laughing in the wrong places at movies, and honking the car horn madly at pedestrians as they started to cross the street. These are small-time adventures, I realize, but difficult to do with real style.

Basically, I had myself a good summer. It's always a pleasure to master a set of skills, and I think I've come close to being an expert pest. I wonder what new thrills lie in wait next summer.

Discussion and Questions

"How I Spent My Summer Vacation." The subject is deadly. To make matters worse, here are two students who spent a remarkably uneventful summer. One blunders along and writes a frightful paper. The other develops a thesis, supports it, and ends with an appealing little paper. It's no candidate for a prize, but it's an appealing little paper. Enough said.

1. In paper A, is "it's hard to write much about my summer vacation" a thesis? Is it a good thesis? Does the writer support it?
2. If both papers have a thesis, are the theses basically the same?
3. What topics mentioned in paper A are not mentioned in paper B? Why?
4. Which paper has a conclusion? Is it effective?
5. Both papers use many specific details. Which uses them better? Why?
6. Which paper has better developed paragraphs?
7. Which paragraphs in paper A do not have topic sentences? Do all the paragraphs in paper B have topic sentences?
8. Which paper handles the argument about lunch better? Why?

Two Freshman English Essays on a Literary Subject

Many freshman English courses devote part of the school year to reading, discussing, and writing about works of literature. One of the most popular and frequently anthologized American works of the twentieth century is Shirley Jackson's short story "The Lottery." It was first published in 1948 and is still a source of critical analysis and controversy. We invite you to read "The Lottery" and then apply the persuasive principle to evaluating two student essays about the story.

THE LOTTERY
Shirley Jackson

1 The morning of June 27th was clear and sunny, with the fresh warmth of a full-summer day; the flowers were blossoming profusely and the grass was richly green. The people of the village began to gather in the square, between the post office and the bank, around ten o'clock; in some towns there were so many people that the lottery took two days and had to be started on June 26th, but in this village, where there were only about three hundred people, the whole lottery took less than two hours, so it could begin at ten o'clock in the morning and still be through in time to allow the villagers to get home for noon dinner.

2 The children assembled first, of course. School was recently over for the summer, and the feeling of liberty sat uneasily on most of them; they tended to gather together quietly for a while before they broke into boisterous play, and their talk was still of the classroom and the teacher, of books and reprimands. Bobby Martin had already stuffed his pockets full of stones, and the other boys soon followed his example, selecting the smoothest and roundest stones; Bobby and Harry Jones and Dickie Delacroix—the villagers pronounced this name "Dellacroy"—eventually made a great pile of stones in one corner of the square and guarded it against the raids of the other boys. The girls stood aside, talking among themselves, looking over their shoulders at the boys, and the very small children rolled in the dust or clung to the hands of their older brothers or sisters.

3 Soon the men began to gather, surveying their own children, speaking of planting and rain, tractors and taxes. They stood together, away from the pile of stones in the corner, and their jokes were quiet and they smiled rather than

laughed. The women, wearing faded house dresses and sweaters, came shortly after their menfolk. They greeted one another and exchanged bits of gossip as they went to join their husbands. Soon the women, standing by their husbands, began to call to their children, and the children came reluctantly, having to be called four or five times. Bobby Martin ducked under his mother's grasping hand and ran, laughing, back to the pile of stones. His father spoke up sharply, and Bobby came quickly and took his place between his father and his oldest brother.

4   The lottery was conducted—as were the square dances, the teen-age club, the Halloween program—by Mr. Summers, who had time and energy to devote to civic activities. He was a round-faced, jovial man and he ran the coal business, and people were sorry for him, because he had no children and his wife was a scold. When he arrived in the square, carrying the black wooden box, there was a murmur of conversation among the villagers, and he waved and called, "Little late today, folks." The postmaster, Mr. Graves, followed him, carrying a three-legged stool, and the stool was put in the center of the square and Mr. Summers set the black box down on it. The villagers kept their distance, leaving a space between themselves and the stool, and when Mr. Summers said, "Some of you fellows want to give me a hand?" there was a hesitation before two men, Mr. Martin and his oldest son, Baxter, came forward to hold the box steady on the stool while Mr. Summers stirred up the papers inside it.

5   The original paraphernalia for the lottery had been lost long ago, and the black box now resting on the stool had been put into use even before Old Man Warner, the oldest man in town, was born. Mr. Summers spoke frequently to the villagers about making a new box, but no one liked to upset even as much tradition as was represented by the black box. There was a story that the present box had been made with some pieces of the box that had preceded it, the one that had been constructed when the first people settled down to make a village here. Every year, after the lottery, Mr. Summers began talking again about a new box, but every year the subject was allowed to fade off without anything's being done. The black box grew shabbier each year; by now it was no longer completely black but splintered badly along one side to show the original wood color, and in some places faded or stained.

6   Mr. Martin and his oldest son, Baxter, held the black box securely on the stool until Mr. Summers had stirred the papers thoroughly with his hand. Because so much of the ritual had been forgotten or discarded, Mr. Summers had been successful in having slips of paper substituted for the chips of wood that had been used for generations. Chips of wood, Mr. Summers had argued, had been all very well when the village was tiny, but now that the population

was more than three hundred and likely to keep on growing, it was necessary to use something that would fit more easily into the black box. The night before the lottery, Mr. Summers and Mr. Graves made up the slips of paper and put them in the box, and it was then taken to the safe of Mr. Summers' coal company and locked up until Mr. Summers was ready to take it to the square next morning. The rest of the year, the box was put away, sometimes one place, sometimes another; it had spent one year in Mr. Graves's barn and another year underfoot in the post office, and sometimes it was set on a shelf in the Martin grocery and left there.

7   There was a great deal of fussing to be done before Mr. Summers declared the lottery open. There were the lists to make up—of heads of families, heads of households in each family, members of each household in each family. There was the proper swearing-in of Mr. Summers by the postmaster, as the official of the lottery; at one time, some people remembered, there had been a recital of some sort, performed by the official of the lottery, a perfunctory, tuneless chant that had been rattled off duly each year; some people believed that the official of the lottery used to stand just so when he said or sang it, others believed that he was supposed to walk among the people, but years and years ago this part of the ritual had been allowed to lapse. There had been, also, a ritual salute, which the official of the lottery had had to use in addressing each person who came up to draw from the box, but this also had changed with time, until now it was felt necessary only for the official to speak to each person approaching. Mr. Summers was very good at all this; in his clean white shirt and blue jeans, with one hand resting carelessly on the black box, he seemed very proper and important as he talked interminably to Mr. Graves and the Martins.

8   Just as Mr. Summers finally left off talking and turned to the assembled villagers, Mrs. Hutchinson came hurriedly along the path to the square, her sweater thrown over her shoulders, and slid into place in the back of the crowd. "Clean forgot what day it was," she said to Mrs. Delacroix, who stood next to her, and they both laughed softly. "Thought my old man was out back stacking wood," Mrs. Hutchinson went on, "and then I looked out the window and the kids was gone, and then I remembered it was the twenty-seventh and came a-running." She dried her hands on her apron, and Mrs. Delacroix said, "You're in time, though. They're still talking away up there."

9   Mrs. Hutchinson craned her neck to see through the crowd and found her husband and children standing near the front. She tapped Mrs. Delacroix on the arm as a farewell and began to make her way through the crowd. The people separated good-humoredly to let her through; two or three people said, in voices just loud enough to be heard across the crowd, "Here comes your Missus, Hutchinson," and "Bill, she made it after all." Mrs. Hutchinson

reached her husband, and Mr. Summers, who had been waiting, said cheerfully, "Thought we were going to have to get on without you, Tessie." Mrs.
Hutchinson said, grinning, "Wouldn't have me leave m'dishes in the sink,
now, would you, Joe?," and soft laughter ran through the crowd as the people
stirred back into position after Mrs. Hutchinson's arrival.

10   "Well, now," Mr. Summers said soberly, "guess we better get started, get
this over with, so's we can go back to work. Anybody ain't here?"

11   "Dunbar," several people said. "Dunbar, Dunbar."

12   Mr. Summers consulted his list. "Clyde Dunbar," he said. "That's right.
He's broke his leg, hasn't he? Who's drawing for him?"

13   "Me, I guess," a woman said, and Mr. Summers turned to look at her.
"Wife draws for her husband," Mr. Summers said. "Don't you have a grown
boy to do it for you, Janey?" Although Mr. Summers and everyone else in the
village knew the answer perfectly well, it was the business of the official of
the lottery to ask such questions formally. Mr. Summers waited with an expression of polite interest while Mrs. Dunbar answered.

14   "Horace's not but sixteen yet," Mrs. Dunbar said regretfully. "Guess I
gotta fill in for the old man this year."

15   "Right," Mr. Summers said. He made a note on the list he was holding.
Then he asked, "Watson boy drawing this year?"

16   A tall boy in the crowd raised his hand. "Here," he said. "I'm drawing for
m'mother and me." He blinked his eyes nervously and ducked his head as several voices in the crowd said things like "Good fellow, Jack," and "Glad to see
your mother's got a man to do it."

17   "Well," Mr. Summers said, "guess that's everyone. Old Man Warner
make it?"

18   "Here," a voice said, and Mr. Summers nodded.

19   A sudden hush fell on the crowd as Mr. Summers cleared his throat and
looked at the list. "All ready?" he called. "Now, I'll read the names—heads of
families first—and the men come up and take a paper out of the box. Keep
the paper folded in your hand without looking at it until everyone has had a
turn. Everything clear?"

20   The people had done it so many times that they only half listened to the
directions; most of them were quiet, wetting their lips, not looking around.
Then Mr. Summers raised one hand high and said, "Adams." A man disen-
gaged himself from the crowd and came forward. "Hi, Steve," Mr. Summers
said, and Mr. Adams said, "Hi, Joe." They grinned at one another humorlessly
and nervously. Then Mr. Adams reached into the black box and took out a
folded paper. He held it firmly by one corner as he turned and went hastily
back to his place in the crowd, where he stood a little apart from his family,
not looking down at his hand.

21   "Allen," Mr. Summers said. "Anderson. . . . Bentham."

22   "Seems like there's no time at all between lotteries any more," Mrs. Delacroix said to Mrs. Graves in the back row. "Seems like we got through with the last one only last week."

23   "Time sure goes fast," Mrs. Graves said.

24   "Clark. . . . Delacroix."

25   "There goes my old man," Mrs. Delacroix said. She held her breath while her husband went forward.

26   "Dunbar," Mr. Summers said, and Mrs. Dunbar went steadily to the box while one of the women said, "Go on, Janey," and another said, "There she goes."

27   "We're next," Mrs. Graves said. She watched while Mr. Graves came around from the side of the box, greeted Mr. Summers gravely, and selected a slip of paper from the box. By now, all through the crowd there were men holding the small folded papers in their large hands, turning them over and over nervously. Mrs. Dunbar and her two sons stood together, Mrs. Dunbar holding the slip of paper.

28   "Harburt. . . . Hutchinson."

29   "Get up there, Bill," Mrs. Hutchinson said, and the people near her laughed.

30   "Jones."

31   "They do say," Mr. Adams said to Old Man Warner, who stood next to him, "that over in the north village they're talking of giving up the lottery."

32   Old Man Warner snorted. "Pack of crazy fools," he said. "Listening to the young folks, nothing's good enough for *them*. Next thing you know, they'll be wanting to go back to living in caves, nobody work any more, live *that* way for a while. Used to be a saying about 'Lottery in June, corn be heavy soon.' First thing you know, we'd all be eating stewed chickweed and acorns. There's *always* been a lottery," he added petulantly. "Bad enough to see young Joe Summers up there joking with everybody."

33   "Some places have already quit lotteries," Mrs. Adams said.

34   "Nothing but trouble in *that*," Old Man Warner said stoutly. "Pack of young fools."

35   "Martin." And Bobby Martin watched his father go forward. "Overdyke. . . . Percy."

36   "I wish they'd hurry," Mrs. Dunbar said to her older son. "I wish they'd hurry."

37   "They're almost through," her son said.

38   "You get ready to run tell Dad," Mrs. Dunbar said.

39   Mr. Summers called his own name and then stepped forward precisely and selected a slip from the box. Then he called, "Warner."

40   "Seventy-seventh year I been in the lottery," Old Man Warner said as he went through the crowd. "Seventy-seventh time."

41   "Watson." The tall boy came awkwardly through the crowd. Someone said, "Don't be nervous, Jack," and Mr. Summers said, "Take your time, son."

42   "Zanini."

43   After that, there was a long pause, a breathless pause, until Mr. Summers, holding his slip of paper in the air, said, "All right, fellows." For a minute, no one moved, and then all the slips of paper were opened. Suddenly, all the women began to speak at once, saying, "Who is it?," "Who's got it?," "Is it the Dunbars?," "Is it the Watsons?" Then the voices began to say, "It's Hutchinson. It's Bill," "Bill Hutchinson's got it."

44   "Go tell your father," Mrs. Dunbar said to her older son.

45   People began to look around to see the Hutchinsons. Bill Hutchinson was standing quiet, staring down at the paper in his hand. Suddenly, Tessie Hutchinson shouted to Mr. Summers, "You didn't give him time enough to take any paper he wanted. I saw you. It wasn't fair!"

46   "Be a good sport, Tessie," Mrs. Delacroix called, and Mrs. Graves said, "All of us took the same chance."

47   "Shut up, Tessie," Bill Hutchinson said.

48   "Well, everyone," Mr. Summers said, "that was done pretty fast, and now we've got to be hurrying a little more to get done in time." He consulted his next list. "Bill," he said, "you draw for the Hutchinson family. You got any other households in the Hutchinsons?"

49   "There's Don and Eva," Mrs. Hutchinson yelled, "Make them take their chance!"

50   "Daughters draw with their husbands' families, Tessie," Mr. Summers said gently. "You know that as well as anyone else."

51   "It wasn't fair," Tessie said.

52   "I guess not, Joe," Bill Hutchinson said regretfully. "My daughter draws with her husband's family, that's only fair. And I've got no other family except the kids."

53   "Then, as far as drawing for families is concerned, it's you," Mr. Summers said in explanation, "and as far as drawing for households is concerned, that's you, too. Right?"

54   "Right," Bill Hutchinson said.

55   "How many kids, Bill?" Mr. Summers asked formally.

56   "Three," Bill Hutchinson said. "There's Bill, Jr., and Nancy, and little Dave. And Tessie and me."

57   "All right, then," Mr. Summers said. "Harry, you got their tickets back?"

58   Mr. Graves nodded and held up the slips of paper. "Put them in the box, then," Mr. Summers directed. "Take Bill's and put it in."

59   "I think we ought to start over," Mrs. Hutchinson said, as quietly as she could. "I tell you it wasn't *fair*. You didn't give him time enough to choose. Everybody saw that."

60   Mr. Graves had selected the five slips and put them in the box, and he dropped all the papers but those onto the ground, where the breeze caught them and lifted them off.

61   "Listen, everybody," Mrs. Hutchinson was saying to the people around her.

62   "Ready, Bill?" Mr. Summers asked, and Bill Hutchinson, with one quick glance around at his wife and children, nodded.

63   "Remember," Mr. Summers said, "take the slips and keep them folded until each person has taken one. Harry, you help little Dave." Mr. Graves took the hand of the little boy, who came willingly with him up to the box. "Take a paper out of the box, Davy," Mr. Summers said. Davy put his hand into the box and laughed. "Take just *one* paper," Mr. Summers said. "Harry, you hold it for him." Mr. Graves took the child's hand and removed the folded paper from the tight fist and held it while little Dave stood next to him and looked at him wonderingly.

64   "Nancy next," Mr. Summers said. Nancy was twelve, and her school friends breathed heavily as she went forward, switching her skirt, and took a slip daintily from the box. "Bill, Jr.," Mr. Summers said, and Billy, his face red and his feet overlarge, nearly knocked the box over as he got a paper out. "Tessie," Mr. Summers said. She hesitated for a minute, looking around defiantly, and then set her lips and went up to the box. She snatched a paper out and held it behind her.

65   "Bill," Mr. Summers said, and Bill Hutchinson reached into the box and felt around, bringing his hand out at last with the slip of paper in it.

66   The crowd was quiet. A girl whispered, "I hope it's not Nancy," and the sound of the whisper reached the edges of the crowd.

67   "It's not the way it used to be," Old Man Warner said clearly. "People ain't the way they used to be."

68   "All right," Mr. Summers said. "Open the papers. Harry, you open little Dave's."

69   Mr. Graves opened the slip of paper and there was a general sigh through the crowd as he held it up and everyone could see that it was blank. Nancy and Bill, Jr., opened theirs at the same time, and both beamed and laughed, turning around to the crowd and holding their slips of paper above their heads.

70   "Tessie," Mr. Summers said. There was a pause, and then Mr. Summers looked at Bill Hutchinson, and Bill unfolded his paper and showed it. It was blank.

71 "It's Tessie," Mr. Summers said, and his voice was hushed. "Show us her paper, Bill."

72 Bill Hutchinson went over to his wife and forced the slip of paper out of her hand. It had a black spot on it, the black spot Mr. Summers had made the night before with the heavy pencil in the coal-company office. Bill Hutchinson held it up, and there was a stir in the crowd.

73 "All right, folks," Mr. Summers said. "Let's finish quickly."

74 Although the villagers had forgotten the ritual and lost the original black box, they still remembered to use stones. The pile of stones the boys had made earlier was ready; there were stones on the ground with the blowing scraps of paper that had come out of the box. Mrs. Delacroix selected a stone so large she had to pick it up with both hands and turned to Mrs. Dunbar. "Come on," she said. "Hurry up."

75 Mrs. Dunbar had small stones in both hands, and she said, gasping for breath, "I can't run at all. You'll have to go ahead and I'll catch up with you."

76 The children had stones already, and someone gave little Davy Hutchinson a few pebbles.

77 Tessie Hutchinson was in the center of a cleared space by now, and she held her hands out desperately as the villagers moved in on her. "It isn't fair," she said. A stone hit her on the side of the head.

78 Old Man Warner was saying, "Come on, come on, everyone." Steve Adams was in the front of the crowd of villagers, with Mrs. Graves beside him.

79 "It isn't fair, it isn't right," Mrs. Hutchinson screamed, and then they were upon her.

Essay topic: Shirley Jackson's "The Lottery" has a longstanding reputation as a story with a powerful surprise ending. Write a 300–500 word essay evaluating the validity of that reputation.

A.

"The Lottery," written by the author Shirley Jackson, takes place on the morning of June 27th. June 27th is the day the lottery is always held, and everything seems normal. But the reader is in for a surprise.

The children assemble first. With school just out, they don't know what to do with themselves and start gathering stones. Then the men come telling quiet jokes. We are told that "they smiled rather than laughed." Then the women come, gossiping and summoning the children.

Finally, it is time for the head of the lottery, Mr. Summers, and we are told about the long history of the lottery: the old black box, the slips of paper, the old rituals, and the complicated procedures for drawing. Tessie Hutchinson's late arrival adds a touch of humor.

All the family names are called in alphabetical order, and there seems to be a little nervous tension in the air. Old Man Warner gets angry when told that other towns are thinking of giving up the lottery.

When the Hutchinson family is chosen, Tessie gets very upset and complains that the drawing was not fair because Bill, her husband, was not given enough time to draw. Bill had as much time as anyone else. Mrs. Delacroix tells Tessie to "be a good sport," and even Bill is embarrassed and says, "Shut up, Tessie."

Then there is a second drawing where each member of the Hutchinson family draws individually. Tessie turns out to have the paper with the spot on it. She has won the lottery.

The surprise comes when we find out that Tessie has been chosen to be executed. She is going to be stoned to death, and we remember the stones from the beginning of the story. "The Lottery" by Shirley Jackson shows how people follow traditions, sometimes bad ones, without ever thinking about what they are doing.

B.

Shirley Jackson's "The Lottery" is a wonderful story, but the only thing that surprised me at the end was the stones. I admit that I had pretty much forgotten about the stones, but I knew long before the ending that something terrible was going to happen. "The Lottery" is a powerful story, certainly, but its reputation for having a "powerful surprise ending" is undeserved.

It takes no more than two pages before we realize that the annual village lottery is more mysterious and sinister than any drawing for a trip to Hawaii or a new Buick. To begin with, there's an air of mystery about the shabby black box: shabby as it is, we are told directly that it represents tradition of some kind, and no one wants to replace it. People nervously hesitate to hold it still while Mr. Summers mixes the paper inside it.

As if the mystery and tradition of the black box were not enough, we learn that the whole institution of the lottery goes back to the "first people" who settled the village and that it involved all sorts of mysterious ceremonies and rituals. There had been some sort of "chant," some sort of "ritual salute." We're not just at a lottery—we're practically going to church.

The sense of church-like solemnity continues when Mrs. Dunbar, whose husband has a broken leg, is asked, "Don't you have a grown boy to do it for you, Janey?" When young Jack Watson, now old enough to draw for his family, walks up to the box, he is told, "Glad to see your mother's got a man to do it." What's going on here? What is so awesome that picking up a slip of paper is considered a job appropriate only for menfolk?

As the drawing proceeds, the story stresses the tension. People wet their lips. If they grin, they do so "humorlessly and nervously."

Any surviving thoughts about the lottery being a pleasant social occasion have to disappear with Old Man Warner's hysterical reaction to the news that some villages are thinking about abandoning the lottery. He calls them a "pack of crazy fools" and virtually predicts the end of the world—"they'll be wanting to go back to living in caves." He quotes an old saying: "Lottery in June, corn be heavy soon." We're dealing with ancient rites and rituals here—famines, and gods of the harvest, and keeping the gods happy.

We're still a long way from the end, but the author keeps pouring it on. The Hutchinson family wins the drawing, and Tessie Hutchinson, instead of packing her bags for Hawaii, complains that "It wasn't fair!" She wants someone else to win because it's obvious that something bad happens to the winner. As the individual members of the Hutchinson family participate in the second drawing, a girl's voice from the crowd says, "I hope it's not Nancy," because the girl knows what happens, too.

Any reader by this time knows from the seriousness of the reactions that we are dealing with matters of life and death. The stones are a surprise, and an important one. They fit into the story well because stoning as a means of execution is ancient, connected to religion, and involves the whole community. The stones are a surprise, but nothing else is.

Discusson and Questions

Students sometimes say that it's easy to bluff when writing an essay examination or at-home essay on a literary subject. Maybe so, but most teachers are as aware of the hazards as anyone else and make a special effort to spot bluffing.

A good, nonbluffing essay on a literary subject, especially on a "What's-your-opinion?" question, can go in many different directions, but it always displays the following characteristics:

A. It discusses the subject assigned, not the one the student wishes had been assigned. Inexperienced or nervous students might see the title "The Lottery" and haphazardly start writing everything they have ever heard or thought about the story. Stick to the subject.

B. It uses specific details to support its thesis. The instructor wants an essay from someone who has read and remembered and understood the story, not from someone who, from all the essay shows, has merely turned up in class and gotten the general drift of what the story must be about.

C. It does not get sidetracked into a plot summary unless the assignment specifically calls for one. Any references to the plot should support a thesis, not tell the story all over again.

1. Which essay has a thesis?
2. Is the thesis supported with specific details?
3. Which essay is mostly a plot summary?
4. Compare first sentences. Which is more directly related to the assignment?
5. Does the writer of the essay that has a thesis keep the thesis in mind throughout, or are there some digressions?
6. Can the relative merits of both essays be determined even by a reader unfamiliar with "The Lottery?"

Narration

"Tell me a story," children say again and again. They're bored or restless, and they know the wonders a good story can perform. "Tell me another story," say the now grown-up children, still bored and restless, as they spend millions on romances and science-fiction fantasies and whodunits. *Narration* is the telling of a story—and from the fairy tales of childhood to the parables of the New Testament, from Aesop's fables to the latest Stephen King novel, the shared experience of the human race suggests that a well-told story has few rivals in lasting fascination.

Telling a story is one of the patterns by which a thesis can be supported. That's by no means the only purpose of narration. Many writers of modern stories are far more interested in conveying a sense of life than in conveying ideas. "Yes," says the reader of these stories, "that's what a family argument"— or a first kiss or being a soldier or having the air conditioner break down—"is really like." A thesis, as such, either does not exist or is so subordinate to other concerns that it may as well not exist. This approach to narration has produced some great fiction, but it's not what your narration theme is about.

Chances are that your narration theme isn't going to be fiction at all. Nothing is wrong with trying your hand at fiction, but most narration themes proceed in far different ways. You'll probably be telling a story about what once really happened to you or to people you know. (Like any good storyteller, you'll emphasize some elements and de-emphasize or ignore others, depending on the point of the story.) All the reading selections in this chapter deal with authentic events in the lives of real people.

Imagine a scene in which some friends are uttering what strikes you as sentimental foolishness about the glories of jogging. You say, "I think jogging is horrible. Let me tell you what happened to me." And you tell your story. That's the essence of the narration paper: a point and a story to back it up.

There are millions of stories and thousands of ways to tell them. *Tell your own story in your own way* is as good a piece of advice as any. As you do so, it's reasonable to remember the various bores you may have listened to or read and try to avoid their mistakes: the bores who worried about what day of the week it was when they were bitten by a snake, who constantly repeated the same phrases *(you know, and then I, you see)*, who went on long after the interesting part of their story had been told. Profit from their examples, but tell your own story in your own way.

That advice has a fine ring to it, but it's certainly on the abstract side. "Your own way" will undoubtedly change from one story to another. To get less abstract, in *most* narration papers *most* of the time, you should keep the following suggestions in mind:

Stress the Story

The story must have a thesis, but the story itself is what gives life to the paper. *Write a story, not a sermon.* Your thesis is usually a sentence or two at the beginning or end of the paper. Sometimes the thesis can be so clearly part of the story itself that it may not even need to be expressed directly. In any event, most of your words should be devoted to the telling of your story, not to lecturing and moralizing.

Remember That a Good
Story Has Conflict

Some critics would be prepared to argue that without conflict it's impossible to have a story at all. In any event, conflict is usually the starting point for readers' interest. Three patterns of conflict are the most common. First, *conflict between people:* You went jogging in the park with a group of friends, and while you were gasping for breath, one friend was driving you mad with lofty philosophical comments about appreciating the outdoors and feeling good about our bodies. Second, *conflict between people and their environment* (a social custom or prejudice, a religious tradition, a force of nature such as a hurricane, and so on): At the end of the jogging trail, after you had managed to survive the intolerably hot weather and a killer pebble that had worked its way into one of your sneakers, your friends happily began to discuss a time and place for jogging the next day; you wanted to say "Never again," but the social pressure was too great to resist, and you went along with the crowd. Third, *conflict within a person:* All through your jogging miseries, one side of you was calling the other side a soft, overcivilized snob, incapable of appreciating the simple pleasures of life. Clearly you do not need to confine your story to only one kind of conflict.

Use Plenty of Convincing Realistic Details

The good story will give a sense of having actually happened, and convincing realistic details are your best device for transmitting that sense, as well as for preventing the sermon from taking over the story. Don't just mention the insect pests that kept bothering you as you jogged through the park—mention mosquitoes. Don't just mention mosquitoes—mention the huge one with blood lust that got onto your neck and summoned up dim memories of a malaria victim in an old Tarzan movie.

Play Fair

Stories of pure innocence versus pure evil, of totally good guys versus totally bad guys, tend to be unconvincing because they are gross distortions of what everyone knows about the complexities of life. Support your thesis energetically, by all means, but don't neglect to show some awareness of the complexities. The paper on jogging, for example, will be more powerful and persuasive if it grudgingly concedes somewhere that the park was beautiful, after all, and that while hating every minute of your journey through it, you were able occasionally to notice the beauty.

WRITING SUGGESTIONS FOR NARRATION THEMES

Choose one of the well-known quotations or proverbs that follow and write a narration that supports it. You will probably draw on personal experience for your basic material, but you should also feel free to decorate or invent whenever convenient. Some of the suggestions might be appropriate for a fable or parable.

1. What a tangled web we weave/When first we practice to deceive.
   —*Walter Scott*
2. Haste makes waste.
3. Don't put all your eggs in one basket.

4. Nobody ever went broke underestimating the intelligence of the American public.—*H.L. Mencken*
5. Faith is believing what you know ain't so.—*Mark Twain*
6. Absence makes the heart grow fonder.
7. The bridge between laughing and crying is not long.—*Jamaican proverb*
8. The way to a man's heart is through his stomach.
9. Few things are harder to put up with than the annoyance of a good example.—*Mark Twain*
10. Patriotism is the last refuge of a scoundrel.—*Samuel Johnson*
11. Genius is one percent inspiration and ninety-nine percent perspiration.—*Thomas A. Edison*
12. Winning isn't the most important thing. It's the only thing.—*Vince Lombardi*
13. No guts, no glory.
14. Those who do not know history are condemned to repeat it.—*George Santayana*
15. Wickedness is a myth invented by good people to account for the curious attractiveness of others.—*Oscar Wilde*
16. There is an exception to every rule.
17. The mass of men lead lives of quiet desperation.—*Henry David Thoreau*
18. Every cloud has a silver lining.
19. Fools and their money are soon parted.
20. Someone who hates dogs and children can't be all bad.—*W.C. Fields*
21. A thing of beauty is a joy forever.—*John Keats*
22. Everything I like is either illegal, immoral, or fattening.—*Alexander Woollcott*
23. In America, nothing fails like success.—*F. Scott Fitzgerald*
24. Luck is the residue of design.—*Branch Rickey*
25. Advice to those about to marry: Don't.—*Punch Magazine*

Readings

Readings in this chapter and in all remaining chapters are intended to provide you with practical models for your own writing. The readings begin with one student-written essay (two essays in Chapter 6 on Comparison and Contrast) together with an outline to stress the importance of careful organization. The student work is followed by a group of professional models with notes and detailed comments and questions on organization, content, and style.

BIKING WITH GRANDMA ROSE
Audrey P. McManus (student)

Thesis: Grandma Rose gave me excellent advice when she told me always to take some money with me when leaving the house.

   I. Biking habits
     A. Long rides
     B. No baggage

  II. The bad ride
     A. Flat tire
     B. No cash

 III. The walk home
     A. Rough neighborhoods
     B. Rain

Conclusion: Grandma Rose was right, and I have now mended my ways.

Always take a jacket. Don't forget to say "thank you." Eat all your vegetables before dessert. Cross your legs at the ankles, not at the knees. Give your seat on the bus to people who need it. My Grandma Rose who raised me had a hundred bits of advice for me. When I was younger, I thought they were all useless relics from ancient history just like her statements about never going to church without a hat and not wearing white shoes after Labor Day. The bit of wisdom that came in for most of my scorn, though, was "Never leave the house without some money in your purse." Grandma Rose explained that a lady could never be sure that her escort would be a gentleman, and she should always have enough money for a phone call and a cab ride home in case he left her stranded. In a time of credit cards, bank machines, and phone cards, I was quite sure Grandma Rose's warning could be safely ignored. I called her last week. I told her I called just to say "hi," but I really called to apologize silently for ever thinking she was wrong.

Here in Chicago I like to take advantage of the beautiful summer days by taking long rides on the lakeside bike path. I ride about twenty miles each time I go out. Because I don't like to be weighed down by a backpack or bothered by a hip sack, all I ever take with me is my Walkman and my apartment key, which I pin to my waistband. I feel free and unfettered that way, and if I stop to take a break along the way, I don't have to worry about leaving anything behind.

Last Tuesday, about ten miles into my bike ride, I suddenly noticed that the ride was unusually bumpy. It didn't take me too much longer to realize that I had a very flat tire. There was no way I could possibly ride my bike home. So there I was, ten miles from home, ten miles from the only bike shop I knew about, and completely without cash. I couldn't catch a cab. I couldn't call a friend to come and pick me up because I had no idea what my phone card number was. I couldn't even take a dollar and a half "El" ride. I didn't have much choice. I started walking.

Now, the bike path I ride on goes through some pretty rough neighborhoods. I don't worry when I'm on my bike and moving quickly, but walking slowly through them was not a terribly pleasant experience. My imagination may be influencing my memory a little, but it seems to me that everywhere I walked, large and unfriendly men looked at me never blinking, never moving—just watching and, well, lurking, I guess. Even worse than that were a few large men who *did* try to get friendly, mostly with language that would have startled and distressed Grandma Rose. The men became fewer and less menacing after a while when that Chicago weather did what Chicago weather always does, and it started to rain. I mean it started to pour.

Eventually I got back to my apartment. I now know it takes me approximately three hours to walk my bicycle ten miles. I changed into some dry clothes, got some cash, went to the bike shop, and had my tire fixed. I'd wasted my whole day, missed two classes, and given myself a serious headache. I'd also convinced myself that Grandma Rose's warning was right. I should always carry some money. Now, when I go bike riding, I pack my newly purchased hip sack with twenty dollars and sixty-six cents. Ten dollars and thirty-one cents for flat tire repair, thirty-five cents for a phone call, and ten dollars for a cab ride. I may not have to worry about being stranded by an ungentlemanly escort like Grandma Rose did, but I certainly have to worry about being stranded by a flat.

COMPUTER GAMES ANONYMOUS

Joanna Connors

Joanna Connors is a newspaper film critic and writer of feature articles. This humorous essay tells a familiar tale about a new kind of addiction.

Words to check:

icon (paragraph 13)   modem (27)

1 My name is Joanna C., and I am a FreeCell addict.

2   It has taken me months to get to this point, where I can admit it. I fight the FreeCell urge every day. Every hour! But if telling my story can help one person stay off the computer game, it will be worth it.

3   It started with Solitaire and a deck of cards. The small stuff. I first played it when I was a kid; my parents showed me how. Right in our own living room! But I don't blame them. They didn't know how powerful the stuff was; they didn't know it could lead to bigger games.

4   Besides, playing Solitaire was different back in the '60s. It wasn't as powerful. Really: I could take it or leave it. I didn't even touch it when I was in college, that's how indifferent I was to it.

5   Then I discovered Solitaire on my first computer. The dealer gave the game to me for free. I was naive. I didn't realize the first games are always free.

6   I started playing, figuring I could handle it. Why not? I had owned cards for years. So what if they were hidden in drawers and cabinets?

7   I played it on my laptop at home. It was fun. Nothing more than fun. I didn't recognize the warning signals: My kids were begging me to stop playing and make dinner. Then they wanted to play. My children! This is so painful to talk about.

8   After a while, I found myself playing it during the day, at work. I'd get stuck on a story, and I'd switch over to Solitaire, just for a little break. It relaxed me, you know? I didn't need it; it just helped me through the day.

9   I was hiding it, though, looking over my shoulder, making sure no one saw me playing. Then I started missing deadlines because I had to play just one more game. I knew I was in trouble when I found myself playing Solitaire . . . alone. It wasn't social Solitaire anymore.

10   It didn't help to know that I wasn't the only one with a problem. I started hearing rumors that companies were checking up on their office workers, monitoring their networks. My own company did the socially responsible thing: It ordered the game removed from all computers.

11   But I still had my laptop.

12   I kept playing. Then one day I realized I wasn't playing Solitaire; it was playing me. To this day I don't know where I found the strength, but I called the company computer expert and asked him how to delete the game from my laptop. I didn't stop to think about what I was doing, I just did it. I went cold turkey.

13   The first week was hard; I kept switching to the Games icon, only to find it empty. But after that, life was good. I was making dinner again, most days anyway. I got slightly closer to making my deadlines. I felt as if I had gotten that Solitaire monkey off my back.

14   Then, I don't know what happened, but I found myself back visiting my old dealer. I needed a new computer. I didn't care how much it cost. He

smiled when he saw me come in; he said he had some great stuff, and he'd even give me a little discount.

15   I told him: No Solitaire. I'm clean. But when I got the computer home and turned it on, the first thing I saw was that seductive Games icon, whispering to me, "Just one . . ."

16   He stuck to his word. The Solitaire was gone. But in its place was Free-Cell, a card game that made Solitaire look like soda pop. One game and I was hooked. It's that strong.

17   FreeCell is the hard stuff. It toys with your mind. You beat it once, twice, even three times, and then it shows you who is really in charge. No way can you beat it every time, no matter what anyone tells you.

18   It keeps you coming back for more, too. If you win a game, it asks: "Do you want to play again?" If you lose a game, it offers to let you play the same one, again. And again. And again. As though you could ever come out on top of FreeCell.

19   I went to a therapist, and it came out that I play FreeCell. I thought I was hiding it, but it turns out she could tell because she plays the game, too! A therapist! I was shocked.

20   She told me her hospital knew the score about FreeCell, and had it removed from the computer network. Of course, a hospital would be on top of these things.

21   But then she told me she'd found FreeCell on the Internet. She actually laughed when she told me. She even showed me the address, so I wouldn't have to go to my old dealer anymore.

22   She told me she can control her habit. "I don't play during the week. But when I'm here writing on the weekend, I'll work for 20 minutes and then I'll let myself play for 10 minutes, like a reward."

23   I looked at her. This was my therapist talking.

24   "Do you really stop at 10 minutes?" I asked, quietly.

25   "Well . . . not always," she said.

26   I left that session lower than I've ever felt before, still clutching the Internet address she'd scribbled for me on an appointment card. Appointment is right. Appointment with the devil!

27   I haven't deleted FreeCell yet from my new computer. I can't do it alone. I need help, someone to tell me how. Besides, even if I remove it, I'll know that it's available, out on the highway, for anyone with a modem and money to spend. Someone has to do something about this virus in our society. Kids are starting to play, and it's leading to other stuff. Minesweeper. Tetris. I caught my son playing computer golf the other night.

28   You can see the signs of the addiction everywhere: Hollow-eyed addicts, some of them so far gone they have braces on their wrists from the stress

injuries the constant computer playing has caused. Does it stop them? Sadly, no.

29   As for me, it has gotten to the point where I hardly remember what we did with our free time before computer games. I guess I made dinner, some nights. I remembered to call my mother once a week. I had friends. We'd actually do things together, like drink wine and smoke cigarettes and talk all night.

30   I want that life back. I want to be free of FreeCell.

31   Right after one little game. After all, I've just written for 20 minutes. I deserve my reward.

WHAT DID THE WRITER SAY AND WHAT DID YOU THINK?

1. What is the thesis? Where is it first expressed?
2. According to the author, what is her purpose in telling her story?
3. What point is established in the last sentence, "I deserve my reward"?
4. What elements in the essay show that the author is not alone in her addiction?

HOW DID THE WRITER SAY IT?

1. Much of the humor in this selection comes from the author's applying language used to deal with serious addictions to a relatively trivial addiction—"the first games are always free," for example. Cite as many instances of this humorous device as you can find.
2. What groups or programs are we meant to be reminded of by the first sentence?
3. Are readers who are afflicted with or familiar with serious addictions likely to be offended by parts of this selection?

WHAT ABOUT <u>YOUR</u> WRITING?

Many good writers try for an informal, conversational tone in their writing. Occasionally, writers go overboard and confuse a conversational *tone* with actual conversation, sometimes even with speechmaking.

Joanna O'Connor may drift into using the language of speechmaking when she writes in paragraph 7, "This is so painful to talk about." No doubt she is trying to imitate the confessional language of testimonials at meetings of addicts. Still, as her last paragraph shows, she is well aware that she is writing rather than addressing a live audience. Does it make sense to pretend otherwise?

This minor lapse, if it's a lapse at all, can become significant when writers become downright delusional:

And now, with your permission, I'd like to turn to another topic . . .
Finally, I simply want to say that . . .
I need to talk with some frankness about this problem.
I hope you'll grant me your kind indulgence while I . . .
I've droned on long enough.

Writing an essay isn't the same as giving a speech. Don't confuse the two.

MY GREATEST DAY IN BASEBALL
Dick Feagler

Dick Feagler, longtime columnist for *The Plain Dealer* (Cleveland), draws on his passions for nostalgia and baseball to comment on the complexities of worldly glory.

Words to check:

wistful (paragraph 2)

1 Every year at this time, I remember my greatest day in baseball. When I was a kid, I read this book called *My Greatest Day in Baseball*, and in it, a bunch of old ball players talked about their greatest days. Babe Ruth talked about calling his shots, and Cy Young talked about pitching his perfect game. They all had their greatest day, and I had mine.

2 It was my dream to be a ball player. The love songs of that day talked a lot about dreams. Men were always dreaming of women they could not have. These days, the songs are about having them and singing about it in the middle of it. But in my youth, it was all right to be wistful. Then, you could dream about things you knew were not attainable.

3 My baseball career was a wistful one. There is no secret about why. You can look up any kid who knew me, and he'll tell you the truth in black and white. I was lousy.

4 When they put me in right field, I stood there praying that nobody would hit one to me. At least not in the air. If it came out on the ground, I could pick

it up, but then I couldn't throw it. I had a sort of natural change-up. I threw change-ups from right field. When I tried to throw a man out at home, I threw so high the infielders had to call for it. My favorite time to come to bat was with two out and nobody on.

5   Now you can ask yourself, if you want to, why, if I was that bad, I still loved the game. Why would I love something that humiliated me? Why would I keep going back for more punishment, day after day?

6   Well, sometimes men in love do that. They do it with women. There is no law that says that you must only love the things that reward you. Though maybe there ought to be.

7   I have read that all good athletes must believe in themselves. But this does not always ensure positive results. I believed in myself. I believed I was lousy. In my whole baseball career, I only had one good day. So naturally, that day was my greatest day in baseball. Let me tell you how it was.

8   It was a day at the very end of my baseball career, though I didn't know it at the time. I had grown up playing lousy and gone through college playing lousy and gone into the Army. And one day in the Army, my company commander decided to schedule a baseball game with a rival company. It was a grimly serious game because the Army gets grimly serious about things like baseball games in off years when there's no war going on and nobody to shoot at. I was picked to start in left field.

9   Here I was among strangers. Nobody had ever seen me play baseball. I trotted out to left field and prayed nobody would hit one to me.

10   The first two batters on the other team grounded out. Then the third guy hit a vicious, slicing, sinking line drive out toward left.

11   I want to tell you that there was no way to catch that ball. When I started after it, I knew I'd never catch it. I ran toward it as fast as I could and then I dove at it. I dove strictly for theatrical reasons. It never occurred to me to even look for the ball. I just dove. And it hit my glove and stuck, and I rolled over and vaulted to my feet and trotted in with it in a kind of state of shock.

12   I was almost to the bench before anybody else on my team had even moved. They couldn't believe I'd caught the ball, and then, all of a sudden they did believe it, and they ran over and slapped me on the back and said things like "fantastic," and "way to go."

13   "I didn't get a very good jump on it," I said. "My timing must be a little off." They looked at me in awe. Awe!

14   We got two men on base next inning, and then two guys popped out. And it was my turn to bat. I had been thinking about things and had decided that since I had made a terrific catch by merely pretending I could catch, I

might be able to get a hit by pretending I could hit. So I went up there and tripled.

15   By the ninth inning of this game, I had tripled, doubled, played errorlessly in the field and struck out twice. The strikeouts were both on called strikes, and, instead of sneering at me, the other guys on the team yelled at the umpire. "Yer blind," they said. In my dignity, I said nothing.

16   This brings us to the ninth.

17   To be honest about it, when I sat down to write about my greatest day in baseball, I considered leaving out the ninth. But I'm going to tell about it as a kind of gift. A kind of gift to any boy who might love baseball but find that despite this love, they are always standing out there praying nobody will hit one to them.

18   We were ahead by one run in the bottom of the inning. They had two outs, but they had a guy on second and a guy on third. We were an out away from a victory and a hit away from a loss. And then their last batter came up and lifted a high pop fly out behind short.

19   I started coming in on it, and our shortstop started backing up. There was something in the way he was backing up that I recognized, and suddenly I knew—just knew—that this shortstop had had a baseball career similar to mine. That he, too, was lousy. That he was praying that he wouldn't have to catch this ball. And I knew that it was really my play and that if he heard me coming from behind him, he would veer off and let me catch it.

20   That ball seemed to hang up in the sky forever. I can see it yet. I can see it now and see the kid backing up toward me and see myself kind of tiptoeing in so he wouldn't hear me coming.

21   I knew as sure as I knew my name that that kid would drop the ball because he was made of the same athletic stuff I was made of and if there was a play that had to be made, he would muff it.

22   But I also knew that this was my greatest day in baseball and if there was ever a day I would be able to catch that ball, this was it.

23   Ah, little kids in right field—little wimps, little losers. Take it from me, life is full of these moments. You don't leave them behind when you retire from baseball. All your life, they keep hitting balls to you that are beyond your abilities to handle. All your life, you have to make a choice whether to try and maybe fail and be the goat or not to try at all and keep your shame private.

24   I let the kid try to catch it, and he dropped it. Two runs scored and we lost the game. That was my greatest day in baseball. Even your greatest days are rarely 100 percent great. You have to live with that and hope that someday, the bad parts fade. It vanished like a summer in my youth, leaving only the memory that once it was there.

WHAT DID THE WRITER SAY AND WHAT DID YOU THINK?

1. In what ways is the title deliberately misleading?
2. Does the author attribute any of his great deeds to skill? If not, to what does he attribute them?
3. What lessons about life does the author feel can be learned from his experiences on his greatest day?

HOW DID THE WRITER SAY IT?

1. Paragraph 23 makes it clear that the author thinks his baseball experiences provide insight into life as a whole. What earlier parts of the essay prepare us to think that the author has more than just baseball on his mind?
2. Does the author intend his observations to apply only to boys (see paragraph 17, for example)?
3. In paragraph 23, are readers being addressed as "little wimps, little losers"? If so, are many readers likely to be offended?

WHAT ABOUT <u>YOUR</u> WRITING?

Dick Feagler writes with great humor, warmth, and thoughtfulness. He does so many hard things well that it's startling to find him committing a common grammatical error in pronoun agreement.

In paragraph 17, Feagler writes that he has decided to describe the horrendous ninth inning as "a kind of gift to any boy who might love baseball but find that despite this love, they are always standing out there praying nobody will hit one to them." Forget about the probably unconscious sexism that seems to assume that only boys love baseball and can profit from the author's insights. That's not grammar. The grammatical problem is that *boy* is singular and that *they* and *them* are plural. The writer needs to choose one or the other.

Singular	Plural
A kind of gift to any boy who might love baseball but find that . . . he is always standing out there praying nobody will hit one to him	A kind of gift to all boys who might love baseball but find that . . . they are always standing out there praying nobody will hit one to them.

It's easy enough to see why the error is so common. "Any boy" is grammatically singular but in meaning could refer to vast numbers. That gives us a reason for the error, but it's still an error. Watch out for similar errors:

Every homeowner is required to recycle their trash.

No one in the theater knew what they should expect.

Each business must meet their responsibilities to the community.

See pages 205–208 for related comments on sexist language.

A CULTURAL DIVORCE

Elizabeth Wong

Elizabeth Wong has written the plays *Letter to a Student Revolutionary*, *Kimchee and Chitlins*, *China Doll*, and *Punk Girls*. Wong's essay about her school days spectacularly avoids the danger of becoming sweetly sentimental about the past: classrooms, the innocence of children, the joys of family life (see pp. 218–219). After you finish this essay, consider whether it can be thought of as a story with an abrupt surprise ending or whether the surprise is anticipated earlier.

Words to check:

stoically (paragraph 1)	kowtow (6)
dissuade (2)	ideographs (7)
flanked (5)	pidgin (10)

1 It's still there, the Chinese school on Yale Street where my brother and I used to go. Despite the new coat of paint and the high wire fence, the school I knew 10 years ago remains remarkably, stoically the same.

2 Every day at 5 P.M., instead of playing with our fourth- and fifth-grade friends or sneaking out to the empty lot to hunt ghosts and animal bones, my brother and I had to go to Chinese school. No amount of kicking, screaming, or pleading could dissuade my mother, who was solidly determined to have us learn the language of our heritage.

3 Forcibly, she walked us the seven long, hilly blocks from our home to school, depositing our defiant tearful faces before the stern principal. My only memory of him is that he swayed on his heels like a palm tree, and he always clasped his impatient twitching hands behind his back. I recognized him

as a repressed maniacal child killer, and knew that if we ever saw his hands we'd be in big trouble.

4   We all sat in little chairs in an empty auditorium. The room smelled like Chinese medicine, an imported faraway mustiness. Like ancient mothballs or dirty closets. I hated that smell. I favored crisp new scents. Like the soft French perfume that my American teacher wore in public school.

5   There was a stage far to the right, flanked by an American flag and the flag of the Nationalist Republic of China, which was also red, white and blue but not as pretty.

6   Although the emphasis at the school was mainly language—speaking, reading, writing—the lessons always began with an exercise in politeness. With the entrance of the teacher, the best student would tap a bell and everyone would get up, kowtow, and chant, "Sing san ho," the phonetic for "How are you, teacher?"

7   Being ten years old, I had better things to learn than ideographs copied painstakingly in lines that ran right to left from the tip of a *moc but*, a real ink pen that had to be held in an awkward way if blotches were to be avoided. After all, I could do the multiplication tables, name the satellites of Mars, and write reports on "Little Women" and "Black Beauty." Nancy Drew, my favorite book heroine, never spoke Chinese.

8   The language was a source of embarrassment. More times than not, I had tried to disassociate myself from the nagging loud voice that followed me wherever I wandered in the nearby American supermarket outside China-town. The voice belonged to my grandmother, a fragile woman in her seven-ties who could outshout the best of the street vendors. Her humor was raunchy, her Chinese rhythmless, patternless. It was quick, it was loud, it was unbeautiful. It was not like the quiet, lilting romance of French or the gentle refinement of the American South. Chinese sounded pedestrian. Public.

9   In Chinatown, the comings and goings of hundreds of Chinese on their daily tasks sounded chaotic and frenzied. I did not want to be thought of as mad, as talking gibberish. When I spoke English, people nodded at me, smiled sweetly, said encouraging words. Even the people in my culture would cluck and say that I'd do well in life. "My, doesn't she move her lips fast," they would say, meaning that I'd be able to keep up with the world outside Chinatown.

10   My brother was even more fanatical than I about speaking English. He was especially hard on my mother, criticizing her, often cruelly, for her pidgin speech—smatterings of Chinese scattered like chop suey in her conversation. "It's not 'What it is,' Mom," he'd say in exasperation. "It's 'What is it, what is it, what is it!'" Sometimes Mom might leave out an occasional "the" or "a," or perhaps a verb of being. He would stop her in midsentence: "Say it again,

Mom. Say it right." When he tripped over his own tongue, he'd blame it on her: "See, Mom, it's all your fault. You set a bad example."

11   What infuriated my mother most was when my brother cornered her on her consonants, especially "r." My father had played a cruel joke on Mom by assigning her an American name that her tongue wouldn't allow her to say. No matter how hard she tried, "Ruth" always ended up "Luth" or "Roof."

12   After two years of writing with a *moc but* and reciting words with multiples of meanings, I finally was granted a cultural divorce. I was permitted to stop Chinese school.

13   I thought of myself as multicultural. I preferred tacos to egg rolls; I enjoyed Cinco de Mayo* more than Chinese New Year.

14   At last, I was one of you; I wasn't one of them.

15   Sadly, I still am.

WHAT DID THE WRITER SAY AND WHAT DID YOU THINK?

1. What is Wong's thesis? Does she state it directly? Does she need to?
2. What are the implications of the last sentence of this reading?
3. When the author was a child she hated speaking Chinese. Why?
4. What are Wong's current feelings about being forced to attend Chinese school?
5. What is the "cruel joke" of the author's mother's name?

HOW DID THE WRITER SAY IT?

1. What specific details does the author use to emphasize her childhood distaste for all that was Chinese and love for all that was American?
2. What does the phrase "a cultural divorce" mean?
3. How and where does Wong indicate that her childhood attitudes have changed?

WHAT ABOUT <u>YOUR</u> WRITING?

Once writers are ready to go beyond the obvious ingredients of grammar, mechanics, and organization, they frequently find themselves working hardest on specific details. That's what they should be doing. Writing that lacks effective specific details is almost always dull and sometimes unclear. Writing that uses effective specific details has energy, character, and conviction. Of course,

---

*May 5, a holiday celebrating the defeat of French troops in Mexico at the Battle of Puebla, 1862.

writers must generalize; a thesis statement is a generalization, after all. To a great extent, however, it's by specific details that the writing lives or dies. Without them, no matter how sensible or important or even brilliant the ideas, a paper is likely to perish from malnutrition.

In "A Cultural Divorce," Elizabeth Wong uses specific details to bring her subject to life. She does not settle for writing accurately but ploddingly, "I was proud of my American schooling and contemptuous of my Chinese schooling." Instead, she makes the same general point with specific details—and the writing becomes twice as interesting, twice as forceful, and twice as convincing: "After all, I could do the multiplication tables, name the satellites of Mars, and write reports on 'Little Women' and 'Black Beauty.' Nancy Drew, my favorite book heroine, never spoke Chinese." Wong does not tell us in general terms that her mother had trouble speaking English. Instead, we see Wong's mother unable to pronounce her own name, and we share some of the pain and embarrassment. We start to care, and we care intensely. And that's why specific details are so important.

SALVATION
Langston Hughes

Poet, playwright, short story writer, and essayist, Langston Hughes (1902–1967) is referred to by the *Encyclopedia Britannica* as "one of the foremost interpreters to the world of the black experience in the United States." Hughes achieved great popularity with readers of all races, and when he died an astonishing twenty-seven of his books were still in print. "Salvation," from the 1940 autobiographical volume *The Big Sea*, shows Hughes' great gift for treating essentially serious subjects with a mixture of sensitivity and humor.

Words to check:

revival (paragraph 1)	knickerbockered (11)
dire (3)	punctuated (14)
gnarled (4)	

1 I was saved from sin when I was going on thirteen. But not really saved. It happened like this. There was a big revival at my Auntie Reed's church. Every night for weeks there had been much preaching, singing, praying, and shouting, and some very hardened sinners had been brought to Christ, and the membership of the church had grown by leaps and bounds. Then just before

the revival ended, they held a special meeting for children, "to bring the young lambs to the fold." My aunt spoke of it for days ahead. That night I was escorted to the front row and placed on the mourners' bench with all the other young sinners, who had not yet been brought to Jesus.

2   My aunt told me that when you were saved you saw a light, and something happened to you inside! And Jesus came into your life! And God was with you from then on! She said you could see and hear and feel Jesus in your soul. I believed her. I have heard a great many old people say the same thing and it seemed to me they ought to know. So I sat there calmly in the hot, crowded church, waiting for Jesus to come to me.

3   The preacher preached a wonderful rhythmical sermon, all moans and shouts and lonely cries and dire pictures of hell, and then he sang a song about the ninety and nine safe in the fold, but one little lamb was left out in the cold. Then he said: "Won't you come? Won't you come to Jesus? Young lambs, won't you come?" And he held out his arms to all us young sinners there on the mourners' bench. And the little girls cried. And some of them jumped up and went to Jesus right away. But most of us just sat there.

4   A great many old people came and knelt around us and prayed, old women with jet-black faces and braided hair, old men with work-gnarled hands. And the church sang a song about the lower lights are burning, some poor sinners to be saved. And the whole building rocked with prayer and song.

5   Still I kept waiting to *see* Jesus.

6   Finally all the young people had gone to the altar and were saved, but one boy and me. He was a rounder's son named Westley. Westley and I were surrounded by sisters and deacons praying. It was very hot in the church, and getting late now. Finally Westley said to me in a whisper: "God damn! I'm tired o' sitting here. Let's get up and be saved." So he got up and was saved.

7   Then I was left all alone on the mourners' bench. My aunt came and knelt at my knees and cried, while prayers and songs swirled all around me in the little church. The whole congregation prayed for me alone, in a mighty wail of moans and voices. And I kept waiting serenely for Jesus, waiting, waiting—but he didn't come. I wanted to see him, but nothing happened to me. Nothing! I wanted something to happen to me, but nothing happened.

8   I heard the songs and the minister saying: "Why don't you come? My dear child, why don't you come to Jesus? Jesus is waiting for you. He wants you. Why don't you come? Sister Reed, what is this child's name?"

9   "Langston," my aunt sobbed.

10   "Langston, why don't you come? Why don't you come and be saved? Oh, Lamb of God! Why don't you come?"

11   Now it was really getting late. I began to be ashamed of myself, holding everything up so long. I began to wonder what God thought about Westley,

who certainly hadn't seen Jesus either, but who was now sitting proudly on the platform, swinging his knickerbockered legs and grinning down at me, surrounded by deacons and old women on their knees praying. God had not struck Westley dead for taking his name in vain or for lying in the temple. So I decided that maybe to save further trouble, I'd better lie, too, and say that Jesus had come, and get up and be saved.

12   So I got up.

13   Suddenly the whole room broke into a sea of shouting, as they saw me rise. Waves of rejoicing swept the place. Women leaped in the air. My aunt threw her arms around me. The minister took me by the hand and led me to the platform.

14   When things quieted down, in a hushed silence, punctuated by a few ecstatic "Amens," all the new young lambs were blessed in the name of God. Then joyous singing filled the room.

15   That night, for the last time in my life but one—for I was a big boy twelve years old—I cried. I cried, in bed alone, and couldn't stop. I buried my head under the quilts, but my aunt heard me. She woke up and told my uncle I was crying because the Holy Ghost had come into my life, and because I had seen Jesus. But I was really crying because I couldn't bear to tell her that I had lied, that I had deceived everybody in the church, that I hadn't seen Jesus, and that now I didn't believe there was a Jesus any more, since he didn't come to help me.

WHAT DID THE WRITER SAY AND WHAT DID YOU THINK?

1. What is the narrative point or thesis in "Salvation"?
2. Do you think that the adults were unfair in their pressures on the children? Why or why not?
3. How does the young Langston define "see"? Why, then, is he disappointed?
4. How is Westley's reaction different from Langston's?
5. Do you think that Hughes wants his essay to be read as a comment about adults' failure to remember the fears of childhood? Explain.

HOW DID THE WRITER SAY IT?

1. Why is Hughes' thesis implied rather than expressed directly?
2. In what order does Hughes present his narrative? Does this order create suspense for the reader? How?
3. Do you think the audience has to be acquainted with the concept of religious revivals in order to comprehend Hughes' narrative? If you think so, what details could support your answer?

4. How do the hymn lyrics contribute to the pressures the young Langston feels?

WHAT ABOUT <u>YOUR</u> WRITING?

Part of the appeal of "Salvation" is its awakening of memories. Reading about the author's childhood, readers return to their own childhoods and remember the relatives, the boredom, the illusions, the ideals. Everything starts coming back.

It's hard to beat nostalgia as subject matter for papers. The friendly trivia contests at parties, the popularity of games like "Trivial Pursuit," and the "Whatever Happened to . . ." and "Remember When?" features in newspapers and magazines, are only superficial signs of that appeal. In the midst of a world seemingly devoted to impermanence and the celebration of "future shock," many people find themselves drawn to keep in touch with, to keep faith with, their pasts.

The writer's age doesn't matter much with nostalgia. Our pasts may be different, but each of us has one. One person will remember Jackie Robinson and Joe DiMaggio, rationing during World War II, and "The Shadow" suspense program on radio. Another will remember the first showing of *Star Wars*, the tragic *Challenger* flight, and the attempted assassination of Presdent Reagan. There are recent and less recent memories, funny ones and tragic ones, memories to treasure and memories to fear—but no normal person ever lived without memories.

Nostalgia can work in almost any paper, but bear one warning in mind: Avoid oozing sentimentality. Don't make the mistake of assuming automatically that everything about the past was glorious and everything about the present terrible. With that warning, though, a nostalgic trip into your own past can often result in a surprisingly easy solution to the problem of being stuck for a subject.

FOUL SHOTS
Rogelio R. Gomez

As you read this narrative about an unforgettably nasty day in the writer's high school years, ask yourself if the thesis is ever explicitly stated, and if it has to do with young men, basketball, prejudice, the power of the past, or all of these together.

Words to check:

barrios (paragraph 2)	dictum (4)	coup (7)
sardonically (3)	reprisal (4)	retrospect (7)
acutely (3)	glib (5)	inherent (10)
cavalier (3)	quashed (6)	deft (11)
psyche (4)	fathomed (7)	

1 Now and then I can still see their faces, snickering and laughing, their eyes mocking me. And it bothers me that I should remember. Time and maturity should have diminished the pain, because the incident happened more than 20 years ago. Occasionally, however, a smug smile triggers the memory, and I think, "I should have done something." Some act of defiance could have killed and buried the memory of the incident. Now it's too late.

2 In 1969, I was a senior on the Luther Burbank High School basketball team. The school is on the south side of San Antonio, in one of the city's many barrios. After practice one day our coach announced that we were going to spend the following Saturday scrimmaging with the ball club from Winston Churchill High, located in the city's rich, white north side. After the basketball game, we were to select someone from the opposite team and "buddy up"—talk with him, have lunch with him and generally spend the day attempting friendship. By telling us that this experience would do both teams some good, I suspect our well-intentioned coach was thinking about the possible benefits of integration and of learning to appreciate the difference of other people. By integrating us with this more prosperous group, I think he was also trying to inspire us.

3 But my teammates and I smiled sardonically at one another, and our sneakers squeaked as we nervously rubbed them against the waxed hardwood floor of our gym. The prospect of a full day of unfavorable comparisons drew from us a collective groan. As "barrio boys," we were already acutely aware of the differences between us and them. Churchill meant "white" to us: It meant shiny new cars, two-story homes with fireplaces, pedigreed dogs and manicured hedges. In other words, everything that we did not have. Worse, traveling north meant putting up a front, to ourselves as well as to the Churchill team. We felt we had to pretend that we were cavalier about it all, tough guys who didn't care about "nothin'."

4 It's clear now that we entered the contest with negative images of ourselves. From childhood, we must have suspected something was inherently wrong with us. The evidence wrapped itself around our collective psyche like a noose. In elementary school, we were not allowed to speak Spanish. The bladed edge of a wooden ruler once came crashing down on my knuckles for violating this dictum. By high school, however, policies had changed, and we

could speak Spanish without fear of physical reprisal. Still, speaking our language before whites brought on spasms of shame—for the supposed inferiority of our language and culture—and guilt at feeling shame. That mixture of emotions fueled our burning sense of inferiority.

5   After all, our mothers in no way resembled the glamorized models of American TV mothers—Donna Reed baking cookies in high heels. My mother's hands were rough and chafed, her wardrobe drab and worn. And my father was preoccupied with making ends meet. His silence starkly contrasted with the glib counsel Jim Anderson offered in "Father Knows Best." And where the Beaver worried about trying to understand some difficult homework assignment, for me it was an altogether different horror, when I was told by my elementary school principal that I did not have the ability to learn.

6   After I failed to pass the first grade, my report card read that I had a "learning disability." What shame and disillusion it brought my parents! To have carried their dream of a better life from Mexico to America, only to have their hopes quashed by having their only son branded inadequate. And so somewhere during my schooling I assumed that saying I had a "learning disability" was just another way of saying that I was "retarded." School administrators didn't care that I could not speak English.

7   As teen-agers, of course, my Mexican-American friends and I did not consciously understand why we felt inferior. But we might have understood if we had fathomed our desperate need to trounce Churchill. We viewed the prospect of beating a white, northside squad as a particularly fine coup. The match was clearly racial, our need to succeed born of a defiance against prejudice. I see now that we used the basketball court to prove our "blood." And who better to confirm us, if not those whom we considered better? In retrospect, I realize the only thing confirmed that day was that we saw ourselves as negatively as they did.

8   After we won the morning scrimmage, both teams were led from the gym into an empty room where everyone sat on a shiny linoleum floor. We were supposed to mingle—rub the colors together. But the teams sat separately, our backs against concrete walls. We faced one another like enemies, the empty floor between us a no man's land. As the coaches walked away, one reminded us to share lunch. God! The mere thought of offering them a taco from our brown bags when they had refrigerated deli lunches horrified us.

9   Then one of their players tossed a bag of Fritos at us. It slid across the slippery floor and stopped in the center of the room. With hearts beating anxiously, we Chicanos stared at the bag as the boy said with a sneer, "Y'all probably like 'em"—the "Frito Bandito" commercial being popular then. And we could see them, smiling at each other, giggling, jabbing their elbows into

one another's ribs at the joke. The bag seemed to grow before our eyes like a monstrous symbol of inferiority.

10   We won the afternoon basketball game as well. But winning had accomplished nothing. Though we had wanted to, we couldn't change their perception of us. It seems, in fact, that defeating them made them meaner. Looking back, I feel these young men needed to put us "in our place," to reaffirm the power they felt we had threatened. I think, moreover, that they felt justified, not only because of their inherent sense of superiority, but because our failure to respond to their insult underscored our worthlessness in their eyes.

11   Two decades later, the memory of their gloating lives on in me. When a white person is discourteous, I find myself wondering what I should do, and afterward, if I've done the right thing. Sometimes I argue when a deft comment would suffice. Then I reprimand myself, for I am no longer a boy. But my impulse to argue bears witness to my ghosts. For, invariably, whenever I feel insulted I'm reminded of that day at Churchill High. And whenever the past encroaches upon the present, I see myself rising boldly, stepping proudly across the years and crushing, underfoot, a silly bag of Fritos.

WHAT DID THE WRITER SAY AND WHAT DID YOU THINK?

1. Explain why tossing the bag of Fritos to the "barrio boys" is an insult.
2. Why does the author say the memory of the insult persists after "more than 20 years"? How has the memory adversely affected the author as an adult?
3. Comment on the meaning or meanings of the title.
4. How, specifically, do Anglos in the essay stereotype Mexican-Americans? Is there any evidence that Mexican-Americans do the same to Anglos?
5. "The road to hell is paved with good intentions." The coaches were apparently trying to foster better relations and only made things worse. What might they have done differently?

HOW DID THE WRITER SAY IT?

1. Why is so much background information necessary before the heart of the narration—the visit to the "north side" school—can begin?
2. What purpose is served by bringing up the diagnosis of a learning disability in paragraph 6?
3. In the last words of this essay, the author refers to the bag of Fritos as "silly." How does that word choice reflect or not reflect his current attitude?

WHAT ABOUT <u>YOUR</u> WRITING?

Many writers in search of a good subject might do well to bear in mind John F. Kennedy's reputed comment about some questionable practices of his political opponents: "Don't get mad. Get even."

Sometime when your mind is a blank and you start to believe that you have nothing to write about, you might consider revenge. Nobody would suggest that revenge is a noble emotion, but it has led to some excellent writing. In "Foul Shots," Rogelio R. Gomez presents some serious reflections on complex issues, but he is also settling old scores, getting his own back, taking revenge for twenty-year-old insults.

Think about some of your own ancient grudges as possible subjects. (They don't all need to be ancient by any means, but you may still be too overwrought by an event that happened yesterday to write about it with sufficient perspective.) Think about prejudice, romantic betrayals, snobbish put-downs, and brush-offs. Think about boring sermons and lectures. Think about the times you forced yourself or were forced by others to be polite to undeserving toads. Think about high-school bullies and in-crowds. Think about unjust accusations, vicious gossip, and bad advice. Then don't get mad. Start writing and get even.

A CRIME OF COMPASSION
Barbara Huttmann

Barbara Huttmann, a medical professional, has written a number of articles and books, among them *Code Blue: A Nurse's True-Life Story* (1982). In "A Crime of Compassion," originally published in *Newsweek*, Huttmann uses personal and professional experience to express her strongly held convictions on a subject of continuing and heated controversy. As you read, notice how even as a passionate advocate of her position, Huttmann lets the powerful story of Mac's life and death do most of the preaching for her.

Words to check:
resuscitate (paragraph 3)	arrogant (11)
haggard (5)	imperative (11)
lucid (10)	pallor (15)

1 "Murderer," a man shouted. "God help patients who get *you* for a nurse."

2 "What gives you the right to play God?" another one asked.

3 It was the Phil Donahue show where the guest is a fatted calf and the audience a 200-strong flock of vultures hungering to pick up the bones. I had told them about Mac, one of my favorite cancer patients. "We resuscitated him fifty-two times in just one month. I refused to resuscitate him again. I simply sat there and held his hand while he died."

4 There wasn't time to explain that Mac was a young, witty, macho cop who walked into the hospital with thirty-two pounds of attack equipment, looking as if he could single-handedly protect the whole city, if not the entire state. "Can't get rid of this cough," he said. Otherwise, he felt great.

5 Before the day was over, tests confirmed that he had lung cancer. And before the year was over, I loved him, his wife, Maura, and their three kids as if they were my own. All the nurses loved him. And we all battled his disease for six months without ever giving death a thought. Six months isn't such a long time in the whole scheme of things, but it was long enough to see him lose his youth, his wit, his macho, his hair, his bowel and bladder control, his sense of taste and smell, and his ability to do the slightest thing for himself. It was also long enough to watch Maura's transformation from a young woman into a haggard, beaten old lady.

6 When Mac had wasted away to a 60-pound skeleton kept alive by liquid food we poured down a tube, IV solutions we dripped into his veins, and oxygen we piped to a mask on his face, he begged us: "Mercy . . . for God's sake, please just let me go."

7 The first time he stopped breathing, the nurse pushed the button that calls a "code blue" throughout the hospital and sends a team rushing to resuscitate the patient. Each time he stopped breathing, sometimes two or three times in one day, the code team came again. The doctors and technicians worked their miracles and walked away. The nurses stayed to wipe the saliva that drooled from his mouth, irrigate the big craters of bedsores that covered his hips, suction the lung fluids that threatened to drown him, clean the feces that burned his skin like lye, pour the liquid food down the tube attached to his stomach, put pillows between his knees to ease the bone-on-bone pain, turn him every hour to keep the bedsores from getting worse, and change his gown and linen every two hours to keep him from being soaked in perspiration.

8 At night I went home and tried to scrub away the smell of decaying flesh that seemed woven into the fabric of my uniform. It was in my hair, the upholstery of my car—there was no washing it away. And every night I prayed that his agonized eyes would never again plead with me to let him die.

9 Every morning I asked the doctor for a "no code" order. Without that order, we had to resuscitate every patient who stopped breathing. His doctor was one of the several who believe we must extend life as long as we have the means and knowledge to do it. To not do it is to be liable for negligence, at least in the eyes of many people, including some nurses. I thought about what it would be like to stand before a judge, accused of murder, if Mac stopped breathing and I didn't call a code.

10 And after the fifty-second code, when Mac was still lucid enough to beg for death again, and Maura was crumbled in my arms again, and when no amount of pain medication stilled his moaning and agony, I wondered about a spiritual judge. Was all this misery and suffering supposed to be building character or infusing us all with the sense of humility that comes from impotence?

11 Had we, the whole medical community, become so arrogant that we believed in the illusion of salvation through science? Had we become so self-righteous that we thought meddling in God's work was our duty, our moral imperative, and our legal obligation? Did we really believe that we had the right to force "life" on a suffering man who had begged for the right to die?

12 Such questions haunted me more than ever early one morning when Maura went home to change her clothes and I was bathing Mac. He had been still for so long, I thought he at last had the blessed relief of coma. Then he opened his eyes and moaned, "Pain . . . no more . . . Barbara . . . do something . . . God, let me go."

13 The desperation in the eyes and voice riddled me with guilt. "I'll stop," I told him as I injected the pain medication.

14 I sat on the bed and held Mac's hands in mine. He pressed his bony fingers against my hand and muttered, "Thanks." Then there was the one soft sigh and I felt his hands go cold in mine. "Mac?" I whispered, as I waited for his chest to rise and fall again.

15 A clutch of panic banded my chest, drew my finger to the code button, urged me to do something, anything . . . but sit there alone with death. I kept one finger on the button, without pressing it, as a waxen pallor slowly transformed his face from person to empty shell. Nothing I've ever done in my forty-seven years has taken so much effort as it took not to press that code button.

16 Eventually, when I was as sure as I could be that the code team would fail to bring him back, I entered the legal twilight zone and pushed the button. The team tried. And while they were trying, Maura walked in the room and shrieked, "No . . . don't let them do this to him . . . for God's sake . . . please, no more."

17   Cradling her in my arms was like cradling myself, Mac, and all those patients and nurses who had been in this place before who do the best they can in a death-denying society.

18   So a TV audience accused me of murder. Perhaps I am guilty. If a doctor had written a no-code order, which is the only *legal* alternative, would he have felt any less guilty? Until there is legislation making it a criminal act to code a patient who has requested the right to die, we will all of us risk the same fate as Mac. For whatever reason, we developed the means to prolong life, and now we are forced to use it. We do not have the right to die.

WHAT DID THE WRITER SAY AND WHAT DID YOU THINK?

1. Define "code blue." Define "no-code."
2. Explain the meaning of the last sentence: "We do not have the right to die."
3. A member of a television audience attacks the author by asking, "What gives you the right to play God?" In paragraph 11, however, the author complains about hospitals "meddling in God's work." Explain what each person means. Which do you think has the better case?
4. What, specifically, is the author advocating? Does she believe in giving a lethal injection to any sick person who requests one?

HOW DID THE WRITER SAY IT?

1. Why bother at the beginning and end of the essay with describing the author's appearance on a television talk show? Would anything be lost by eliminating the description?
2. How does the title suggest the author's thesis? Of what common phrase is it a variation?
3. Why is it necessary to give so many specific details about the physical horrors undergone by the patient?

WHAT ABOUT <u>YOUR</u> WRITING?

We write about what we know and what means something to us. That's natural and sensible, but with controversial material it can lead the reader to worry about ingrained bias. Is the writer a trustworthy observer, or have the writer's views been unduly shaped by special influences and concerns?

In "A Crime of Compassion," for example, we see that Barbara Huttmann is a medical professional who ministers to terminally ill patients who plead for death. Huttmann has agonizingly had to follow the rules rather than the dictates of her heart or conscience. That is surely how she became so concerned with her subject. That is why she knows so much about it. That is why she is so fiercely in favor of "the right to die." But has her closeness to the sweat and the screams and her own pain interfered with her ability to present her case as fairly and reasonably as warranted by complex life and death issues?

The problem is universal. A student paper advocating the elimination of grades pushes the issues of human dignity and human rights, but the reader suspects personal bias: the student is having difficulty in physics and doesn't want to flunk. A weapons manufacturer presents a closely reasoned argument against a new piece of gun control legislation; solid as the argument may be, the reader hesitates to endorse it, speculating that the manufacturer may be worried more about personal income than about public safety.

Huttmann's approach is almost certainly the best. State right out whatever your personal involvement may be, and state it early. Get that out of the way, and then press your strong points for all they're worth.

After acknowledging your involvement, turn it to your advantage, if you can; the nightmare of some deaths is more than a mere abstraction for Huttmann. The student who wants to eliminate grades might as well grant at the outset any elements of pure self-interest—the danger of a poor grade in physics or the tensions of parental nagging, for example. With these elements out of the way, the student can proceed and perhaps even suggest that only a student can have an authentic realization of the psychological damage that the grading system can do.

Don't cover up or conceal. An honest acknowledgement of personal involvement will earn an honest reader's respect.

Description

Description is nothing new. You undoubtedly noted the descriptions you encountered in the previous narration chapter. Narrative writing draws much of its life from descriptive details. In "Foul Shots" when Rogelio R. Gomez wrote "My mother's hands were rough and chafed, her wardrobe drab and worn," and in "Salvation" when Langston Hughes wrote of a friend ". . . swinging his knickerbockered legs and grinning down at me, surrounded by deacons and old women on their knees praying," these authors were using descriptive details to help the reader see a specific image. If you have already written a narrative essay, you, too, probably relied on description to help bring the narration to life. In your essays to come, you will also find that description is essential. Description is not new, but devoting an entire paper to it is new and demands separate consideration.

Some descriptions can be completely *objective:* they can describe the size and color of measles spots, the size and speed of a missile. Objective descriptions make no judgments about the ugliness of the spots or the morality of the missile. Ordinarily intended to meet special needs, objective descriptions are not within the province of this chapter.

The *impressionistic* or *interpretive* description paper is our basic concern. The writer of this paper uses description to convey an attitude. Any objective description of measles spots, for instance, is subordinate here to convincing the reader of the ugliness or triviality or seriousness of the spots.

Rules, guidelines, and handy hints are of less practical value than usual when writing the comparatively freewheeling description paper. Only three major points need to be stressed, and none of them is especially restrictive.

Emotional Appeal

Description papers tend to rely more than others on a direct appeal to the reader's emotions. A description of a room will more probably have a thesis like *The room was frightening* than *The room was big*. To make their emotional appeal, description papers also tend to concentrate more than others on using colorful language. Such hard-to-pin-down elements as mood and tone tend to be major concerns. These generalizations don't apply to all description papers, and they certainly shouldn't be interpreted as implying that other patterns of writing can't or shouldn't appeal to emotions, use colorful language, and so on. As a whole, however, good description papers do receive praise more for their insight and sensitivity than for their masterful logic.

Nobody can teach you how to make your writing tingle with deep perceptions. Insight and sensitivity come from within. It might help, however, to suggest a few approaches that can give your writing a push in the right direction toward attaining the lively emotional appeal of good description.

Try a Deliberately Unconventional Thesis

If a room would strike ninety-nine people out of a hundred as ugly, try pointing out its hidden beauties. If everyone agrees that a young woman is painfully shy, try showing that she really has a superiority complex. Don't lie and don't attempt to support a thesis you believe is idiotic; do see if you can make a case for an unconventional idea.

Show Your Powers of Observation by Stressing Specific Details

Virtually all good writing uses specifics, lots of them. A description paper absolutely depends on them. Try to take a seemingly trivial detail and show its surprising relevancy. Demonstrate that you had the ability to notice the detail in the first place and then to have its significance register on your mind. If you write a paper attempting to show that a certain man pays no attention to his appearance, don't just say that he looks messy; bring up the bread crumbs in his moustache and the toe protruding through the hole in his tennis sneaker. Too trivial? Not at all. As long as the details support the thesis, they add life to the paper.

Use Specific Language

Another principle of most good writing is of particular importance in description. The effect of a specific detail can be weakened if the language used to present the detail is not itself specific. *There were bread crumbs in his mustache* shows observation of specific details. *Forgotten bread crumbs, slowly hardening in his mustache, had the same revolting inappropriateness as mustard stains on a silk blouse* shows observation of specific details dramatized by specific language.

Stress the Psychological Impact of What You Describe

A good description will be accurate, but it will be exciting, too. Your description of a dusty old room won't convey a sense of immediacy by itemizing the locations of all the clumps of dust; your reader should have not only a picture of what the room looks like but also a strong sense of how depressed or indignant or philosophical the room made you feel.

So much for emotional appeal.

Organization

Choose an appropriate organizing principle, and stick to it. Some authorities suggest that in describing the appearance of a person, the writer might start with the head and go down to the toes (or vice versa). In describing a landscape, the writer might start with objects farthest away and progress to those closest. Many writers should be able to do better. The authorities want to achieve order but sometimes seem to invite rigidity.

Still, they have a case, and cautious agreement with them is the only reasonable course. Nobody wants rigidity, but chaos is even worse. Certainly, a writer needs enough of a predetermined organizing principle to decide which descriptive details come first and which come last. It's easy to understand hesitation about the cut-and-dried mathematics of top-to-bottom or far-to-near, but not all the formulas need to be that definite. Some description papers may be organized on a looser principle like attractive features/unattractive features, first impressions/second impressions, impact on senses like sight, touch, and hearing. Structure of some kind is necessary. In addition, even the top-to-bottom and far-to-near principles seldom turn out to be as dreary as they sound. A good writer, after all, doesn't ordinarily make formal announcements like "moving down from the forehead, I shall now discuss the nose" or "The next closest object is . . ." Don't adopt an organizing principle that makes a prisoner of you and your reader, but do adopt a principle. There's freedom of choice, but you have to make a choice.

Persuasive Principle

The description paper must commit itself to the discipline of the persuasive principle. With all this material on freedom and emotional appeal, this last point is particularly important. It's precisely because of the relatively free-form nature of much descriptive writing that the persuasive principle has to be insisted on so strongly. Freedom and sloppiness are not the same. Thesis and support of thesis are the main ingredients for holding the description paper together. Without a thesis, a process paper (see Chapter 5) can still trace a process. Without a thesis, a description paper goes off in all directions and disintegrates into a shapeless mass. It doesn't describe; it simply takes inventory. Without a thesis, a description paper has no backbone and, like a body without a backbone, has no freedom to do or be anything.

There's not much this book can say about the general nature of the persuasive principle that it hasn't already said. Throughout much of Chapter 1, the book showed how a paper on education was narrowed down to a description of Professor X with the thesis "Professor X is an incompetent teacher." On page 11, a sample opening paragraph showed how such a paper might begin. A description paper doesn't merely benefit from a thesis. It needs one in order to exist.

WRITING SUGGESTIONS FOR DESCRIPTION THEMES

Some of the suggested topics that follow are more specific than usual. Don't feel hemmed in. Use them only as starting points for your own ideas. Notice that many topics can be treated in two different ways. You can write a description of a general or composite type of airline flight attendant or lifeguard or hospital waiting room, having no one specific person, place, or thing in mind; you can also write a description of an *individual* person, place, or thing: flight attendant Susan Early, lifeguard John Braun, the waiting room at St. Luke's.

1. Homeless people
2. Know-it-all car mechanics
3. Traffic jams
4. Lifeguards
5. Spoiled children
6. Haunted houses
7. People eating lobster or corn on the cob
8. Thunderstorms
9. Dentists
10. Animals in the zoo
11. Bus drivers

12. Airline flight attendants
13. Video game fanatics
14. Normally busy places, now deserted
15. People with speech impediments
16. Disadvantaged children
17. Drunks
18. Hospital waiting rooms
19. The contents of a pocketbook
20. Overcommercialized tourist attractions
21. Housing developments
22. Amusement parks
23. Vans or campers
24. Sports stadiums

THE GLORIOUS FOURTH

Allen Robertson (student)

Thesis: When I was a kid, the Fourth of July was the best holiday there was.

    I. Daytime
       A. Playing games
       B. Lying in the hammock

   II. Evening
       A. Barbecuing
       B. Playing with sparklers
       C. Eating dinner

  III. Night
       A. Waiting for the fireworks
       B. Watching fireworks

Conclusion: I still try to hold on to the beauty and excitement that was the
           Fourth of July.

When I was a kid, the Fourth of July was the best holiday there was. It was better than Easter or Christmas because I didn't have to waste any of the day in church. It was better than Thanksgiving because there was more to do. And it was better than a birthday because absolutely everybody was celebrating with me.

    We always spent the sunlit half of the day doing very little. Maybe we would run through the sprinkler, or have a water fight, or play catch in the street, or maybe we'd just lie in the hammock and watch the green leaves and the gold sunshine and the blue shadows changing shape above our heads.

Around five o'clock, Dad would light the barbecue, and the tingly smoke would creep out to wherever my brothers and I were playing. We'd start feeling hungry and wander on home. To keep us out of his way while he cooked the spicy, smoky barbecued chicken, Dad would give us sparklers. He'd light the ends of these mysterious gray metal sticks with his cigarette lighter. We watched impatiently, waiting for them to burst into a waterfall of golden sparks that always seemed to last just five seconds short of long enough.

One or more of us always tried to sneak a sparkler into the kitchen to share with Mom, but she always chased us out, sending us off to clean up for dinner. We moved pretty fast when we heard the word dinner, because there was never anything better than a plate filled with Dad's barbecued chicken and Mom's once-a-year-and-I-only-do-it-because-I-love-you potato salad.

After dinner, when the dishes were cleaned up and put away, and the sky was getting dark and the bugs were coming out, and just when we kids were starting to worry that we might miss the main event, Mom and Dad would pile us into the car. Like all the other families from our neighborhood, we drove out to the top of the hill overlooking the town. We kids climbed up on the roof of the car for the best possible view, and Mom and Dad handed up cookies and lemonade when they weren't talking with old friends. Then, as the night got darker and quieter, we'd wait for the fireworks.

When the fireworks started and everyone else oohed and aahed, I would lie on my back on the top of the car, on the top of the world, and try to hang on to all the beauty and excitement. I knew they couldn't last, not any more than the sparks that made the fireworks could, but I still tried to hang on.

WINSTEAD'S BEST BURGERS

Sarah Bryan Miller

Sarah Bryan Miller lets a new generation in on an old pleasure by celebrating in mouth-watering detail the continuing excellence of a Kansas City institution.

Words to check:

colloquially
  (paragraph 3)
Elysian (3)

extraneous (4)
aesthetic (5)
in situ (5)

repast (7)
brusque (8)

1   They do not sell their hamburgers by the billion. You cannot "supersize" your meal. They are a household word only in Kansas City. But Calvin Trillin was right:[1] Winstead's has the world's best hamburgers.

2   Mr. Trillin, the famed foodie, made his claim nearly 30 years ago, but time has not diminished its essential truth. Winstead's makes a hamburger (or, more properly, steakburger) that is blessedly pure in its simplicity: Fresh-ground high-quality lean beef—no additives!—is grilled, greaselessly, and placed upon a plain toasted bun. You may choose between a single ($1.65), a double ($2.75) or a triple ($3.25), cheese and lettuce extra; the patties are thin, the double is recommended. The steakburger does not come automatically loaded with slop, but ask and you shall receive. It is served half-wrapped in paper, the better to consume it without soiling one's hands, upon a sturdy china plate.

3   But the steakburger is not quite complete without its perfect complement, "the exclusive Winstead drink you eat with a spoon." Known officially as the "special chocolate malt" and colloquially as a "frosty"—a name that predates the Wendy's chain by a generation or two—the frosty is thick, chocolaty and delicious. Take a bite of steakburger; follow it with a spoonful of frosty, alternating the salty and textured with the sweet and smooth. The cholesterol police will swoon, but the sensation is Elysian.

4   The menu is limited, and not much changed since Winstead's opened in 1940. They now serve breakfast, and you can get what my 11-year-old daughter, a connoisseur of fast food, assures me is the best grilled cheese sandwich of her ample experience. The french fries, served in a boat-shaped china dish, are respectable and the onion rings highly thought of by those who cherish such things; the dessert menu seems extraneous to one in post-frosty bliss. Green stuff has also been added to the menu, but going to Winstead's and ordering a salad is like going to a microbrewery and ordering a Coke.

5   Winstead's original restaurant, topped by its distinctive art deco spire, sits just north of the Country Club Plaza and conveniently near another of Kansas City's centers of aesthetic excellence, the Nelson-Atkins art gallery. When Winstead's first opened, the brainchild of Katherine Winstead and her sister and brother-in-law, Nelle and Gordon Montgomery, the emphasis was on the drive-in. Drivers would pull into empty spaces, flash their lights

---

[1] Calvin Trillin's many articles about food have been collected in the books *American Fried, Alice, Let's Eat,* and *Third Helpings.* Trillin fans can feast on all three books in *The Tummy Trilogy* (1994).

for service, and carhops would come up and take their orders, which were then consumed in situ. "When it opened, it immediately became a gathering spot," recalls my father, Tom Miller, a third-generation Kansas Citian who as a student at nearby Southwest High School was present at the creation.

6   "We went on 'good-time' dates—a group of us would go to a movie and sit in the cheaper seats; then we'd head over to Winstead's and get a steak-burger and a frosty. It was 'see and be seen'; people would go from car to car and visit, and then everybody would pull out with a grand squeal of tires. During the war, if you were lucky enough to get a furlough, the first thing you did was head for Winstead's. In spite of the wartime regulations, they kept up the quality."

7   I was introduced to the joy of frosties at the age of eight months, I am reliably informed, and never looked back; throughout childhood, a meal at Winstead's was a special treat, invariably consumed in the car, a repast dispensed from a metal tray hanging on the driver's side window. When my father decided that we would not partake of a single hamburger on a marathon car trip to and from California—just to prove that it could be done, and, perhaps, from a bit of simple cussedness—we marked the end of our journey with a celebratory feast at Winstead's. "And during the years we lived in Chicago," notes my father, who returned to Kansas City from his northern exile upon taking early retirement, "we always came to Winstead's when we were back on visits—and we always saw somebody we knew."

8   The original restaurant (Winstead's is now a chain, with a total of 12 outlets; the quality is most reliable at the flagship) has been remodeled and enlarged; the yellow tile exterior remains, along with the spire. The old convenience of the drive-in is gone, replaced by an office building and the new convenience of a drive-through window. But the current owners, the Haddad Restaurant Group, have kept standards up. The feel of the place is much the same, from the booths to the deco light fixtures; the juke box still offers Glenn Miller, albeit on compact disk. The lunchtime crowd includes high school kids, older folks (my father, true to form, spots a classmate), construction workers, mothers with toddlers. The waitresses still wear pastel uniform dresses with white trim and little caps, and they are still brusque and prone to wisecracking.

9   Connie Llamas started as a carhop at the age of 18; she's been at Winstead's for 25 years. "I had more fun at the curb; you could flirt with the boys. But the place is pretty much the same. It just got bigger. People who retired and moved away come back on vacations—they think Winstead's is the place to be. And it is."

WHAT DID THE WRITER SAY AND WHAT DID YOU THINK?

1. In addition to the hamburgers, what menu items make Winstead's so outstanding?
2. Is the author's enthusiasm about the food limited in any way?
3. What does Winstead's offer beyond excellent food?
4. Are there any suggestions that Winstead's, good as it is, may no longer be all that it used to be?

HOW DID THE WRITER SAY IT?

1. Who are the "cholesterol police" in paragraph 3?
2. Why is Chicago described as a place of "northern exile" in paragraph 7?
3. How does the author make a reference to the Nelson-Atkins art gallery relevant to the rest of the essay?

WHAT ABOUT YOUR WRITING?

An allusion is a reference, usually brief and often indirect, to a character, event, activity, work of art, and so on, distinct from what is being discussed. In paragraph 2 of Sarah Bryan Miller's hymn of praise to Winstead's, Miller alludes to the New Testament when she writes, "The steakburger does not come automatically loaded with slop, but ask and you shall receive." In the next paragraph, she alludes to the Elysian Fields, the paradise of Greek mythology, to describe the combined taste of a burger and frosty. These references purposefully suggest an amusing connection between true divinity and the truly divine food at Winstead's. Well-managed allusions, employed sparingly—don't use them for mere showing off—can add depth to a writer's style and thought. They can reveal unsuspected resemblances, relate unfamiliar material to material the reader knows, make abstract subjects seem more specific, and help establish confidence in a writer's range of knowledge. You don't need to be an expert in any particular field to add an occasional allusion to your writing; anyone with ordinary education and some experience of life has a rich fund on which to draw:

Television: My father reminds me of Dan Rather. Whenever I see him, he's talking.

History: The teacher gave unannounced quizzes throughout the term. Every week was another Pearl Harbor.

Movies: The stranger had Antonio Banderas eyes, a Tom Hanks smile, and a Woody Allen physique.

Famous quotes: It's true that nothing is more powerful than an idea whose time has come, but saving the environment with electric cars is an idea whose time has gone.

Sports: The administration has given up. Its game plan can be summed up in one word: Punt.

Literature: The lawyers indicated at first that we would be entitled to a beautiful tax deduction. Then they told us about Catch-22.

Advertisements: The senator can't help being embarrassed. He hasn't exactly broken the law, but he has surely been discovered to have a bad case of ring around the collar.

SAY NOW, THAT WAS MILO

Cheryl Heckler-Feltz

Cheryl Heckler-Feltz writes for the New York Times Syndicate, usually on the subjects of women and religion. She also co-authored *The Carpenter's Apprentice: The Spiritual Biography of Jimmy Carter* (1996). Here she writes a touching description of Milo Mailer, a "town character," with some reflections on town characters in general.

Words to check:

marginalized (paragraph 15)   irascible (17)   societal (16)

1   I was walking down Main St. of our little town one day several years ago when Milo Mailer came lumbering out of the alley right behind the bank.

2   "Say now," he said. "What kind of doctor are you?"

3   I was dressed in blue jeans and a sweatshirt, and he was a confused, harmless old man. "I'm not a doctor. I'm Cheryl," I said.

4   "Squirrel? What kind of name is that?"

5   "Not squirrel. Cher-ill."

6   "Oh. Well, where you headed?"

7   This began one of the most colorful and memorable relationships I've ever had, and I'm ashamed to say that in the early days I spent so much time thinking Milo would never go away that I had no appreciation for him.

8   I never really felt we were part of the same conversation. He rambled in a whiny, nasally voice, and I tried to keep pace. His sentences always started

abruptly with "Say now," and to the day Milo died, I had no evidence that he knew my real name.

9   "Say now, can you wind this pocket watch for me?"

10 "Sure, Milo."

11 "Say now, who is your husband, and what does he do?"

12 "He's Glenn. He's a psychologist."

13 "Say now, could he fix my back?"

14 "No, Milo."

15 In larger cities they are the marginalized, the powerless, the homeless, but in smaller communities they can be elevated to the rank of "town character," and as best I can tell, Milo was a classic.

16 To be a town character you have to have an odd name, a very crooked nose and absolutely no use for societal norms regarding what you wear or how often you shower. You prefer the downtown area for the distraction it provides in the form of passing motorists and old newspapers.

17 You ramble but don't hallucinate. You are irascible but not violent. You know which crew at the fire department fries up the best sidemeat, and every police officer and church secretary in the city has given you a ride home sometime this year.

18 "Poor" becomes a permanent part of your name when you are out of ear shot.

19 "Poor Milo," women inevitably asked as they passed him on the street. "Does anyone take care of him?"

20 As a town character, you have great fondness for one particular piece of clothing, like a flannel shirt or a frayed VFW cap. For Milo, it was the long denim apron that hung around his neck, never got tied in the back and draped all the way to his ankles.

21 Sometimes he wore jeans. Sometimes work clothes, but it was his apron, his ridiculous winter hats and his grating voice that distinguished him.

22 Unlike Blanche DuBois,* Milo never depended on the kindness of strangers. He knew his mark for every day of the week. The Presbyterian women met Tuesday mornings and would save him doughnuts. The Lutheran women met for lunch on Thursday and saved him cookies. He could get a free copy of yesterday's paper from Mr. Carmazzi at the newsstand, and every bank teller in town handed him at least three free calendars every single year in what they called "the Milo Ritual."

23 He'd walk into the bank lobby and select a teller he hadn't seen lately.

24 "Say now, Ma'am, do you have calendars left?"

---

*Character in *A Streetcar Named Desire* (1947) by Tennessee Williams.

25   "Yes, Mr. Mailer, I have one right here for you."

26   He'd thank her and lumber away, getting just outside the door before someone—a teller, a secretary or even a customer—would ask, "What does he do with all of them?"

27   There are unwritten rules of interacting with these characters. Children walking downtown alone naturally avoided Milo. In groups they mocked him—hurting only themselves, incidentally, because to his own benefit, Milo Mailer was oblivious to societal disdain. It was my favorite thing about him.

28   "He's not so creepy once you get to know him," my daughter said. "I think he knows more than he lets on."

29   Perhaps the most important rule about town characters is that we are more comfortable talking to them when someone has taught us how.

30   My first lesson came at the hand of my father when I was no more than 10. We were downtown running errands when he stopped abruptly on the street corner to talk to the most hideous man I thought I'd ever see in person.

31   My father's 6-foot frame and broad farmer's shoulders towered over the hunched, painfully thin figure of Poor Bobby. It was an absurd picture—until I saw the gentleness shared by these two men.

32   "Why did you give him money?" I asked my father later.

33   "Because it was the right thing to do," he said. "Life can fall apart for anyone." (As I watched my father struggle unsuccessfully with the instability of his own health and lifestyle in his final years, I thought often of this comment.)

34   My most memorable Milo moment happened in church. He lumbered in during the first hymn, and then walked up and down the aisle looking for just the right seat. My son and I waved to him, and Milo came and sat beside me. He didn't seem very interested in the service, but Milo knew there was a potluck dinner after church.

35   During the final hymn, a couple in our congregation walked toward the altar with a request for prayers. Ron was dying of cancer. The treatments had failed. Joyce was about to become a widow, and everyone knew it. I nearly choked on my own tears. My husband quietly handed me his handkerchief, but Milo, in his absurdity and innocence reached over and roughly patted my cheek.

36   God's comic relief, I thought. Milo wants to see if these tears are real.

37   But when I looked at him, his eyes revealed clarity and warmth and an element I had never seen there before—understanding.

38   "She's your friend, and her husband's dying." His voice was gentle and pleasant, and I wondered who this man was standing beside me. His nose even seemed a little straighter.

39   I nodded, and Milo put his arm around me. "Say now, but you are okay kid, and I'm really sorry you're sad." I was stunned that he was capable of such a normal, appropriate comment.

40   As the final hymn ended I turned to ask him a question, but Milo was zipping down the aisle wanting to be the first in line for the potluck. In the most grating, whiny voice, he belted out, "Say now, Mr. Michael, do you have any extra potatoes from your garden I could have?"

41   Several months later we were sitting in church when we learned that Milo was in the hospital and not expected to live through the week. In fact, he died that very afternoon—about the same time I arrived at the hospital to see him.

42   As I rounded the corner to his room, I found the circuit court judge, the hospital president, and the mayor standing in the hallway, staring at the floor and quietly comforting each other with their favorite Milo stories.

43   "When I ran for office, I swear to God Milo was the only voter in this city who actually asked me why I was running and what I hoped to achieve," the mayor said. "My wife heard that and said, 'Now who are the oddballs in this town, Sam?'"

44   The judge spoke of Milo's visits to his court chamber with little gifts of calendars and cookies, and the hospital president said Milo came by every single weekday to see which friends were on the inpatient unit.

45   I had little to offer this conversation because at that moment I was profoundly struck by the obvious lesson of Milo's life: The town character sees more, hears more and knows more than most of us can realize. He also probably deserves more respect than we have given.

46   After all, do you expect the judge, the mayor and the hospital president to see you off someday?

WHAT DID THE WRITER SAY AND WHAT DID YOU THINK?

1. What is the thesis? Where is it presented?
2. Where is there evidence that Milo truly does know "more than he lets on"?
3. What justifies the author's assertion that Milo "deserves more respect than we have given"?
4. According to the author, what are the characteristics of town characters in general?
5. Milo is no misunderstood saint. What are some of his less appealing qualities?
6. Why is Milo better off in a small town than in a large city?
7. What terms other than "town character" could be used to describe Milo?

HOW DID THE WRITER SAY IT?

1. Is the anecdote about the author's father (paragraphs 30–33) important enough to be included in the essay?
2. Explain the phrase "Milo moment" in paragraph 34.

WHAT ABOUT <u>YOUR</u> WRITING?

Watch out for *very*. Of all the trouble-making words in the language, *very* has possibly contributed most to sloppy writing. *Very* is an intensifier. You can smack it in front of nearly any adjective and strengthen—intensify—the meaning: *very pretty, very silly,* and so forth. The trouble is that the strengthening tends to be so generalized and imprecise that usually little of any substance is actually added to meaning. Sometimes meaning is even diminished or confused.

Few readers will object to Cheryl Heckler-Feltz describing Milo's nose as "very crooked" in paragraph 16, but wasn't she perhaps settling for convenient writing rather than effective writing? Tossing in *very* takes a tenth of a second. Finding a more precise term, however, may be worth the extra time and bother. What about *grotesquely crooked* or *startlingly crooked* or *hideously crooked* or *crooked as the nose of a Halloween witch?* Nobody suggests that the word *very* be outlawed, but in your own writing you'd do well to avoid it whenever you can. Start by looking for one-word synonyms: Instead of *very pretty,* try *beautiful;* instead of *very silly,* try *ridiculous.*

Really is another overused intensifier, particularly when intended as the equivalent of *very. Very* may not mean much, but at least it means itself. *Really* doesn't even have that much going for it in the following sentences:

They ate a really fine dinner.

The stairs are really steep.

The new furniture was really expensive.

So watch out for *really,* too. Its only legitimate use occurs when the writer has in mind a distinction between what is factual or *real* in opposition to what is false or imaginary.

The seemingly bizarre accusations of child abuse were really accurate.

When she says tomorrow, she doesn't mean next week. She really means tomorrow.

A GOOD PCA IS HARD TO FIND

Lorenzo W. Milam

Lorenzo W. Milam has been active in community radio and in working for rights for the disabled. He is the author of *The Radio Papers: From KRAB To KCHU (Essays on the Art and Practice of Radio Transmission)* and *Cripzen: A Manual for Survival*, as well as a host of print and online articles. As you read this essay, originally published in *Personal Mobility* magazine, notice how Milam combines his interest in public issues with lively description of an individual.

Words to check:

orthopedic (4)   gyosa (5)   sashimi (5)

1 We crips are always on the lookout for a good personal care attendant (PCA), aren't we? One who isn't slovenly or snarly, who doesn't complain, who will come to work when he's supposed to. One who doesn't drink, doesn't smoke, and doesn't stick needles in his arm.

2 One like Raul, whom I found six months ago.

3 I think you'd like Raul. Neat and pleasant, he's as good a PCA as you could ask for. When we get to the store, he has my wheelchair ready in seconds. He's very strong.

4 If I'm too tired to go, he takes the car and my grocery list, and when he comes back he puts everything away, washes the dishes, and sweeps out the kitchen. Then he vacuums the house, puts my clothes in the dryer, irons them, folds them, and places them in the dresser. When one of my orthopedic corsets needed fixing the other day, he sewed it up for me.

5 He'll make me my favorite sandwich for lunch, and if I want to go out to a Japanese restaurant for supper, he'll get me inside the restaurant and park me at the table. Then he'll talk to me cheerfully during dinner—even though he doesn't much care for gyosa or sashimi.

6 When it's time to go to bed, he helps me get my clothes off, handling me very carefully, almost tenderly. His one diversion, when there's nothing else to do, is watching TV. He always asks politely if it's OK. And he always keeps the sound down.

7 He's a dynamite worker.

8 And he robs me blind.

9 It first happens after he's been here a month, while I'm taking a shower. He helps me take off my pants and hangs them on a hook, just out of my line of sight. He lifts me onto the shower chair and pulls the curtain. The water is running, so I can't see my pants, or him. Anyway, when I'm taking a shower, I'm not thinking about my pants, or him, or the wallet in my pants.

10   Later, we go to Target to buy some shirts for me—and one for him, too, because he's poor and his clothes are a bit shabby. At the cash register, I notice that I don't have as many $20 bills as I thought I had.

11   I don't habitually count my money, but it seems that over the next couple of weeks, I'm always a bit more broke than usual.

12   Once, when I send Raul to the supermarket, he comes back with a package of chicken, some vegetables, bread, milk, and cheese. The bill is almost $50. "Did you get a receipt'?" I ask. "No," Raul says.

13   The issue finally comes out in the open because of Jennifer, the woman who lives next door. We share the house, and her kitchen is connected to mine. One day, while Jennifer is at work, I send Raul over to her place to look for some books I lent her. When Jennifer comes home, she bangs on the door, steaming, and says to me, "Ask Raul if he stole my $35."

14   "What?"

15   "I had $35 on my desk," she says. "Now it's gone. Ask him if he did it." Since no one else goes in and out of her place except her dog and me, Raul is the obvious suspect.

16   "Now?" I ask.

17   "Now."

18   Raul speaks only Spanish, which means she can't cross-examine him directly. I ask him, "Robaste $35 de la habitacion de Jennifer?"

19   I look at that thin pale handsome face of his, the small mustache, the ruddy cheeks (even ruddier right now), and he says no.

20   Jennifer now locks the door between her part of the house and mine. She doesn't visit anymore.

21   I don't fire Raul. How in hell can I fire the best worker I've ever had? Instead, I start acting as if I am under siege. I never let my wallet out of my sight. When Raul goes to the grocery or hardware store for me, or puts gas in the car, I always ask him to bring me a receipt with the correct change.

22   When I fly to Florida to visit my family, I hide the checkbooks just in case he's a check forger, too.

23   When I come back from my trip, I go through the checks, one by one, thinking, "I hate being a policeman." But none of the checks is missing, not even from the middle of the checkbook. That's where my last PCA stole them from.

24   Then Jennifer tells me that Raul was using my car while I was in Florida.

25   "Well," I say to myself, "at least he didn't sell it for parts or run into a tree, or rob a bank, or run home to Mexico with it." But now—finally—Raul and I will have to talk.

26   "Look, Raul," I say, "I really like having you around. You're a great worker. You're willing, and you do what I ask, and you never complain.

27   "But I think there are two Rauls working here. One is clean and neat and a nice worker. This Raul I like. Then there is another who takes things from me and from Jennifer without asking. That one I don't care for."

28   He smiles his winning, shy smile, shrugs his shoulders, and looks at me innocently. He says nothing. My hands are shaking. I drop the subject.

29   Until I get a call from the long-distance telephone service. They're terribly sorry, the operator says, but they have to cut off my calling privileges because of the excessive number of long-distance calls to Mexico.

30   I say nothing to Raul because in a few days the telephone bill will be here. For the first time, I will have proof—written proof—that he is a thief. Proof that I really don't want.

31   Meanwhile, I've just sent him to the store in my $20,000 van to get us some steaks for supper. He and I will cook them, to celebrate his sixth month of working for me. We'll eat together, and we'll talk. I'll have some wine. He doesn't drink, so he'll have a Fresca.

32   He'll tell me about his family in Mexico City—his poor family, with scarcely enough food in the house, not enough clothes for his eight brothers and sisters.

33   And maybe I'll tell him about the time when I was a kid when I, too, was two people. When I used to steal from my family, driving them crazy with my thievery. I was good at it—as good as Raul.

34   But, you ask, what am I going to do about him? Easy. When the telephone bill comes, I'll show it to him, tell him I'm taking the money out of his salary. We'll spread the payments out so it won't be too much of a hardship for him. And I'll tell him he shouldn't do it again.

35   Because in Raul I've got a jewel. A jewel with just a few flaws. And I am not going to lose him unless he steals my computer, totals my car, burns down the house, or sells me into white slavery.

36   Meanwhile, I'll try to explain to Raul that it's better not to risk his security, and our future relationship, for his instant gratification. I'm going to try to teach him that self-pity—and I am convinced that thievery is a rank form of self-pity—is not the answer to his problems.

37   I'm going to send Raul to school, the University of Lorenzo, where I'll try to give him classes in humanity, try to convince him to treasure Raul the Worker, instead of Raul the Robber.

38   And isn't a good PCA worth his weight in gold?

WHAT DID THE WRITER SAY AND WHAT DID YOU THINK?

1. Express the thesis in your own words. Does the author ever state the thesis directly? If so, where?

2. Explain the difference between Jennifer's reaction to Raul's thefts and the author's reaction.
3. How does Raul react when confronted by the author?
4. Does the author suggest that there may be any excuses for Raul's actions?
5. If you had been in the author's predicament, would you have handled the problem any differently? Explain.

HOW DID THE WRITER SAY IT?

1. Note the publication in which this selection first appeared. Who is the primary intended audience? Explain the use of the slangy, even derogatory term "crips" in paragraph 1.
2. What descriptive details about Raul are stressed in paragraphs 1 through 7?
3. Explain the phrase "classes in humanity" in paragraph 37.

WHAT ABOUT YOUR WRITING?

The normal body paragraph in an essay has a topic sentence and a varying number of additional sentences that develop or support the topic sentence. Specialized one-sentence transitional paragraphs are acceptable for their own special purpose—"Now that we have finished the mixing, we are ready to bake," for example. Written dialogue has its own paragraphing conventions, too (see pp. 114–115).

"A Good PCA Is Hard to Find" by Lorenzo W. Milam has a number of short one-sentence paragraphs, including the second and last ones—not transitional paragraphs by any stretch of the imagination. Note especially paragraphs 7 and 8, two one-sentence paragraphs in a row. How is it that such a clearly solid, well-written essay can break, or seem to break, so many basic rules?

If Milam had been writing for a newspaper instead of a magazine, one part of the answer would be obvious because newspaper paragraphs have to be kept short no matter what textbooks say. The words in a newspaper appear in narrow columns. A normal-sized paragraph in that narrow column would present readers with an excessively long solid block of print with no convenient place for the eyes to rest. Physical reality has to take precedence over rules. Readers with eyestrain don't stay readers for long.

The reason for one-sentence paragraphs in Milam's essay is that they stand out—and that's just what the author wants. Precisely because most paragraphs most of the time are much longer—and for good cause—readers will tend to pay special attention to unexpected, dramatic exceptions to the usual. Milam does not want the two central facts about Raul, his job skills and his thievery, to be lost in the middle of a paragraph. He wants them to stand out.

Like this.

Rules let us know what works for *almost* all writers *almost* all the time. Rules can save us painful years of effort, because without them we are forced to discover all the basic truths for ourselves. Rules are not meant to enslave us, however.

Don't let them enslave you.

HUSH, TIMMY—THIS IS LIKE A CHURCH
Kurt Andersen

Kurt Andersen is editor-in-chief of *New York* magazine, co-founder and editor of *Spy* magazine, a columnist for *The New Yorker*, and author of the novel *Turn of the Century* (1999). The following description of the Vietnam Veterans Memorial was written while Andersen was architecture and design critic for *Time* magazine.

Words to check:

vapid (paragraph 1)	salutary (3)	maudlin (5)
uncowed (1)	simpering (3)	pique (5)
millenniums (2)	rustic (4)	distended (5)
whim (2)	aboriginal (4)	dugs (5)
fawn (2)	bathetic (4)	dankest (5)
insipid (2)	lumbering (4)	cranny (5)
adheres (2)	ponderousness (4)	void (5)

1 The veteran and his wife had already stared hard at four particular names. Now the couple walked slowly down the incline in front of the wall, looking at rows of hundreds, thousands more, amazed at the roster of the dead. "All the names," she said quietly, sniffling in the early-spring chill. "It's unreal, how many names." He said nothing. "You have to see it to believe it," she said.

2 Just so. In person, close up, the Vietnam Veterans Memorial—two skinny black granite triangles wedged onto a mound of Washington sod—is some kind of sanctum, beautiful and terrible. "We didn't plan that," says John Wheeler, chairman of the veterans' group that raised the money and built it. "I had a picture of seven-year-olds throwing a Frisbee around on the grass

in front. But it's treated as a spiritual place." When Wheeler's colleague Jan Scruggs decided there ought to be a monument, he had only vague notions of what it might be like. "You don't set out and *build* a national shrine," Scruggs says. "It *becomes* one."

3   Washington is thick with monuments, several of them quite affecting. But as the Vietnam War was singular and strange, the dark, dreamy, redemptive memorial to its American veterans is like no other. "It's more solemn," says National Park Service Ranger Sarah Page, who has also worked at the memorials honoring Lincoln, Washington, and Jefferson. "People give it more respect." Lately it has been the most visited monument in the capital: 2.3 million saw it in 1984, about 45,000 a week, but it is currently drawing 100,000 a week. Where does it get its power—to console, and also to make people sob?

4   The men who set up the Vietnam Veterans Memorial Fund wanted something that would include the name of every American killed in Vietnam, and would be contemplative and apolitical. They conducted an open design competition that drew 1,421 entries, all submitted anonymously. The winner, Maya Ying Lin, was a Chinese-American undergraduate at Yale: to memorialize men killed in a war in Asia, an Asian female studying at an old antiwar hotbed.

5   Opposition to Lin's design was intense. The opponents wanted something gleaming and grand. To them, the low-slung black wall would send the same old defeatist, elitist messages that had lost the war in the '60s and then stigmatized the veterans in the '70s. "Creating the memorial triggered a lot of old angers and rage among vets about the war," recalls Wheeler, a captain in Vietnam and now a Yale-trained government lawyer. "It got white hot."

6   In the end, Lin's sublime and stirring wall was built, 58,022 names inscribed. As a compromise with opponents, however, a more conventional figurative sculpture was added to the site last fall (at a cost of $400,000). It does not spoil the memorial, as the art mandarins had warned. The three U.S. soldiers, cast in bronze, stand a bit larger than life, carry automatic weapons and wear fatigues, but the pose is not John Wayne-heroic: these American boys are spectral and wary, even slightly bewildered as they gaze southeast toward the wall. While he was planning the figures, sculptor Frederick Hart spent time watching vets at the memorial. Hart now grants that "no modernist monument of its kind has been as successful as that wall. The sculpture and the wall interact beautifully. Everybody won." Nor does Lin, his erstwhile artistic antagonist, still feel that Hart's statue is so awfully trite. "It captures the mood," says Lin. "Their faces have a lost look." Out at the memorial last week, one veteran looked at the new addition and nodded: "That's us."

7   But it is the wall that vets approach as if it were a force field. It is at the wall that families of the dead cry and leave flowers and mementos and

messages, much as Jews leave notes for God in the cracks of Jerusalem's Western Wall. Around the statue, people talk louder and breathe easier, snap vacation photos unselfconsciously, eat Eskimo Pies and Fritos. But near the wall, a young Boston father tells his rambunctious son, "Hush, Timmy—this is like a church." The visitors' processionals do seem to have a ritual, even liturgical quality. Going slowly down toward the vertex, looking at the names, they chat less and less, then fall silent where the names of the first men killed (July 1959) and the last (May 1975) appear. The talk begins again, softly, as they follow the path up out of the little valley of the shadow of death.

8   For veterans, the memorial was a touchstone from the beginning, and the 1982 dedication ceremony a delayed national embrace. "The actual act of being at the memorial is healing for the guy or woman who went to Vietnam," says Wheeler, who visits at least monthly. "It has to do with the felt presence of comrades." He pauses. "I always look at Tommy Hayes' name. Tommy's up on panel 50 east, line 29." Hayes, Wheeler's West Point pal, was killed 17 years ago this month. "I know guys," Wheeler says, "who are still waiting to go, whose wives have told me, 'He hasn't been able to do it yet.'" For those who go, catharsis is common. As Lin says of the names, chronologically ordered, "Veterans can look at the wall, find a name, and in a sense put themselves back in that time." The war has left some residual pathologies that the memorial cannot leach away. One veteran killed himself on the amphitheatrical green near the wall. A second, ex-Marine Randolph Taylor, tried and failed in January. "I regret what I did," he said. "I feel like I desecrated a holy place."

9   The memorial has become a totem, so much so that its tiniest imperfections make news. Last fall somebody noticed a few minute cracks at the seams between several of the granite panels. The cause of the hairlines is still unknown, and the builders are a little worried.

10   Probably no one is more determined than Wheeler to see the memorial's face made perfect, for he savors the startlingly faithful reflections the walls give off: he loves seeing the crowds of visitors looking simultaneously at the names and themselves. "Look!" he said the other day, gesturing at panel 4 east. "You see that plane taking off? You see the blue sky? No one expected that."

WHAT DID THE WRITER SAY AND WHAT DID YOU THINK?

1. What is Andersen's thesis? Does he have one?
2. Does the author find the choice of Maya Ying Lin as the memorial's designer ironic? How do you know?
3. Why does Andersen feel that the Vietnam memorial is so special?

4. Why does the author include stories of suicide and attempted suicide at the memorial?

HOW DID THE WRITER SAY IT?

1. What effect does the author's frequent use of quotations have?
2. Is the title appropriate? Why or why not?
3. The author pays a good deal of attention to numbers and statistics. Does this help support his thesis, or is it a detraction?
4. Andersen writes of "the little valley of the shadow of death." To what work is this an allusion? Why is it fitting?
5. What specific details are used to emphasize the difference between the Vietnam memorial and other memorials?

WHAT ABOUT <u>YOUR</u> WRITING?

"'We didn't plan that,' says John Wheeler, chairman of the veteran's group that raised the money and built it."

"'It's more solemn,' says National Park Service Ranger Sarah Page, who has also worked at the memorials honoring Lincoln, Washington, and Jefferson. 'People give it more respect.'"

One way of backing up a thesis is by *citation of authority*. A writer reinforces a point by quoting or referring to sources whose view the reader must take seriously. A writer on religion quotes the Bible. A writer on psychoanalysis quotes Freud. A writer on art quotes Picasso. A writer on the Vietnam Memorial quotes the head of the group that built it and a guard who studies visitors every day and has studied visitors at other memorials. "The people who should know agree with me," says the writer, no longer an isolated voice, but a voice with authority. In addition, the writer conveys the valuable impression of having done a certain amount of serious research before arriving at an opinion.

The citation of authority must be combined with taste and judgment. An authority in one special field, removed from that field, is no longer an authority. Freud's endorsement of an aftershave lotion would be of limited worth. A former star quarterback's comments about a football coach merit attention, but his feelings about instant tea or shampoos are another matter.

Comments of authorities must also be kept in context. Quoting a Supreme Court decision that the Supreme Court itself reversed ten years later is flatly irresponsible. Finally, assuming that even within the proper field and context the authority must always be right is another danger. Most people agree that

Thomas Jefferson was a great president, but his decision to make the Louisiana Purchase without consulting Congress was not necessarily correct. Citations of authority can strengthen a point; they can't prove it.

With all these necessary warnings, your own writing can profit from an occasional citation of authority. In Emerson's words, "Next to the originator of a good sentence is the first quoter of it."

I AM A CATHOLIC
Anna Quindlen

Anna Quindlen has published two collections of her *New York Times* columns: *Living Out Loud* (1988) and *Thinking Out Loud* (1993). Recipient of a Pulitzer Prize in 1992, she has also written the best-selling novels *Object Lessons* (1991) and *One True Thing* (1994) which recently became a movie. Her most recent novel is *Black and Blue* (1998). In "I Am a Catholic," Quindlen describes a person—herself—not by physical appearances or actions but by inner beliefs, her complex attitudes as a "cultural Catholic" toward her faith.

Words to check:

bona fides (paragraph 1)	tenets (3)
manifestation (2)	absolution (4)
misogyny (2)	

1   *Dominus vobiscum. Et cum spiritu tuo.*[1] These are my bona fides: a word, a phrase, a sentence in a language no one speaks anymore. *Kyrie eleison. Confiteor dei.*[2] I am a Catholic. Once at a nursing home for retired clergy, I ate lunch with a ninety-year-old priest, a man who still muttered the Latin throughout the English Mass and ate fish on Fridays. When he learned how old I was, he said with some satisfaction, "You were a Catholic when being a Catholic still meant something."

2   What does it mean now? For myself, I cannot truly say. Since the issue became material to me, I have not followed the church's teaching on birth control. I disagree with its stand on abortion. I believe its resistance to the ordination of women as priests is a manifestation of a misogyny that has been

---

[1] The Lord be with you. And with your spirit.

[2] Lord have mercy. I confess to God.

with us much longer than the church has. Yet it would never have occurred to my husband and me not to be married in a Catholic church, not to have our children baptized. On hospital forms and in political polls, while others leave the space blank or say "none of your business," I have no hesitation about giving my religion.

3   We are cultural Catholics. I once sneered at that expression, used by Jewish friends at college, only because I was not introspective enough to understand how well it applied to me. Catholicism is to us now not so much a system of beliefs or a set of laws but a shared history. It is not so much our faith as our past. The tenets of the church which I learned as a child have ever since been at war with the facts of my adult life. The Virgin Birth. The Trinity. The Resurrection. Why did God make me? God made me to know Him, to love Him, and to serve Him in this world and to be happy with Him forever in the next. I could recite parts of the Baltimore Catechism in my sleep. Do I believe those words? I don't know. What I do believe are those guidelines that do not vary from faith to faith, that are as true of Judaism or Methodism as they are of Catholicism: that people should be kind to one another, that they should help those in need, that they should respect others as they wish to be respected.

4   And I believe in my own past. I was educated by nuns, given absolution by priests. My parents were married in a Catholic church, my grandparents and mother buried from one. Saturday afternoons kneeling on Leatherette pads in the dim light of the confessional, listening for the sound of the priest sliding back the grille on his side. Sunday mornings kneeling with my face in my hands, the Communion wafer stuck to the roof of my dry mouth. These are my history. I could no more say I am not Catholic than say I am not Irish, not Italian. Yet I have never been to Ireland or Italy.

5   Some of our Jewish friends have returned to the ways of their past, to Shabbat without automobiles and elevators, to dietary laws and the study of Hebrew. We cannot do the same. There is no longer a Latin Mass, no Communion fast from midnight on. Even the inn is gone from the Bible; now Mary and Joseph are turned away from "the place where travelers lodged."

6   The first time my husband and I went to midnight mass on Christmas Eve in our parish church, we arrived a half-hour early so we would get a seat. When the bells sounded twelve and the priest came down the center aisle, his small acolytes in their child-size cassocks walking before him, the pews were still half empty. We were thinking of a different time, when the churches were packed, when missing Mass was a sin, when we still believed that that sort of sin existed—sins against rules, victimless sins.

7   There are more families coming to that church now, families like us with very small children who often have to leave before the Gospel because of tears, fatigue, temper tantrums. (I remember that, when I was growing up, my family's parish church was shaped like a cross, and one of the short arms was for the women with babies. It had a sheet of glass walling it off and was soundproof. And through the glass you could see the babies, as though in a movie with no audio, their little mouths round, their faces red. Inside that room, the noise was dreadful. But missing Mass was a sin.)

8   I think perhaps those families are people like us, people who believe in something, although they are not sure what, people who feel that in a world of precious little history or tradition, this is theirs. We will pass down the story to our children: There was a woman named Mary who was visited by an angel. And the angel said, "Do not be afraid" and told her that though she was a virgin she would have a child. And He was named Jesus and was the Son of God and He rose from the dead. Everything else our children learn in America in the late twentieth century will make this sound like a fairy tale, like tales of the potato famines in Ireland and the little ramshackle houses with grape arbors on hillsides in Italy. But these are my fairy tales, and so, whether or not they are fact, they are true.

9   I was born a Catholic and I think I will die one. I will ask for a priest to give me Extreme Unction, as it was given to my mother, and to her mother before her. At the end, as in the beginning, I will ask for the assistance of the church, which is some fundamental part of my identity. I am a Catholic.

WHAT DID THE WRITER SAY AND WHAT DID YOU THINK?

1. Explain in your own words the meaning of Quindlen's phrase in paragraph 4, "I believe in my own past."
2. Explain the phrase in paragraph 8, "These are my fairy tales, and so, whether or not they are fact, they are true."
3. With what teachings of the Church does the author disagree?
4. Contrast the difference in meaning if the title were "I *Am* a Catholic" or "I Am *a* Catholic." Which meaning comes closer to the author's actual feeling?

HOW DID THE WRITER SAY IT?

1. In paragraph 1, Quindlen uses Latin phrases she knows many readers will not understand. What is her probable purpose?
2. In paragraph 5, Quindlen expresses her disdain for modern translations of the Bible in which "inn," for example, is rendered as "the place where

travelers lodged." How does her attitude on this limited issue of style reflect her general attitude toward her religion?

3. Quindlen calls herself a "cultural Catholic." What terms other than "cultural" might be used by Catholics who are unsympathetic to her position? What terms might the author use to describe Catholics with more traditional beliefs than hers?

WHAT ABOUT <u>YOUR</u> WRITING?

"Never begin a sentence with *and*." The only real problem with that rule is that it shouldn't be a rule at all. It's good enough *advice*, as far as it goes. When readers see *and* at the start of a sentence, their first thought is likely to be that the word introduces a tacked-on idea that logically should be part of the previous sentence. More often than not, they are right.

Still, there's no rule. Precisely because most sentences don't and shouldn't begin with *and*, many good writers sometimes use the word to single out a sentence for special notice and dramatic emphasis. Anna Quindlen does it in the first sentence of paragraph 4. Abraham Lincoln does it in his "Second Inaugural Address":

> Both parties deprecated war; but one of them would make war rather than let the nation survive; and the other would accept war rather than let is perish. And the war came.

In the powerful last paragraph of Edgar Allan Poe's "The Masque of the Red Death," we find a virtual festival of *ands*, here used not only for dramatic force, but to suggest the eloquence of the King James version of the Bible—many sentences of which also begin with *and*:

> And now was acknowledged the presence of the Red Death. He had come like a thief in the night. And one by one dropped the revellers in the blood-bedewed halls of their revel, and died each in the despairing posture of his fall. And the life of the ebony clock went out with that of the last of the gay. And the flames of the tripods expired. And Darkness and Decay and the Red Death held illimitable dominion over all.

The moral is simple: Sentences shouldn't begin with *and* except in special circumstances. In special circumstances, *and* can be effective. When it is effective—clearly effective—use it.

GOOD USED CARS
John Steinbeck

Although attacked by some critics for sentimentality and occasional preten-
tiousness, John Steinbeck (1902–1968) is the author of a number of popular
and still supremely readable novels and novelettes, among them *Tortilla Flat*
(1935), *In Dubious Battle* (1936), *Of Mice and Men* (1937), *The Grapes of
Wrath* (1939), *Cannery Row* (1945), and *East of Eden* (1952). Steinbeck received the Nobel Prize for Literature in 1962. "Good Used Cars" is the title
given here to Chapter 7 of *The Grapes of Wrath*, Steinbeck's moving account
of the "Okies," former farmers and tenant farmers of Oklahoma and surrounding states who were forced in the 1930s by the drought-created Dust
Bowl to seek employment as migrant workers in the fields of California.
"Good Used Cars" presents a disturbing and impassioned description of the
effort to purchase affordable transportation for the thousand-mile journey
westward.

Words to check:

blazoned (paragraph 1)	jalopy (3)
sheaf (2)	Zephyr (43)

1 In the towns, on the edges of the towns, in fields, in vacant lots, the used car
yards, the wreckers' yards, the garages with blazoned signs—Used Cars, Good
Used Cars. Cheap transportation, three trailers. '27 Ford, clean. Checked cars,
guaranteed cars. Free radio. Car with 100 gallons of gas free. Come in and
look. Used cars. No overhead.

2 A lot and a house large enough for a desk and chair and a blue book.[1]
Sheaf of contracts, dog-eared, held with paper clips, and a neat pile of unused
contracts. Pen—keep it full, keep it working. A sale's been lost 'cause a pen
didn't work.

3 Those sons-of-bitches over there ain't buying. Every yard gets 'em.
They're lookers. Spend all their time looking. Don't want to buy no cars; take
up your time. Don't give a damn for your time. Over there, them two people—no, with the kids. Get 'em in a car. Start 'em at two hundred and work
down. They look good for one and a quarter. Get 'em rolling. Get 'em out in
a jalopy. Sock it to 'em! They took our time.

4 Owners with rolled-up sleeves. Salesmen, neat, deadly, small intent eyes
watching for weaknesses.

---

[1] A booklet listing the standard dollar value of used cars.

5   Watch the woman's face. If the woman likes it we can screw the old man. Start 'em on the Cad'. Then you can work 'em down to that '26 Buick. 'F you start on the Buick, they'll go for a Ford. Roll up your sleeves an' get to work. This ain't gonna last forever. Show 'em that Nash while I get the slow leak pumped up on that '25 Dodge. I'll give you a Hymie[2] when I'm ready.

6   What you want is transportation, ain't it? No baloney for you. Sure the upholstery is shot. Seat cushions ain't turning no wheels over.

7   Cars lined up, noses forward, rusty noses, flat tires. Parked close together.

8   Like to get in to see that one? Sure, no trouble. I'll pull her out of the line.

9   Get 'em under obligation. Make 'em take up your time. Don't let 'em forget they're takin' your time. People are nice, mostly. They hate to put you out. Make 'em put you out, an' then sock it to 'em.

10   Cars lined up, Model T's, high and snotty, creaking wheel, worn bands. Buicks, Nashes, De Sotos.

11   Yes, sir. '22 Dodge. Best goddamn car Dodge ever made. Never wear out. Low compression. High compression got lots a sap for a while, but the metal ain't made that'll hold it for long. Plymouths, Rocknes, Stars.

12   Jesus, where'd that Apperson come from, the Ark? And a Chalmers and a Chandler—ain't made 'em for years. We ain't sellin' cars—rolling junk. Goddamn it, I got to get jalopies. I don't want nothing for more'n twenty-five, thirty bucks. Sell 'em for fifty, seventy-five. That's a good profit. Christ, what cut do you make on a new car? Get jalopies. I can sell 'em fast as I get 'em. Nothing over two hundred fifty. Jim, corral that old bastard on the sidewalk. Don't know his ass from a hole in the ground. Try him on that Apperson. Say, where is that Apperson? Sold? If we don't get some jalopies we got nothing to sell.

13   Flags, red and white, white and blue—all along the curb. Used cars. Good Used Cars.

14   Today's bargain—up on the platform. Never sell it. Makes folks come in, though. If we sold that bargain at that price we'd hardly make a dime. Tell 'em it's jus' sold. Take out that yard battery before you make delivery. Put in that dumb cell. Christ, what they want for six bits? Roll up your sleeves— pitch in. This ain't gonna last. If I had enough jalopies, I'd retire in six months.

15   Listen, Jim, I heard that Chevvy's rear end. Sounds like bustin' bottles. Squirt in a couple quarts of sawdust. Put some in the gears, too. We got to move that lemon for thirty-five dollars. Bastard cheated me on that one. I offer ten an' he jerks me to fifteen, an' then the son-of-a-bitch took the tools out. God Almighty! I wisht I had five hundred jalopies. This ain't gonna last.

---

[2]A special look or gesture, a secret signal.

He don't like the tires? Tell 'im they got ten thousand in 'em, knock off a buck an' a half.

16 Piles of rusty ruins against the fence, rows of wrecks in back, fenders, grease-black wrecks, blocks lying on the ground and a pig weed growing up through the cylinders. Brake rods, exhausts, piled like snakes. Grease, gasoline.

17 See if you can't find a spark plug that ain't cracked. Christ, if I had fifty trailers at under a hundred I'd clean up. What the hell is he kickin' about? We sell 'em, but we don't push 'em home for him. That's good! Don't push 'em home. Get that one in the Monthly, I bet. You don't think he's a prospect? Well, kick 'im out. We got too much to do to bother with a guy that can't make up his mind. Take the right front tire off the Graham. Turn that mended side down. The rest looks swell. Got tread an' everything.

18 Sure! There's fifty thousan' in that ol' heap yet. Keep plenty oil in. So long. Good luck.

19 Lookin' for a car? What did you have in mind? See anything attracts you? I'm dry. How about a little snort a good stuff? Come on, while your wife's lookin' at that La Salle. You don't want no La Salle. Bearings shot. Uses too much oil. Got a Lincoln '24. There's a car. Run forever. Make her into a truck.

20 Hot sun on rusted metal. Oil on the ground. People are wandering in, bewildered, needing a car.

21 Wipe your feet. Don't lean on that car, it's dirty. How do you buy a car? What does it cost? Watch the children, now. I wonder how much for this one? We'll ask. It don't cost money to ask. We can ask, can't we? Can't pay a nickel over seventy-five, or there won't be enough to get to California.

22 God, if I could only get a hundred jalopies. I don't care if they run or not.

23 Tires, used, bruised tires, stacked in tall cylinders; tubes, red, gray, hanging like sausages.

24 Tire patch? Radiator cleaner? Spark intensifier? Drop this little pill in your gas tank and get ten extra miles to the gallon. Just paint it on—you got a new surface for fifty cents. Wipers, fan belts, gaskets? Maybe it's the valve. Get a new valve stem. What can you lose for a nickel?

25 All right, Joe. You soften 'em up an' shoot 'em in here. I'll close 'em, I'll deal 'em or I'll kill 'em. Don't send in no bums. I want deals.

26 Yes, sir, step in. You got a buy there. Yes, sir! At eighty bucks you got a buy.

27 I can't go no higher than fifty. The fella outside says fifty.

28 *Fifty. Fifty?* He's nuts. Paid seventy-eight fifty for that little number. Joe, you crazy fool, you tryin' to bust us? Have to can that guy. I might take sixty. Now look here, mister, I ain't got all day. I'm a business man but I ain't out to stick nobody. Got anything to trade?

29 Got a pair of mules I'll trade.

30   *Mules!* Hey, Joe, hear this? This guy wants to trade mules. Didn't nobody tell you this is the machine age? They don't use mules for nothing but glue no more.

31   Fine big mules—five and seven years old. Maybe we better look around.

32   Look around! You come in when we're busy, an' take up our time an' then walk out! Joe, did you know you was talkin' to pikers?

33   I ain't a piker. I got to get a car. We're goin' to California. I got to get a car.

34   Well, I'm a sucker. Joe says I'm a sucker. Says if I don't quit givin' my shirt away I'll starve to death. Tell you what I'll do—I can get five bucks apiece for them mules for dog feed.

35   I wouldn't want them to go for dog feed.

36   Well, maybe I can get ten or seven maybe. Tell you what we'll do. We'll take your mules for twenty. Wagon goes with 'em, don't it? An' you put up fifty, an' you can sign a contract to send the rest at ten dollars a month.

37   But you said eighty.

38   Didn't you never hear about carrying charges and insurance? That just boosts her a little. You'll get her all paid up in four—five months. Sign your name right here. We'll take care of ever'thing.

39   Well, I don't know.

40   Now, look here. I'm givin' you my shirt, an' you took all this time. I might a made three sales while I been talkin' to you. I'm disgusted. Yeah, sign right there. All right, sir. Joe, fill up the tank for this gentleman. We'll give him gas.

41   Jesus, Joe, that was a hot one! What'd we give for that jalopy? Thirty bucks—thirty-five wasn't it? I got that team, an' if I can't get seventy-five for that team, I ain't a business man. An' I got fifty cash an' a contract for forty more. Oh, I know they're not all honest, but it'll surprise you how many kick through with the rest. One guy came through with a hundred two years after I wrote him off. I bet you this guy sends the money. Christ, if I could only get five hundred jalopies! Roll up your sleeves, Joe. Go out an' soften 'em, an' send 'em in to me. You get twenty on that last deal. You ain't doing bad.

42   Limp flags in the afternoon sun. Today's Bargain. '29 Ford pickup, runs good.

43   What do you want for fifty bucks—a Zephyr?

44   Horsehair curling out of seat cushions, fenders battered and hammered back. Bumpers torn loose and hanging. Fancy Ford roadster with little colored lights at fender guide, at radiator cap, and three behind. Mud aprons, and a big die on the gear-shift lever. Pretty girl on tire cover, painted in color and named Cora. Afternoon sun on the dusty windshields.

45   Christ, I ain't had time to go out an' eat! Joe, send a kid for a hamburger.

46   Spattering roar of ancient engines.

47   There's a dumb-bunny lookin' at that Chrysler. Find out if he got any jack in his jeans. Some a these farm boys is sneaky. Soften 'em up an' roll 'em in to me, Joe. You're doin' good.

48   Sure, we sold it. Guarantee? We guaranteed it to be an automobile. We didn't guarantee to wet-nurse it. Now listen here, you—you bought a car, an' now you're squawkin'. I don't give a damn if you don't make payments. We ain't got your paper. We turn that over to the finance company. They'll get after you, not us. We don't hold no paper. Yeah? Well you jus' get tough an' I'll call a cop. No, we did not switch the tires. Run 'im outa here, Joe. He bought a car, an' now he ain't satisfied. How'd you think if I bought a steak an' et half an' try to bring it back? We're runnin' a business, not a charity ward. Can ya imagine that guy, Joe? Say—looka there! Got a Elk's tooth![3] Run over there. Let 'em glance over that '36 Pontiac. Yeah.

49   Square noses, round noses, rusty noses, shovel noses, and the long curves of streamlines, and the flat surfaces before streamlining. Bargains Today. Old monsters with deep upholstery—you can cut her into a truck easy. Two-wheel trailers, axles rusty in the hard afternoon sun. Used Cars. Good Used Cars. Clean, runs good. Don't pump oil.

50   Christ, look at 'er! Somebody took nice care of 'er.

51   Cadillacs, La Salles, Buicks, Plymouths, Packards, Chevvies, Fords, Pontiacs. Row on row, headlights glinting in the afternoon sun. Good Used Cars.

52   Soften 'em up, Joe. Jesus, I wisht I had a thousand jalopies! Get 'em ready to deal, an' I'll close 'em.

53   Goin' to California? Here's jus' what you need. Looks shot, but they's thousan's of miles in her.

54   Lined up side by side. Good Used Cars. Bargains. Clean, runs good.

WHAT DID THE WRITER SAY AND WHAT DID YOU THINK?

1. State the thesis of "Good Used Cars" in your own words.
2. Is the author describing one particular used car lot or used car lots in general?
3. What dirty tricks do the lot owners play on the customers?
4. Do you feel that the author may overstate his case? Are the owners too evil to believe, the customers too gullible?
5. "Good Used Cars" was written about sixty-five years ago. Apart from the mention of cars no longer manufactured, is the reading selection out of date in any important way?

---

[3] Symbol of membership in the Benevolent and Protective Orders of Elks, a prestigious fraternal organization.

HOW DID THE WRITER SAY IT?

1. The author does not write an explicit thesis statement. Why?
2. Why aren't quotation marks used around the "spoken" passages?
3. Why are there so many deliberate sentence fragments?
4. What words and phrases are repeated throughout the selection to intensify dramatic effects?

WHAT ABOUT <u>YOUR</u> WRITING?

An old cartoon shows two college students talking to each other. "Well," says one, "I think I'll have to write this story as stream-of-consciousness. It's due tomorrow."

Stream-of-consciousness writing, or its close cousin *impressionism*, whether in fiction or nonfiction, abandons the idea of an author or narrator as a helpful intermediary between the reader and the thoughts or experiences being described. We normally expect the author to be our guide—to select, organize, analyze, interpret. Stream-of-consciousness writing attempts to communicate more directly. We usually don't think in complete sentences, for example, so stream-of-consciousness writing often doesn't bother with complete sentences. Our thoughts don't come to us complete with the logic of neatly chosen transitional words and phrases. An overheard scrap of conversation registers on our ears while our thoughts continue their erratic course. As we read a book or watch television, a jumbled mass of past memories, present concerns, and future anticipations jostle each other to get our attention.

Imagine suddenly being placed in the middle of the frenzy and chaos of Steinbeck's used-car lot. How can the experience be conveyed authentically? A hundred scattered impressions assault our senses at once. A sign here and there, the words of a salesperson, a worried family group, an unfocused awareness of colors and fenders and rust—these are what hit us, not intellectual general statements like "The scene was chaotic" or "The dealers cheat the customers."

Steinbeck's success with stream-of-consciousness, or impressionism, may inspire you to use the same techniques in descriptive writing of your own. If you're tempted, keep the following suggestions in mind:

1. Get your instructor's approval. Your course is set up primarily to teach you to master more conventional forms of writing.
2. Be sure that your choice of subject and approach to the subject make stream-of-consciousness appropriate. A description of shopping on

Christmas Eve might work well, but it's hard to see how a stream-of-consciousness description of a new dining room set could make much sense.

3. Consider limiting stream-of-consciousness to one or two sections of your description. The beginning of the Christmas shopping piece, for example, might benefit from the dramatic punch of stream-of-consciousness, but you may choose to describe the rest of the scene with more traditional techniques.

4. Above all, remember that the student in the cartoon who thought that stream-of-consciousness writing could be dashed off the night before class was dead wrong. Stream-of-consciousness may sometimes give the illusion of disorder, but it needs to be put together with at least as much care as any other kind of good writing. Beneath the illusion of disorder in Steinbeck's "Good Used Cars" is the reality of extremely tight organization. A strong thesis runs through the entire selection, and specific details support the thesis everywhere. Repetition of key phrases and a carefully balanced pattern of spoken words alternating with descriptive passages provide additional structure. Anyone who thinks Steinbeck wrote "Good Used Cars" without thoughtful planning hasn't read it carefully enough.

———

Examples

An example is a single item drawn from a larger group to which it belongs. An example is also often viewed as one of a number of specific cases in which a generalization turns out to be true. Smog is one of many possible examples of pollution. Chicken pox is an example of a childhood disease. The egg yolk on Bill's necktie is an example of his sloppy eating habits. The bald eagle is an example that backs up the generalization that endangered species can sometimes be preserved. The French Reign of Terror is an example that supports the idea that violent revolutions often bring about further violence. (The preceding five sentences are examples of examples.)

It's hard to write a good paper of any kind without using at least some examples. Examples *clarify* a writer's thought by bringing remote abstractions down to earth:

> The American Civil War was not all the romantic valor we read about in storybooks. It was the horrors of trench warfare, the medical nightmare of wholesale amputations, and for the South, at least, the agony of slow starvation.

Examples also *add interest:* The most humdrum generalization can take on new life if supported by effective examples. Specific details described in specific language are at the heart of almost all good writing, and examples by their very nature are specific:

> Professor Smathers' course in Shakespeare was the worst I have ever taken. Once we spent a whole week listening to students recite—or mumble—sonnets they had been forced to memorize. Another time Professor Smathers devoted an entire period to attacking one of the footnotes in our edition of *Hamlet*. And I never understood the true meaning of boredom until the great day that I heard him discourse on Shakespeare's preference for daisies over roses.

Examples help *persuade.* Without the help of examples, many perfectly valid statements can be perceived as dismal echoes of ideas the author has heard somewhere but has never thought about seriously. If the writer of the following paragraph had omitted the examples, there would be no way to evaluate the merits of the complaint:

> Routine city services are in a terrible state. The freeway from West 50th Street to the Downtown exit has been filled with gaping chuckholes since early spring. Rat-infested, condemned, and abandoned buildings still line Water Street despite three-year-old promises to tear them down. Last week the papers reported the story of a man who called the police about a burglar entering his home—and got a busy signal.

An example essay is one that relies entirely on examples to support its thesis. The ordinary pattern for an example essay is elementary, though bear in mind that no pattern should be followed blindly. A first paragraph presents the thesis. A varying number of paragraphs—depending on the subject, complexity of thesis, and material available to the writer—then establishes through examples the validity of the thesis. A concluding paragraph reinforces or advances the thesis. The pattern seems simple, and it is.

What isn't quite so simple is seeing to it that all the examples are relevant and persuasive.

Are There Enough Examples to Support Your Thesis?

Three examples may sometimes be enough. A hundred may be too few (and in that case you've made a poor choice of thesis for an example essay). Common sense is your best guide. Three in-depth examples of overly sentimental deathbed scenes from Dickens' novels may be enough to establish that Dickens had trouble with deathbed scenes. A hundred examples of middle-aged men with protruding stomachs will not even begin to establish that most middle-aged men have potbellies. As a general rule for a paper of five hundred words or so, choose a thesis that can be supported adequately with no more than fifteen examples, unless your instructor tells you otherwise. Don't use fewer than three examples unless you're extremely confident about the virtues of your paper. Remember, too, that the fewer the examples, the more fully each needs to be developed.

Are the Examples Fairly Chosen?

Your reader must be convinced that the examples represent a reasonable cross-section of the group you're dealing with. Choose typical examples. Anyone can load the dice. You may have an imposing number of dramatic examples showing that the downtown business area of a city is deserted and dying, but if you drew all the examples from only one street or from visiting the area on a Sunday afternoon, you would not have played fair. Plan your paper with the notion of a cross-section constantly in mind. If you're generalizing about teachers in your school, try to pick examples from different departments, age groups, sexes, and so on. If you're attacking television commercials, make sure your examples include significantly different products; otherwise, you might wind up convincing your reader that only ads for soaps and detergents are bad.

Have You Stuck to Your Thesis?

One way of losing sight of your thesis has just been described. Poorly selected examples, besides creating an impression of unfairness, may support only part of the thesis; one writer demonstrates that only a single block is deserted and dying, not the whole downtown area; another shows that commercials about laundry products are offensive, not commercials in general.

A second, but equally common, way of drifting off is to forget you are writing an example paper. A writer starts out well by providing examples establishing the idea that "routine city services are in a terrible state." Halfway through the paper, the writer gets sidetracked into a discussion of the causes for this condition and the steps the average citizen can take to remedy it. The writer thus manages to produce a paper that is 50 percent irrelevant to the declared thesis.

Have You Arranged Your Examples to Produce the Greatest Impact?

In planning your paper, you've limited your subject, developed a thesis, and jotted down many examples. You've eliminated irrelevant and illogical examples. Now how do you handle those that are left? Which comes first? Which comes last?

Unless you're superhuman, some of the examples you're going to use will be clearly superior to others. As a general principle, try to start off with a bang. Grab the attention of your reader as soon as possible with your most dramatic or shocking or amusing or disturbing example. If you have two unusually effective examples, so much the better. Save one for last: Try to end with a bang, too.

A large number of exceptionally strong examples can also lead to a common variation on the orthodox pattern of devoting the first paragraph to a presentation of the thesis. Use the first paragraph instead to present one of the strongest examples. (Humorous anecdotes often work particularly well.)

Stimulate curiosity. Arouse interest. Then present the thesis in the second paragraph before going on to the other examples.

Paragraphing itself is important throughout the essay to help the reader understand the nature of your material and the logic of your argument. With a few well-developed examples, there's no problem. Each should get a paragraph to itself. With a great number of examples, however, there's some potential for difficulties. Each example will probably be short—one or two sentences, let's say—because you're writing an essay of only a few hundred words, not a term paper. If each of these short examples gets a separate paragraph, the paper is likely to be extremely awkward and choppy to read. But even without that burden, the physical appearance alone of the page can bother most readers: Before getting to the actual reading, they will have thought of the paper as a collection of separate sentences and thoughts rather than as a unified composition.

The solution to this paragraphing problem is to gather the many examples together into a few logical groups and write a paragraph for each group, not for each example. Suppose you have fifteen good examples of declining city services. Instead of writing fifteen one-sentence paragraphs, you observe that four examples involve transportation; five, safety; three, housing; and the rest, pollution and sanitation. Your paragraphing problems are over.

¶ 1 Thesis: *Routine city services are in a terrible state.*

¶ 2 *Transportation*

    Example 1—Higher fares for same or worse service

    Example 2—No parking facilities

    Example 3—Poor snow removal

    Example 4—Refusal to synchronize traffic lights downtown

¶ 3 *Safety*

    Example 1—Unrepaired chuckholes

    Example 2—Unrepaired traffic lights

    Example 3—Busy signals at police station

    Example 4—Slow response when police do come

    Example 5—Releasing of dangerous criminals because of overcrowding
        at city jail

¶ 4 *Housing*

    Example 1—Decaying public projects

    Example 2—Abandoned buildings not torn down

    Example 3—Housing codes not enforced in some neighborhoods

¶ 5 *Pollution and Sanitation*

    Example 1—Flooded basements

    Example 2—Litter in public parks

    Example 3—Increase in rats

¶ 6 *Conclusion*

WRITING SUGGESTIONS FOR EXAMPLE ESSAYS

Write an example essay supporting one of the following statements or a related statement of your own.

1. Life in [your town] is not as bad as it's cracked up to be.
2. Some teachers try too hard to identify with their students.
3. Junk food has many virtues.
4. Corruption is part of the American way of life.
5. Teenage marriages are likely to end unhappily.
6. People express their personalities through the clothes they wear.
7. The generation gap is a myth.
8. Children's television programs display too much violence.
9. A student's life is not a happy one.
10. Nuns and/or priests are complex human beings, not plaster saints.
11. You can tell a lot about people from their table manners.
12. Student government is a farce.
13. Apparent nonconformists are sometimes the worst conformists.
14. Everyone loves to gossip.
15. Many people never learn from their mistakes.
16. The effort to succeed is more satisfying than success itself.
17. Even at their best, most people are basically selfish.
18. The road to hell is paved with good intentions.
19. Taking care of a pet can be a great educational experience for children.
20. Newspapers rarely bother to report good news.

DAN'S NEW MINIVAN
Britt Teller (student)

Thesis: My husband, Dan, chose the new family minivan because of its great number of gadgets.

    I. Technological wonders

        A. CD player

        B. Compass and thermometer

    C. Power everything

    D. Remote control

    E. Burglar alarm

  II. Nonhigh-tech wonders

    A. Storage compartments

    B. Holder for garage door opener

    C. Sun visors

  III. Deluxe cupholders

Conclusion: To be honest, I really like the car, too.

My husband, Dan, just bought a new minivan. He spent months poring over shiny brochures from car companies, checking out safety features and mileage statistics, reading and rereading critical reviews in *Consumer Reports* and *Car and Driver,* and talking with friends, neighbors, and perfect strangers about their own minivans. He talked to me and the kids about our preferences in size, color, seating, and a host of other details. He paid for computerized services itemizing dealer costs and sticker prices. He spent ages visiting dealers and practicing his negotiating skills. (I swore off accompanying him on those trips to dealers fifteen years and three cars ago.) Finally the big day came. My husband went out to buy the minivan he had scientifically determined to be the best for our family. He came home with the van with the most gadgets.

    Our new van has scores of technological wonders. It has a CD player that my eleven-year-old daughter had to show her father how to use and for which we own no CDs. It has separate heating and air conditioning controls for the driver's seat, the passenger's seat, and the bench seats in the back. In case Dan gets lost while driving around the corner to pick up a carton of milk, the new van has a digital compass that constantly flashes the direction he's heading, and as a bonus also shows the current outside temperature in Celsius and Fahrenheit, plus the total trip distance in miles and kilometers. So no one in the family gets wrist strain, the van has power locks, power windows, and power seats with memories. So no one gets finger strain, it has a key chain gizmo that locks and unlocks the doors through remote control. It has a built-in burglar alarm—that I hate and which was accidentally set off three times in the first week that we had it.

    Other gadgets in the minivan are not as high tech, but they are just as much fun for my husband to play with. The new van has a secret locking storage compartment beneath the passenger seat. And if anyone should need to store anything else, there are at least six more storage areas tucked in convenient and inconvenient places all around the van. To allay panic when one is trying to open the garage door, the new van even has a special holder for the garage door opener that lets Dan press the magic button without any fumbling. Even the sun visors are miracles. They have built-in extenders to block the sun at the trickiest angles. They have vanity mirrors with built-in lights. And the lights themselves are adjustable. (I'm not making this up.)

But the very best thing about the van, Dan's favorite thing about his brand new car, the thing he shows off to all the neighbors—is the cupholders! There are fourteen cupholders. Fourteen! In a minivan that seats only seven, that's quite an accomplishment. They are in armrests and under the dashboard. They are attached to doors. They are on the backs of seats. They pull out from under other seats. Two of them are adjustable, for heaven's sake. They fit the cups better than my clothes fit me.

To be honest, I really am pleased with Dan's choice of minivan. I'm grateful that we can somehow afford the darned thing, of course. It gets surprisingly good mileage. It's easy to park and fun to drive, and now that I've got the hang of the burglar alarm, even that isn't too bad. I know my husband only bought it for the gadgets, and I know it's not the most practical thing he's ever done, but he's very happy, and I always have some place to put my coffee.

COUPLE LIES

Adair Lara

Domestic tranquility in the nation sometimes requires the U.S. government, according to the Constitution, but for domestic tranquility in marriage, "couple lies" often come in handy. Has Adair Lara, a columnist for the *San Francisco Chronicle*, discovered a new kind of lie, found a new name for an old lie, or merely dramatized a harmless aspect of human relations into seeming like a lie? Whatever the answer, married students among Lara's readers may find themselves checking the coffee and laundry in new and different ways.

Words to check:

abashed (paragraph 1)   chronically (7)
lapse (4)   squeamish (8)

1 I discovered one morning that my husband, Bill, who buys and brews the beans for our morning coffee, had switched to decaf months ago. He had the grace to look abashed when I stormed into his bathroom and confronted him. "I didn't think you'd notice," he said, blushing.

2 The night before, I was feeling tired just as a late meeting was about to start and had the inspiration of getting a coffee bean to chew on. To my surprise, all three of our white bags of beans were marked decaf: Swiss, Columbian, Hazelnut Creme. "When were you planning to tell me?" I asked.

3   "Well, never," he said. He admitted he had reduced the amount of caffeine we were drinking gradually, over months, before cutting it out completely. "You never make the coffee, so how would you know? I had no idea you'd do a crazy thing like eat a coffee bean. I was afraid if I did tell you, you'd want the caffeine back, and I've been feeling so much better since I stopped drinking it. You're not mad, are you?"

4   Mad? Me? Of course not! I'm just glad to have an explanation for all those puzzling health problems I've been experiencing—like pounding headaches and a tendency to lapse into unconsciousness before noon.

5   It's easy to see how this sort of thing can happen. As couples march in lockstep toward the boneyard, disagreements are bound to arise. You can't agree on everything, and maybe one of you wants to give up coffee but the other either might not be ready to or hasn't thought about it. So while the two of you drink out of the same pot, one stealthily reduces the caffeine yet doesn't tell the other. As Oscar Wilde said, "If one tells the truth, one is sure, sooner or later, to be found out."

6   This is marital lying. It's not a white lie, meant to spare your feelings. It's a pink lie, a couple lie. It means: I'll make the decisions, Angelface; you just drink the coffee.

7   Everybody tells couple lies. A woman I know fills the Mountain Valley bottles with tap water when they're empty and puts them back in the fridge. Her husband never catches on. Another friend, Donna, exasperated that her mate, Michael, kept absentmindedly walking off with the Papermate she kept next to the grocery list in the kitchen, now hides the pen in the silverware drawer. And my friend Dirk tells his chronically late girlfriend they have to be everywhere a half hour before they actually do.

8   I myself used to slip polyester shirts in my then-boyfriend's wardrobe to make the ironing easier. I must say, despite his contention that he could wear only pure cotton, I didn't see him tearing off his button-downs in the middle of the morning, swearing he couldn't breathe. He also claimed he was allergic to garlic, but I figured he meant he was squeamish about the smell or that he associated garlic with a three-day beard—I added it anyway, and the food tasted so much better.

9   A couple lie is, in reality, close to an omission. Bill didn't actually tell me an untruth. I never said to him, "Morning, Sweetie, coffee have caffeine in it today?" Michael never said to Donna, as he searched futilely for the pen that used to be there, "You aren't by any chance hiding it in the silverware drawer, are you, Honeybunch?"

10   Since we're all guilty, sooner or later, of a little pink omission, I've decided I'm not mad about the coffee. And I know Bill won't mind if I admit that sometimes, after I do the laundry and discover one of the socks still

behind the hamper—and wanting to keep the pair together but unwilling to wash the clean one all over again—I let him go off to work wearing one dirty sock and one laundered one. It's not lying. He didn't, after all, ask me if both his socks were clean.

WHAT DID THE WRITER SAY AND WHAT DID YOU THINK?

1. What is a couple lie? Does Lara ever explicitly define the term?
2. What is the difference between a white lie and a couple lie?
3. What is the thesis? Is it ever directly stated?
4. What seems to motivate most couple lies?
5. What kept Lara from getting even angrier than she did about the coffee episode?
6. Are couple lies necessarily limited to married couples?

HOW DID THE WRITER SAY IT?

1. Are there enough examples? Do they represent a "reasonable cross section" (see p. 100)?
2. The couples in this essay use several supersweet terms of endearment such as "Honeybunch" and "Angelface." Does Lara mean this dialogue to be realistic?
3. Why does the essay begin with a story about a couple lie rather than with a definition of the term or a thesis statement?

WHAT ABOUT <u>YOUR</u> WRITING?

"Couple Lies" is a good example of why-didn't-I-think-of-saying-that writing. Now that the author mentions it, who doesn't know how often married couples—or parents and children, brothers and sisters, even best friends—make life easier by not telling the "truth"? Who hasn't distinguished between telling direct lies and simply not volunteering information? What does this author know that we don't know? Many readers probably see in the Lara essay a main idea that has occurred to them, read insights that they themselves have probably had, and mutter, "Why didn't I think of saying that?" Maybe they didn't think of it because they were too busy lamenting that they didn't have anything to write about. More likely, they had drifted into the habit of not taking their own ideas seriously.

In "Self-Reliance," Ralph Waldo Emerson presents this moral more memorably when he complains of the person who "dismisses without notice his thought, because it is his. In every work of genius we recognize our own rejected thoughts: they come back to us with a certain alienated majesty." You don't have to believe that Lara's article is a work of genius to agree with Emerson's conclusion: We "should learn to detect and watch that gleam of light which flashes across the mind. . . . Else, tomorrow a stranger will say with masterly good sense precisely what we have thought and felt all the time, and we shall be forced to take with shame our own opinion from another."

HOW TO SPEAK OF ANIMALS
Umberto Eco

Umberto Eco, respected scholarly writer and lecturer, is the author of numerous popular novels, such as *The Name of the Rose* (1983), *Foucault's Pendulum* (1989), and *The Island of the Day Before* (1995). Here, Eco considers the problems of "toyifying" nature and its creatures.

Words to check:

subproletariat (paragraph 2)	*per se* (5)	lemming (6)
sporadic (4)	carnivorous (5)	viper (6)
	benevolent (5)	equilibrium (6)

1   Central Park. The zoo. Some kids are playing near the polar bear tank. One dares the others to dive into the tank and swim alongside the bears; to force them to dive in, the challenger hides the others' clothes; the boys enter the water, splashing past a big male bear, peaceful and drowsy; they tease him, he becomes annoyed, extends a paw, and eats, or rather chomps on, two kids, leaving some bits lying around. The police come quickly, even the mayor arrives, there is some argument about whether or not the bear has to be killed, all admit it's not his fault; some sensational articles appear in the press. It so happens that the boys have Hispanic names: Puerto Ricans, perhaps black, perhaps newcomers to the city, in any event, accustomed to feats of daring, like all slum kids who hang out in packs.

2   Various interpretations ensue, all fairly severe. The cynical reaction is fairly widespread, at least in conversation: natural selection, if they were stupid enough to mess with a bear, they got what they deserved; even when I was five, I had enough sense not to jump into a bear tank. Social interpretation: areas of poverty, insufficient education, alas, the subproletariat has a tendency to act on impulse, without thinking. But, I ask you, what's all this talk about insufficient education? Even the poorest child watches TV, or

has read a schoolbook in which bears devour humans and hunters therefore kill bears.

3   At this point I began to wonder if the boys didn't venture into the pool
precisely because they do watch TV and go to school. These children were
probably victims of our guilty conscience, as reflected in the schools and the
mass media.

4   Human beings have always been merciless with animals, but when humans became aware of their own cruelty, they began, if not to love all animals
(because, with only sporadic hesitation, they continue eating them), at least
to speak well of them. As the media, the schools, public institutions in general, have to explain away so many acts performed against humans by humans, it seems finally a good idea, psychologically and ethically, to insist on
the goodness of animals. We allow children of the Third World to die, but we
urge children of the First to respect not only butterflies and bunny rabbits
but also whales, crocodiles, snakes.

5   Mind you, this educational approach is *per se* correct. What is excessive is
the persuasive technique chosen: to render animals worthy of rescue they are
humanized, toyified. No one says they are entitled to survive *even* if, as a rule,
they are savage and carnivorous. No, they are made respectable by becoming
cuddly, comic, good-natured, benevolent, wise, and prudent.

6   No one is more thoughtless than a lemming, more deceitful than a cat,
more slobbering than a dog in August, more smelly than a piglet, more hysterical than a horse, more idiotic than a moth, more slimy than a snail, more
poisonous than a viper, less imaginative than an ant, and less musically creative than a nightingale. Simply put, we must love—or, if that is downright
impossible, at least respect—these and other animals for what they are. The
tales of earlier times overdid the wicked wolf, the tales of today exaggerate
the good wolves. We must save the whales, not because they are good, but because they are a part of nature's inventory and they contribute to the ecolog-
ical equilibrium. Instead, our children are raised with whales that talk, wolves
that join the Third Order of St. Francis, and, above all, an endless array of
teddy bears.

7   Advertising, cartoons, illustrated books are full of bears with hearts of
gold, law-abiding, cozy, and protective—although in fact it's insulting for a
bear to be told he has a right to live because he's only a dumb but inoffensive
brute. So I suspect that the poor children in Central Park died not through
lack of education but through too much of it. They are the victims of our unhappy conscience.

8   To make them forget how bad human beings are, they were taught too
insistently that bears are good. Instead of being told honestly what humans
are and what bears are.

WHAT DID THE WRITER SAY AND WHAT DID YOU THINK?

1. Before presenting his own explanation for the boys' behavior, the author rejects some other explanations. Summarize those other explanations.
2. Who are the main culprits in misleading the boys about the nature of animals?
3. What do the animals listed at the start of paragraph 6 have in common?
4. Express the thesis in your own words.

HOW DID THE WRITER SAY IT?

1. Define the invented word "toyified" in paragraph 5.
2. In paragraph 4, why is "bunny rabbits" a better choice of words than "bunnies" or "rabbits?"

WHAT ABOUT <u>YOUR</u> WRITING?

One of the fundamental ingredients of English style is *parallelism:* using the same (parallel) grammatical forms to express elements of approximately the same (parallel) importance. This definition may seem more formidable than it really is. Parallelism is so fundamental that we use it all the time.

Three parallel adjectives:

The man was *tall, dark,* and *handsome.*

Four parallel nouns:

We have to buy a *rug,* a *sofa,* two *chairs,* and a *lamp.*

Three parallel prepositional phrases:

. . . *of the people, by the people, for the people.*

Three parallel independent clauses:

I want you. I need you. I love you.

Two parallel imperatives:

Sit down and *relax.*

Four parallel infinitives:

To strive, to seek, to find, and not *to yield.*

The parallel grammatical forms point to and reinforce the parallels in thought and importance. Moreover, parallelism is what readers normally expect; it's the normal way that words are put together. Notice how a breakdown in expected parallelism adversely affects these sentences:

The man was tall, dark, and an athlete.

. . . of the people, by the people, and serving the people.

To strive, to seek, to find, and we must not yield.

We can find frequent and effective use of parallelism throughout "Speaking of Animals." We find parallel nouns in paragraph 4: "whales, crocodiles, snakes." We find parallel adjectives in paragraph 5: "cuddly, comic, good-natured, benevolent, wise, and prudent." Take a special look at the long list beginning paragraph 6. The parallel phrasing here is not just a technicality. It reinforces the idea that the animals *are* parallel in their behavior, that they all have undesirable characteristics that many people would rather ignore.

Bear three points in mind for your own writing:

1. Parallelism isn't just a matter of sterile correctness. It can contribute to genuine stylistic distinction. Some of the most memorable phrases in the language draw much of their strength from parallelism:

   Friends, Romans, countrymen . . .

   I have nothing to offer but blood, sweat, toil, and tears.

   . . . life, liberty, and the pursuit of happiness.

   I came, I saw, I conquered.

   . . . with malice toward none, with charity for all.

2. Occasional modifying words do not break the basic parallelism and can sometimes help avoid the danger of monotony. These sentences still show parallelism:

   He was tall, dark, and astonishingly handsome.

   We have to buy a rug, a sofa, two chairs, and most of all a fancy new lamp.

3. Parallelism works only when each member of the parallel series is roughly equivalent in importance. It leads to absurdity in the following cases:

   My teacher has knowledge, enthusiasm, concern, and sinus trouble.

   We must protect society from murderers, sexual predators, kidnappers, and litterbugs.

DARKNESS AT NOON

Harold Krents

Harold Krents was active for many years in working for fair employment practices for handicapped people. A graduate of Harvard College and Harvard Law School, he worked as a lawyer from 1971 until his death in 1986. Harold Krents was the model for the blind protagonist in the play and movie *Butterflies Are Free*, and his autobiography *To Chase the Wind* inspired the film *To Race the Wind*.

Words to check:

narcissistic (paragraph 1)
enunciating (2)
conversely (2)
retina (3)

graphically (5)
intoned (12)
cum laude (15)
mandate (17)

1   Blind from birth, I have never had the opportunity to see myself and have been completely dependent on the image I create in the eye of the observer. To date it has not been narcissistic.

2   There are those who assume that since I can't see, I obviously also cannot hear. Very often people will converse with me at the top of their lungs, enunciating each word very carefully. Conversely, people will also often whisper, assuming that since my eyes don't work, my ears don't either.

3   For example, when I go to the airport and ask the ticket agent for assistance to the plane, he or she will invariably pick up the phone, call a ground hostess and whisper: "Hi, Jane, we've got a 76 here." I have concluded that the word "blind" is not used for one of two reasons: Either they fear that if the dread word is spoken, the ticket agent's retina will immediately detach, or they are reluctant to inform me of my condition of which I may not have been previously aware.

4   On the other hand, others know that of course I can hear, but believe that I can't talk. Often, therefore, when my wife and I go out to dinner, a waiter or waitress will ask Kit if "*he* would like to drink" to which I respond that "indeed *he* would."

5   This point was graphically driven home to me while we were in England. I had been given a year's leave of absence from my Washington law firm to study for a diploma in law degree at Oxford University. During the year I became ill and was hospitalized. Immediately after admission, I was wheeled down to the X-ray room. Just at the door sat an elderly woman—elderly I would judge from the sound of her voice. "What is his name?" the woman asked the orderly who had been wheeling me.

6   "What's your name?" the orderly repeated to me.

7   "Harold Krents," I replied.

8   "Harold Krents," he repeated.

9   "When was he born?"

10   "When were you born?"

11   "November 5, 1944," I responded.

12   "November 5, 1944," the orderly intoned.

13   This procedure continued for approximately five minutes at which point even my saint-like disposition deserted me. "Look," I finally blurted out, "this is absolutely ridiculous. Okay, granted I can't see, but it's got to have become pretty clear to both of you that I don't need an interpreter."

14   "He says he doesn't need an interpreter," the orderly reported to the woman.

15   The toughest misconception of all is the view that because I can't see, I can't work. I was turned down by over forty law firms because of my blindness, even though my qualifications included a cum laude degree from Harvard College and a good ranking in my Harvard Law School class.

16   The attempt to find employment, the continuous frustration of being told that it was impossible for a blind person to practice law, the rejection letters, not based on my lack of ability but rather on my disability, will always remain one of the most disillusioning experiences of my life.

17   Fortunately, this view of limitation and exclusion is beginning to change. On April 16, [1978] the Department of Labor issued regulations that mandate equal-employment opportunities for the handicapped. By and large, the business community's response to offering employment to the disabled has been enthusiastic.

18   I therefore look forward to the day, with the expectation that it is certain to come, when employers will view their handicapped workers as a little child did me years ago when my family still lived in Scarsdale.

19   I was playing basketball with my father in our backyard according to procedures we had developed. My father would stand beneath the hoop, shout, and I would shoot over his head at the basket attached to our garage. Our next-door neighbor, aged five, wandered over into our yard with a playmate. "He's blind," our neighbor whispered to her friend in a voice that could be heard distinctly by Dad and me. Dad shot and missed; I did the same. Dad hit the rim: I missed entirely: Dad shot and missed the garage entirely. "Which one is blind?" whispered back the little friend.

20   I would hope that in the near future when a plant manager is touring the factory with the foreman and comes upon a handicapped and nonhandicapped person working together, his comment after watching them work will be, "Which one is disabled?"

WHAT DID THE WRITER SAY AND WHAT DID YOU THINK?

1. What is the thesis? Is it ever stated directly?
2. Into what categories does the author divide the sighted people he meets?
3. What is a "76"?
4. Why does Krents feel that discrimination against the handicapped in the workplace will change?
5. What is important about the way the neighbor's friend reacts to Krents and his father?
6. Do you think that the author is overly sensitive?

HOW DID THE WRITER SAY IT?

1. Most of the essay is written in a very casual tone. One section, however, is much more formal. Where is it, and why is it so different?
2. Why is the tone of cheerfulness and good humor so important to the success of this essay?
3. How does Krents relate his basketball experience to his main point?

WHAT ABOUT <u>YOUR</u> WRITING?

"Look . . . this is absolutely ridiculous. Okay, granted I can't see, but it's got to have become pretty clear to both of you that I don't need an interpreter."

"He says he doesn't need an interpreter," the orderly reported to the woman.

Good dialogue, a few lines or a lengthy conversation, can add life to almost any writing, nonfiction as well as fiction. The sense of immediacy can be remarkable. These are the words the people spoke, and readers are on their own. The author may mention a tone of voice or a gesture or may drop in an occasional *he said* or *she said* so that readers can keep track of the speaker, but essentially the author butts out. Good dialogue is direct, dramatic, persuasive. Apart from anything else, it gives the reader a pleasurable sense of recognition: "This is the way people talk," the reader says. "This is authentic."

Among the less obvious uses of dialogue could be its occasional use in original and lively introductions.

"Did you have a good time on your date, Dear?"
"Aw, Mom."
"Was she a nice girl?"
"Aw, Mom."

"What does her father do?"

"Aw, Mom."

The generation gap—in my house, at least—is more than a myth.

"So what should we do about protecting the environment?" my teacher asks. If I had the nerve, I'd like to answer, "First of all, let's stop talking about it every single minute. Enough is enough."

Many creative writing teachers are inclined to feel that writing good dialogue is a gift. You have it or you don't. You were born with an ear for dialogue or you weren't. Still, some elementary pointers might be helpful.

Keep Your Comments Simple

Confine yourself to *he said, she said, he asked, she answered,* and similar phrases. Avoid fancy variations like *he asserted, he expostulated, she queried, she gasped, he hissed.*

Don't Worry about Standard English

If the person who's talking would swear, say *ain't,* confuse *who* and *whom,* make the person talk that way. Don't, whatever you do, use swear words to show off how tough and courageous and unflinchingly honest you are. Just be accurate.

Change Paragraphs with Each Speaker

You'll find violations of this advice among some of the best writers, but it seems ordinary common sense. Changing paragraphs makes the dialogue easier to follow by giving the reader a direct visual indication that there's been a change of speaker.

FRUITFUL QUESTIONS

James Sollisch

James Sollisch is an advertising copywriter and a freelance writer. Here, with examples ranging from children in a food fight to one of the world's greatest astronomers, he helps explain the nature of creative thinking and issues a call for more of it.

Words to check:

paradigm (paragraph 1)   potent (7)
linear (1)   critique (8)
parameters (1)

1 The other night at the dinner table, my three kids—ages 9, 6 and 4—took time out from their food fight to teach me about paradigm shifts, and limitations of linear thinking and how to refocus parameters.

2   Here's how it happened: We were playing our own oral version of the Sesame Street game, "What Doesn't Belong?," where kids look at three pictures and choose the one that doesn't fit. I said, "OK, what doesn't belong, an orange, a tomato or a strawberry?"

3   The oldest didn't take more than a second to deliver his smug answer: "Tomato because the other two are fruits." I agreed that this was the right answer despite the fact that some purists insist a tomato is a fruit. To those of us forced as kids to eat them in salads, tomatoes will always be vegetables. I was about to think up another set of three when my 4-year-old said, "The right answer is strawberry because the other two are round and a strawberry isn't." How could I argue with that?

4   Then my 6-year-old said, "It's the orange because the other two are red." Not to be outdone by his younger siblings, the 9-year-old said, "It could also be the orange because the other two grow on vines."

5   The middle one took this as a direct challenge. "It could be the strawberry because it's the only one you put on ice cream."

6   Something was definitely happening here. It was messier than a food fight and much more important than whether a tomato is a fruit or vegetable. My kids were doing what Copernicus did when he placed the sun at the center of the universe, readjusting the centuries-old paradigm of an Earth-centered system. They were doing what Reuben Mattus did when he renamed his Bronx ice cream Haagen-Dazs and raised the price without changing the product. They were doing what Edward Jenner did when he discovered a vaccination for smallpox by abandoning his quest for a cure.

7   Instead of studying people who were sick with smallpox, he began to study people who were exposed to it but never got sick. He found that they'd all contracted a similar but milder disease, cow pox, which vaccinated them against the deadly smallpox.

8   They were refocusing the parameters. They were redefining the problems. They were reframing the questions. In short, they were doing what every scientist who's ever made an important discovery throughout history

has done, according to Thomas Kuhn, in his book, "The Structure of Scientific Revolutions": They were shifting old paradigms.

9   But if this had been a workbook exercise in school, every kid who didn't circle tomato would have been marked wrong. Every kid who framed the question differently than "Which is not a fruit?" would have been wrong. Maybe that explains why so many of the world's most brilliant scientists and inventors were failures in school, the most notable being Albert Einstein, who was perhaps this century's most potent paradigm-shifter.

10   This is not meant to be a critique of schools. Lord knows, that's easy enough to do. This is, instead, a reminder that there are real limits to the value of information. I bring this up because we seem to be at a point in the evolution of our society where everyone is clamoring for more technology, for instant access to ever-growing bodies of information.

11   Students must be on-line. Your home must be digitally connected to the World Wide Web. Businesses must be able to download volumes of data instantaneously. But unless we shift our paradigms and refocus our parameters, the super information highway will lead us nowhere.

12   We are not now, nor have we recently been suffering from a lack of information. Think how much more information we have than Copernicus had four centuries ago. And he didn't do anything less Earth-shattering (pun intended) than completely change the way the universe was viewed. He didn't do it by uncovering more information—he did it by looking differently at information everyone else already had looked at. Edward Jenner didn't invent preventive medicine by accumulating information; he did it by reframing the question.

13   What we need as we begin to downshift onto the information highway is not more information but new ways of looking at it. We need to discover, as my kids did, that there is more than one right answer, there is more than one right question and there is more than one way to look at a body of information. We need to remember that when you have only a hammer, you tend to see every problem as a nail.

WHAT DID THE WRITER SAY AND WHAT DID YOU THINK?

1. Sollisch humorously uses elevated language in paragraph 1: His children taught him about "paradigm shifts, the limitations of linear thinking and how to refocus parameters." Express the same idea or ideas in everyday language. Does the author ever attempt to do this himself?

2. Why does the author believe the Haagen-Dazs founder belongs in the same group as Copernicus and Jenner? What did Sollisch's children do to deserve membership in the group?

3. What diseases other than smallpox have been conquered by abandoning the quest for a cure and instead finding ways to prevent them?
4. What is the author's main complaint about schools and computers?
5. Can the kind of thinking Sollisch wants actually be taught or is it an inborn gift or talent?

HOW DID THE WRITER SAY IT?

1. Why is the title particularly effective?
2. What makes the elevated language in paragraph 1 especially amusing?
3. How does the last sentence relate logically to the rest of the essay?

WHAT ABOUT <u>YOUR</u> WRITING?

Effective repetition of words and phrases—sometimes exact repetition, sometimes repetition with slight variations—is one of a writer's most direct means of driving home a point and achieving a touch of stylistic power. In paragraph 6, James Sollisch uses repetition to show the importance of his children's thinking and to connect that thinking to great accomplishments of the past: "My kids were doing what Copernicus did. . . . They were doing what Reuben Mattus did . . . They were doing what Edward Jenner did. . . ." Note also the repetition for emotional emphasis of sentences beginning with "they" in paragraph 8 and the repetition of "didn't do" phrases in paragraph 12.

Repetition can be abused. Handled poorly, it can become monotonous and irritating. If *every* sentence in Sollisch's essay began with "they," for example, his readers would lose their patience and their minds. Used properly, however, repetition has produced some of the most memorable phrases in the language:

Gentlemen may cry peace, peace—but there is no peace.

We have nothing to fear but fear itself.

It was the best of times, it was the worst of times.

Good bread, good meat, good God, let's eat!

AMERICA: THE MULTINATIONAL SOCIETY

Ishmael Reed

Twice nominated for National Book Awards, Ishmael Reed has written numerous novels, plays, essays, and songs and has taught at Harvard, Yale, Dartmouth, and the University of California at Berkeley. Among his novels are *The Freelance Pall Bearers* (1967), *Mumbo Jumbo* (1978), and *Reckless Eyeballing (1986)*. Volumes of essays include *Shrovetide in New Orleans (*1979) and *Writin' Is Fightin'* (1988). As you read "America: The Multinational Society," observe how careful Reed is to distribute his examples over as wide an area as possible (see p. 100), not merely to pour on a great number of examples.

Words to check:

mosques (paragraph 2)	monolithic (6)	patriarchs (10)
ostracism (4)	cubists (6)	lecterns (10)
monocultural (4)	surrealists (6)	calypso (11)
bouillabaisse (6)	dissidents (7)	meticulous (12)
entity (6)	archetypal (9)	repository (15)
	incarceration (9)	bereft (15)

1   At the annual Lower East Side Jewish Festival yesterday, a Chinese woman ate a pizza slice in front of Ty Thuan Duc's Vietnamese grocery store. Beside her a Spanish-speaking family patronized a cart with two signs: "Italian Ices" and "Kosher by Rabbi Alper." And after the pastrami ran out, everybody ate knishes.

(*New York Times*, 23 June 1983)

2   On the day before Memorial Day, 1983, a poet called me to describe a city he had just visited. He said that one section included mosques, built by the Islamic people who dwelled there. Attending his reading, he said, were large numbers of Hispanic people, forty thousand of whom lived in the same city. He was not talking about a fabled city located in some mysterious region of the world. The city he'd visited was Detroit.

3   A few months before, as I was leaving Houston, Texas, I heard it announced on the radio that Texas' largest minority was Mexican American, and though a foundation recently issued a report critical of bilingual education, the taped voice used to guide the passengers on the air trams connecting terminals in Dallas Airport is in both Spanish and English. If the trend continues, a day will come when it will be difficult to travel through some sections of the country without hearing commands in both English and Spanish;

after all, for some western states, Spanish was the first written language and the Spanish style lives on in the western way of life.

4   Shortly after my Texas trip, I sat in an auditorium located on the campus of the University of Wisconsin at Milwaukee as a Yale professor—whose original work on the influence of African cultures upon those of the Americas has led to his ostracism from some monocultural intellectual circles—walked up and down the aisle, like an old-time southern evangelist, dancing and drumming the top of the lectern, illustrating his points before some serious Afro-American intellectuals and artists who cheered and applauded his performance and his mastery of information. The professor was "white." After his lecture, he joined a group of Milwaukeeans in a conversation. All of the participants spoke Yoruban,[1] though only the professor had ever traveled to Africa.

5   One of the artists told me that his paintings, which included African and Afro-American mythological symbols and imagery, were hanging in the local McDonald's restaurant. The next day I went to McDonald's and snapped pictures of smiling youngsters eating hamburgers below paintings that could grace the walls of any of the country's leading museums. The manager of the local McDonald's said, "I don't know what you boys are doing, but I like it," as he commissioned the local painters to exhibit in his restaurant.

6   Such blurring of cultural styles occurs in everyday life in the United States to a greater extent than anyone can imagine and is probably more prevalent than the sensational conflict between people of different backgrounds that is played up and often encouraged by the media. The result is what the Yale professor, Robert Thompson, referred to as a cultural bouillabaisse, yet members of the nation's present educational and cultural Elect still cling to the notion that the United States belongs to some vaguely defined entity they refer to as "Western civilization," by which they mean, presumably, a civilization created by the people of Europe, as if Europe can be viewed in monolithic terms. Is Beethoven's Ninth Symphony, which includes Turkish marches, a part of Western civilization, or the late nineteenth- and twentieth-century French paintings, whose creators were influenced by Japanese art? And what of the cubists, through whom the influence of African art changed modern painting, or the surrealists, who were so impressed with the art of the Pacific Northwest Indians that, in their map of North America, Alaska dwarfs the lower forty-eight in size?

7   Are the Russians, who are often criticized for their adoption of "Western" ways by Tsarist dissidents in exile, members of Western civilization? And

---

[1] Language of the Yoruba people, who live mainly in southwest Nigeria

what of the millions of Europeans who have black African and Asian ancestry, black Africans having occupied several countries for hundreds of years? Are these "Europeans" members of Western civilization, or the Hungarians, who originated across the Urals in a place called Greater Hungary, or the Irish, who came from the Iberian Peninsula?

8   Even the notion that North America is part of Western civilization because our "system of government" is derived from Europe is being challenged by Native American historians who say that the founding fathers, Benjamin Franklin especially, were actually influenced by the system of government that had been adopted by the Iroquois hundreds of years prior to the arrival of large numbers of Europeans.

9   Western civilization, then, becomes another confusing category like Third World, or Judeo-Christian culture, as man attempts to impose his small-screen view of political and cultural reality upon a complex world. Our most publicized novelist recently said that Western civilization was the greatest achievement of mankind, an attitude that flourishes on the street level as scribbles in public restrooms: "White Power," "Niggers and Spics Suck," or "Hitler was a prophet," the latter being the most telling, for wasn't Adolph Hitler the archetypal monoculturalist who, in his pig-headed arrogance, believed that one way and one blood was so pure that it had to be protected from alien strains at all costs? Where did such an attitude, which has caused so much misery and depression in our national life, which has tainted even our noblest achievements, begin? An attitude that caused the incarceration of Japanese-American citizens during World War II, the persecution of Chicanos and Chinese Americans, the near-extermination of the Indians, and the murder and lynchings of thousands of Afro-Americans.

10   Virtuous, hardworking, pious, even though they occasionally would wander off after some fancy clothes, or rendezvous in the woods with the town prostitute, the Puritans are idealized in our schoolbooks as "a hardy band" of no-nonsense patriarchs whose discipline razed the forest and brought order to the New World (a term that annoys Native American historians). Industrious, responsible, it was their "Yankee ingenuity" and practicality that created the work ethic. They were simple folk who produced a number of good poets, and they set the tone for the American writing style, of lean and spare lines, long before Hemingway. They worshiped in churches whose colors blended in with the New England snow, churches with simple structures and ornate lecterns.

11   The Puritans were a daring lot, but they had a mean streak. They hated the theater and banned Christmas. They punished people in a cruel and inhuman manner. They killed children who disobeyed their parents. When they came in contact with those whom they considered heathens or aliens, they

behaved in such a bizarre and irrational manner that this chapter in the American history comes down to us as a late-movie horror film. They exterminated the Indians, who taught them how to survive in a world unknown to them, and their encounter with the calypso culture of Barbados resulted in what the tourist guide in Salem's Witches' House refers to as the Witchcraft Hysteria.

12   The Puritan legacy of hard work and meticulous accounting led to the establishment of a great industrial society; it is no wonder that the American industrial revolution began in Lowell, Massachusetts, but there was the other side, the strange and paranoid attitudes toward those different from the Elect.

13   The cultural attitudes of that early Elect continue to be voiced in everyday life in the United States: the president of a distinguished university, writing a letter to the *Times*, belittling the study of African civilizations; the television network that promoted its show on the Vatican art with the boast that this art represented "the finest achievements of the human spirit." A modern up-tempo state of complex rhythms that depends upon contacts with an international community can no longer behave as if it dwelled in a "Zion Wilderness" surrounded by beasts and pagans.

14   When I heard a schoolteacher warn the other night about the invasion of the American educational system by foreign curriculums, I wanted to yell at the television set, "Lady, they're already here." It has already begun because the world is here. The world has been arriving at these shores for at least ten thousand years from Europe, Africa, and Asia. In the late nineteenth and early twentieth centuries, large numbers of Europeans arrived, adding their cultures to those of the European, African, and Asian settlers who were already here, and recently millions have been entering the country from South America and the Caribbean, making Yale Professor Bob Thompson's bouillabaisse richer and thicker.

15   One of our most visionary politicians said that he envisioned a time when the United States could become the brain of the world, by which he meant the repository of all of the latest advanced information systems. I thought of that remark when an enterprising poet friend of mine called to say that he had just sold a poem to a computer magazine and that the editors were delighted to get it because they didn't carry fiction or poetry. Is that the kind of world we desire? A humdrum homogenous world of all brains but no heart, no fiction, no poetry; a world of robots with human attendants bereft of imagination, of culture? Or does North America deserve a more exciting destiny? To become a place where the cultures of the world crisscross. This is possible because the United States is unique in the world: The world is here.

WHAT DID THE WRITER SAY AND WHAT DID YOU THINK?

1. What is Reed's thesis?
2. Where is the thesis first stated?
3. Why does the author have difficulty accepting the traditional definition of "Western Civilization?"
4. Who, according to the author, forms the "Cultural Elect?"
5. What, according to Reed, is offensive about the statement, "Western civilization is the greatest creation of mankind"?
6. Does Reed like or dislike the American Puritans? Does he have mixed feelings?

HOW DID THE WRITER SAY IT?

1. Why does Reed frequently cite other people in order to support his points?
2. Why does the author emphasize the good qualities of the Puritans as well as the bad?
3. How does the tone of the last paragraph differ from the tone in the rest of the essay?

WHAT ABOUT **YOUR** WRITING?

In his last paragraph, Ishmael Reed asks a series of *rhetorical questions:* "Is that the kind of world we desire? A humdrum homogenous world of all brains but no heart, no fiction, no poetry; a world of robots with human attendants bereft of imagination, of culture? Or does North America deserve a more exciting destiny?"

A rhetorical question is a question that either expects no reply or clearly calls for one desired reply. It is not a genuine inquiry like "Who was the thirteenth president of the United States?" Reed is confident that he has proven his case that cultural, racial, and ethnic diversity is one of America's greatest glories. Nevertheless, a flat statement to this effect may simply sound too flat—a dull summary, a bit of needless repetition. Rhetorical questions, in this case, can help remind us of the main point without needing to repeat it.

As long as they are not overused, rhetorical questions can also be a powerful device for establishing a dramatic atmosphere, particularly in conclusions. Rhetorical questions of this kind must be handled with restraint or they become forced and artificial, but a good writer should feel free to use them.

Can all these blunders really be honest mistakes? Isn't it possible that we've let ourselves be duped again? And isn't it time to act?

Doctors get paid only for their patients' being ill, not for their patients' staying healthy. Is that practical? Is that smart? Is that even sane?

Is life so dear, or peace so sweet, as to be purchased at the price of chains and slavery? Forbid it, Almighty God! I know not what course others may take; but as for me, give me liberty, or give me death.

———

Process

In its most familiar form, writing about a process provides instructions. This kind of process paper tells readers the series of steps they must perform to achieve a particular result. At its simplest level, the process paper is a how-to-do-it paper: how to cook Beef Wellington, how to drive from town to Camp Wilderness (see p. 16), how to install wall paneling, how to operate a home computer, how to put together a child's bike on Christmas morning. Writing simple, clear instructions makes many demands on a writer, and people who are good at it often earn excellent salaries. Ask those parents struggling with that bike on Christmas morning how many dollars they would offer for easy-to-read and easy-to-follow instructions.

The conventional how-to-do-it paper sometimes can lend itself to humor, as when a writer deliberately gives instructions on what no one wants to learn: how to flunk out of school, how to have a heart attack, and so forth. Besides drawing on the appeal of humor, such papers can also have serious instructional purposes by telling the reader, between the lines, how to do well in school or how to avoid coronaries. Other humorous pieces give instructions on what many people *do* want to learn but don't usually want to acknowledge: *How to Succeed in Business Without Really Trying* and *Gamesmanship, or The Art of Winning Games Without Actually Cheating* are titles of two successful books.

Several other variations on the how-to-do-it paper are also fairly common. A how-it-works paper explains the functioning of anything from an electric toothbrush to the system for ratifying a new constitutional amendment. A how-it-*was*-done paper might trace the process by which Stonehenge or the Pyramids were built or of how the chase scenes in the old Keystone Kops movies were filmed. A how-*not*-to-do-it paper might trace the process by which the writer did everything wrong in reshingling the roof or buying a used car.

At a more advanced level, process papers can study the course of social, political, scientific, and cultural developments: the process that led to the discovery of the polio vaccine, the decision of Napoleon to invade Russia, the spread of Christianity, Franklin D. Roosevelt's proposal to increase the membership of the Supreme Court. Process writing can also be a powerful instrument of literary analysis: the process by which Frederic Henry in *A Farewell to Arms* comes to desert the army, or Captain Ahab in *Moby-Dick* associates the white whale with evil, or Iago persuades Othello that Desdemona has been unfaithful.

How does the persuasive principle apply to process writing? If you're writing a straightforward how-to-do-it paper, for example, why not simply list the steps and forget about a thesis? You don't have a point to make as such, do you? Aren't you saying only that these are the things one must do to paint a room or change a flat tire or study for an exam? So why not just list them?

These questions are legitimate, and it's certainly possible to write a process paper without a thesis. In most cases, though, the paper won't be as good as it could be and ought to be. Apart from the advantages of writing with a thesis as described in Chapter 1, you're writing a how-to-do-it paper, after all, for people who don't yet know "how to do it." (If they knew, they'd have no reason to read the paper.) A mere long list of things to do, each step considered separately, can both bore readers and confuse them. A thesis helps readers get solidly oriented at the outset and enables them to see each separate step as part of a coherent pattern.

But what kind of thesis makes sense in the humble little paper on how to paint a room? All kinds.

Painting a room is much easier than it seems.

Painting a room is much harder than it seems.

Painting a room is great fun.

Painting a room is horrible drudgery.

Painting a room is easy compared to preparing the room to be painted.

Painting a room takes less time than most people suppose.

Painting a room takes more time than most people suppose.

Any one of these ideas, not to mention many more imaginative ones, could give unity and interest to a how-to-do-it paper. The writer, in addition to making each step convey the necessary raw information, would connect each step or group of related steps to the thesis.

¶ 1—Presentation of thesis: Painting a room is much easier than it seems.

Start of ¶ 2—To prepare the room, you need only a dust cloth, lots of masking tape, spackling paste . . .

Start of ¶ 3—If preparing the room was easy, the painting itself is child's play . . .

Start of ¶ 4—Cleaning up is the easiest part of all . . .

With the desirability of a thesis in mind, it's no massive project to think up promising theses for some other subjects:

Every step of the way, Napoleon's decision to invade Russia was based on foolish overconfidence.

Franklin D. Roosevelt's proposal to pack the Supreme Court came in response to a long series of legislative frustrations.

Frederic Henry's desertion of the army in *A Farewell to Arms* is the last step in a gradually accelerating process of disillusionment.

The dramatic discovery of the polio vaccine came as the result of a fiercely competitive race to be first.

The seemingly spontaneous, mad chase scenes in Keystone Kops movies were actually the product of careful planning of every detail.

The process by which the pyramids were built shows an astonishing knowledge of the laws of modern physics.

Once you set up a thesis, the significant issues are the mechanics of writing about the process itself.

Be Sure You Are Writing About a Process

The words "How to" or "How" in your title guarantee nothing. A process is a series, a sequence, an orderly progression. One step or event follows another: first this, then that, then something else. A happy-go-lucky collection of handy hints is not a process. Chapter 1 of this book followed a necessary sequence in the description of the process of *first* starting with a general subject, *then* limiting the subject, *then* devising a thesis and thesis statement, *then* incorporating the thesis into the whole paper. Chapter 4, on the other hand, while telling "how to" write an example paper, presented a bundle of miscellaneous suggestions on what to think about in looking over the examples; the

suggestions followed no particularly rigid order and therefore did not consti-
tute a real process.

Follow Strict Chronological Order

The rule to follow strict chronological order seems obvious, but in fact it is
unique to process writing. In other patterns, you try to begin with your most
important or dramatic or amusing material. In process writing, you begin
with step one. You try to make all the steps of the process as interesting as
possible to your reader, but you have no choice about the order in which you
discuss them.

Before Describing the First Step of the Process, Indicate Any Special Ingredients or Equipment That Will Be Needed

Recipes, for example, almost always begin with a list of ingredients.

Be Sure the Process Is Complete

In a how-to-do-it paper, you're describing a process that you probably can do
automatically, and it's easy to omit some obvious steps because you don't
consciously think about them at all. They are not so obvious to your reader. If
you're telling the reader how to stop a leak in the kitchen sink, for instance,
don't forget to have the poor soul shut off the water supply before removing
the faucet and replacing the washer.

Try to Anticipate Difficulties

First, warn the reader in advance if a notably tough step is coming up:

Now comes the hard part.
The next step is a bit tricky.
Be extremely careful here.

Second, advise the reader of what can be done to make the process easier
or more pleasant. You're an insider, and you have an insider's information. The
process of changing a flat tire does not require anyone to put the lugs into the
inverted hubcap so they won't get lost, but it's a technique insiders use to
head off trouble before it starts. Painting a room does not require anyone to

wear an old hat, but your mentioning the advisability of an old hat might be appreciated by anyone who prefers paint-free hair.

Third, tell the reader what to do if something goes wrong. Don't terrify the reader, but be frank about common foul-ups:

If any paint should get on the window . . .
If the hubcap is hard to replace . . .

If You Need to Handle Many Separate Steps, Arrange Them into Groups When Possible

Even a simple process may involve a large number of steps. The process paper is far less intimidating if the steps are presented in manageable bunches. On page 127, the writer divided the process of painting a room into preparation, painting, and cleaning up. Each division received a paragraph, and the reader got the impression of having only three major areas to worry about instead of fifty separate steps. Even as uninspired a grouping of steps as Phase I, Phase II, Phase III, or Beginning, Middle, End, is preferable to none at all. The more steps in the process, the more essential it becomes to collect them into groups.

Define Unfamiliar Terms

Definitions of unfamiliar terms are needed in all writing, but they're especially important in the how-to-do-it paper because the instructions are for an audience that must be assumed to know nothing about the subject.

Two final recommendations about your choice of topics are worth brief notes.

Avoid Highly Technical Processes

Because you must define all unfamiliar terms, you don't want to choose an obscure scientific subject with such a specialized vocabulary that most of your energy will be spent providing definitions rather than presenting a process.

Avoid Subjects for Which Pictures Work Better Than Words

Some processes, often but not always the highly technical ones, can best be explained with a few diagrams and almost as few words. Consider instructions on how to tie shoelaces. Pictures are the only way to go. Depending solely or almost solely on words would create pointless trouble for the writer and confusion for the reader. Since you are in a writing class, not an art class, you should avoid such processes.

———————

WRITING SUGGESTIONS FOR PROCESS ESSAYS

Many topics have already been mentioned in this chapter. The suggestions here are meant to provide some further inspiration. Suggestions have been grouped into two categories: General Areas for Exploration (with examples) and Specific Topics.

General Areas for Exploration
1. Do-it-yourself repairs: bikes, cars, radios, television sets, broken windows.
2. Routine chores: gardening, cooking, shopping.
3. School and business: studying, taking notes, registering, applying to colleges, applying for jobs, creating a good impression at job interviews.
4. Sports, games, and other recreational activities: how to win at poker, bridge, Monopoly, Tetris; how to watch a football game, throw Frisbees, water-ski; how to plan a trip.
5. Finances: budgeting, borrowing, investing.
6. Hobbies: how to start a stamp, coin, tropical fish collection; how to work at a particular art or craft; how a magic trick is performed.
7. Children and pets: baby-sitting, toilet training, safety, housebreaking, traveling.
8. Personal care: grooming, breaking a bad habit, treating a cold, curing a hangover.
9. Humor: how to be a bore, worrywart, nag; how to get out of housework, butter up teachers, call in sick; how to die at thirty.
10. How it works: power steering, air conditioning, CD players, zippers.
11. The past: how a battle was fought, a crime was committed, a structure was built, a law was passed, a disease was conquered.
12. Literature: how an author prepares the reader for a surprise ending, how a character makes a crucial decision.

Specific Topics
1. What to do if arrested.
2. What to do if in a car accident.

3. How to find a rich husband or wife.
4. How to diet.
5. How to exercise.
6. How to drive defensively.
7. How to apply first aid for snake bites.
8. How to protect oneself in a natural disaster (tornado, hurricane, flood).
9. How to waste time.
10. How to plan for a holiday or other special occasion: Thanksgiving dinner, Passover seder, birthday party, bar mitzvah or confirmation party, Easter egg hunt, wedding.
11. How to live on nothing a year.
12. How to pack a suitcase.
13. How to stop smoking.
14. How to hitch a ride.
15. How to give oneself a perfect shave.

NO BOWS ON THE BUTT: CHOOSING YOUR WEDDING GOWN

Jennifer Simms-Collins (student)

Thesis: Four important steps can help you find the wedding gown you want.

    I. Be Prepared
       A. Do some thinking
       B. Know what kind of wedding you'll have
       C. Know what kind of person you are

   II. Be Adventurous
       A. Try on a few things you hate
       B. Learn useful things
       C. Take chances while you can

  III. Be Practical
       A. Know how much money you can spend
       B. Try on expensive gowns
       C. Think about less expensive options like less formal gowns

  IV. Be Self-Indulgent
       A. Bring family members or friends along
       B. Try on a veil
       C. Imagine how your fiancé and father will react
       D. Enjoy being a bride

PROCESS

Conclusion: These four steps won't solve every problem, but you'll find the dress you want and probably survive the experience.

I got married about six months ago. Just before my wedding one of my two closest friends got engaged. Just after my wedding the other one followed suit. So, I've recently been involved in the selection and purchase of no fewer than three wedding gowns. This makes me something of an expert on how to find the perfect gown. And, while I'm tempted to summarize all my fine suggestions in the single piece of advice, "No bows on the butt," I won't. Instead, I'll tell you the four crucial steps to finding the gown you really want.

The most important thing to remember is to be prepared. Do some thinking before you shop. Know when and where your wedding will take place. Know if it's going to be a big formal wedding, or a small and casual one. Know whether you'll have the wedding inside or outside. All of these things will affect the kind of gown that will be ideal for your own specific wedding. But no preparation is more important than your knowing the kind of person that you are. Are you a snow-boarding, mountain-biking, martial arts expert? Even if you're having a big traditional wedding, you may not be very comfortable in a gown that tries to make you look like a fairy princess. And if you are the fairy princess type, you probably won't be very happy with a subdued white sheath, even if your wedding is going to be a small and quiet one. Know your wedding and know yourself before you even set foot in a bridal store, and you'll be on your way to a perfect gown.

Next, when you're ready to begin trying things on, it's vital to be adventurous. Just because you do know who you are and what kind of a wedding you'll be having doesn't mean that you can't try on a few wildly inappropriate gowns. One of my friends, in fact, told me that my reward for helping her shop would be that she would try on any dress I told her to, no matter how much she hated it. What she found out was that even if the dress as a whole was terrible there were often small details she liked—a waistline, some embroidery—that she could look for as part of a dress that she liked more. You never know what you'll discover. Besides, when will you ever again have a chance to try on a dress that's wider than you are tall?

While you're being adventurous, though, it's important to remember the third step: Be practical. It is shockingly easy to spend a small fortune on a wedding dress. This is great if you've got the money. My friends and I didn't have that kind of money. We did, however, have math skills, and we decided that we'd divide our gown prices by the number of hours we'd spend wearing them, and see if the cost per hour made us shudder or not. Most of the time we shuddered. So we tried on and sighed over a lot of very expensive and beautiful dresses and then found less expensive ones that were just as beautiful. I wore a bridesmaid's dress that I ordered in white. It was about 10% of the price of my other favorite dress. One of my friends wore what the sales clerk called "an informal," a simpler wedding dress that was just perfect for her small outdoor wedding. The other had a lavish dress made for her, which wasn't cheap, but which still cost less than buying the designer gown she'd longed for. We all loved our dresses, and we didn't have to break the bank or force our wedding guests to eat pizza in order to do it.

Last and most important, when you're shopping for your wedding dress, don't be afraid to be a little self-indulgent. Take your mother, your grandmother, your sister, your best friend along with you. They're guaranteed to coo lovingly and admire you. Try on a veil, even if you think you don't want to wear one. Cry. Look at how beautiful you are. Imagine your fiancé's face, your father's face, when they see you in your dress for the first time. Enjoy being a bride.

I can't promise you that following these steps will mean that you won't have a few frustrations with your dress. Fittings have been known to drive otherwise rational brides entirely around the bend. Shopping for shoes to go with the dress is a challenge I never want to live through again. And even my vast bridal shopping experience has not taught me how to cope with all those super-perky people who work in bridal stores. However, if you follow my four steps, you will be on your way to being a well-dressed bride. And you'll probably even survive the experience.

HOW CAN I MAKE MY HOUSE LOOK GOOD IN A HURRY?

Don Aslett

Don Aslett is the author of numerous books on cleaning, including, most recently, *The Cleaning Encyclopedia* (1999). Here he combines the fun of making a house look perfect with the additional joy of setting records for speed.

Words to check:

strewn (paragraph 8)	aura (10)
diorama (8)	squander (10)

1 The phone rings, and it's Mike and Marsha; they just happen to be driving through. She was Immaculate Homemaker of the Year last year, and he's dean of organizational science at Georgia Tech. They co-host a radio talk show that tells all. You have ten minutes, max, before they "drop by."

2   This happens to every one of us, and we all dread it. Don't panic and don't just shovel the bulk of the junk quickly into the nearest closet.

3   1. First turn up all the lights! Yes, brighter not dimmer helps a dirty house look clean. There's a tendency to try to hide cobwebs, dust, and dropped popcorn by subduing the light, but the opposite is true. Darkness causes shadows, mystery, suspicion. Your place, even clean, will give guests a

"cover up" feeling if it's darkened. Brightly lit homes feel good and visitors feel better and they'll remember that nice feeling and forget the sweat sock or dog bone sticking out from under the sofa.

4 2. Then clean yourself up—a little makeup or quick shave, new shirt or blouse or sweater. A quick upgrade of your appearance goes a long way toward making things seem under control—after all, they'll be seeing a lot more of you than they will of the house.

5 3. Enlist all the help you can, quick—but don't force or threaten anyone into it—they're likely to retaliate by saying something to the guest like, "Boy, if you don't believe in resurrection, you should have seen this place fifteen minutes ago."

6 4. How small a part of the house can you confine them to?—it'll help a lot if you can target your efforts. If it's at least 60 degrees, you can stay on the porch or deck or terrace, outside. Otherwise stick with the living room or kitchen or at least the lower story. Close all the other doors and decide now what you're going to say when they ask for the grand tour of the house—and the kid with the messiest bedroom acts like he's going to take them up on it.

7 5. Cast your eye over the entrance area—porch, door, entryway, steps, even the sidewalk leading up to it. This is what gives that fatal first impression and sets the tone for the whole abode. Remove any out-of-season ornaments and anything crooked or rusty and scoop up all those chewed bones, broken toys, muddy boots, dirty doormats, grubby pet dishes, dead plants, and half-composted shopping flyers.

8 6. Dejunk—especially any empty food containers, strewn clothes, garbage, etc. Merely removing all the loose litter and rearranging everything out of place will do wonders. But do leave reading material and half-done projects out. They make you look industrious and intellectual and will give the guest a complex that will help keep his mind off the "wash me" etched in the dust on the TV screen. If nothing's out there already, spread your one-quarter-done quilt, the first draft of the family history, some seed catalogs, or the kids' salt-dough diorama of the moon out in the middle of the living room floor—"in progress" excuses the most unimaginable messes.

9 7. Hide the dog and cat. If they don't see an animal they never look for animal mess.

10 8. Floors play a big part in an overall aura of cleanliness. So do squander a few minutes sweeping or vacuuming. If you're really rushed, you don't even have to haul out the vacuum—just hand-pick all the obvious stuff off the carpet.

11   9. Next hit the mirrors and glass doors and any picture windows or glass furniture tops within the target area. They look so good when they're sparkling clean and so bad when they're even slightly streaked, hand-printed, or spotted. You get a lot of mileage from a quick glass cleaning.

12 10. If you don't have a dishwasher to stash undone dishes in, pile them in a sinkful of sudsy water. You can also leave a vacuum, dust cloth, and maybe a bottle of furniture polish out in plain sight. Explain at some length when they first arrive how you were just in the middle of the weekly cleaning.

13 11. Run in the kitchen and prepare a fresh drink of lemonade in your prettiest pitcher. They'll notice it more than anything else—just don't feed or refresh them too much or they'll have to use the bathroom. The bathroom, by the way, is the next place to hit quickly, if there's still time. Pull the shower curtain shut; hit the sink, faucets, toilet; neaten up the towels. Even if they don't use it, the relaxation will show in your facial muscles and you'll be a better hostess.

14   Whatever you do, don't apologize for the condition of the house. When they ask how are things, take a deep breath and say, "We've been rather busy between our jobs, our exercise program, our night classes at the college, and church and scout leadership activities, and the time we like to devote to volunteer trail building, historic landmark preservation, and voter registration. Plus we had to take a few extra hours out to make hot meals for all our neighbors. We haven't used the living room for weeks, but we're really glad you happened by at the same time." Be sure to find the TV knob and get the set turned off before you launch into this.

WHAT DID THE WRITER SAY AND WHAT DID YOU THINK?

1. What is the thesis? Is it ever specifically stated?
2. How does the limited subject differentiate this essay from the usual set of housecleaning instructions?
3. Does the "don't apologize" advice in the last paragraph contradict the advice in paragraph 12 to say that "you were just in the middle of the weekly cleaning?"
4. Do you disagree with any of the instructions—cleaning up the bathroom only if there's still time, for example?

HOW DID THE WRITER SAY IT?

1. Does the author follow strict chronological order? If not, where not and why not?

2. Where does the author follow this book's advice (pp. 128–129) to "try to anticipate difficulties?"
3. The last paragraph seems mostly a final step: Don't apologize. Would the essay have benefited from a more traditional concluding paragraph?
4. Many readers may find evidence of unconscious sexism in paragraph 13. Explain.

WHAT ABOUT <u>YOUR</u> WRITING?

According to Mary Poppins, "A spoonful of sugar makes the medicine go down." Think of humor as sugar. When you are dealing with stodgy material—or sometimes presenting a point of view that many readers may find discomforting or hotly controversial—nothing can get your audience on your side faster than a few touches of humor. Who enjoys housecleaning? Whose eyelids don't get heavy at the prospect of reading some well-intentioned directions on making the task easier? Don Aslett uses humor effectively to make his serious instructions more pleasant to read. His references, among others, to a dog bone under the sofa, a "wash me" sign on the TV screen, and imaginary lists of philanthropic family activities not only make us smile but help win our confidence: Here is a sympathetic friend who knows what we are going through. For humor, readers will pardon a stretch of dullness, accept or at least bear with a point they strongly oppose, and generally let the writer get away with more than the writer would ever think of asking for.

There are dangers, of course. You don't want your readers to feel that your point isn't important, that beneath the humor you yourself don't take it seriously. You don't want to distract your reader from the significant intellectual content of your work. You don't want to come through as a crude smart aleck. With all these warnings, however, humor is a major resource for many good writers. Be cautious with it, but don't be shy.

CORN BREAD WITH CHARACTER
Ronni Lundy

Ronni Lundy works as a feature writer for the *Louisville Courier Journal* where her special interests in bluegrass and traditional music often appear in her commentary. She has published three cookbooks, the most recent of which is *Butterbeans to Blackberries: Harvest of the South* (1999), and she has also done free-lance writing for such national magazines as *Esquire* in which "Corn Bread with Character" was first published.

Words to check:

homogenized (paragraph 2)	facet (5)	pulverize (11)
cracklings (2)	impart (7)	scotch (11)
forebear (3)	improvise (7)	instinctive (12)
wield (3)	heady (8)	facsimile (14)
	throes (8)	

1 There are those who will tell you that real corn bread has just a little sugar in it. They'll say it enhances the flavor or that it's an old tradition in the South. Do not listen to them. If God had meant for corn bread to have sugar in it, he'd have called it cake.

2 *Real* corn bread is not sweet. Real corn bread is not homogenized with the addition of flour or puffed up with excessive artificial rising agents. Real corn bread rises from its own strength of character, has substance, crust, and texture. Real corn bread doesn't depend on fancy cornmeal, buttermilk, or cracklings for its quality. Real corn bread is a forthright, honest food as good as the instincts of its cook and the pan it is baked in.

3 That pan had best be a cast-iron skillet, preferably one inherited from a forebear who knew how to wield it. My mother, who made real corn bread almost every day of my growing-up life, has a great pan, a square cast-iron skillet given by a great aunt. She also has an eight-slot corn stick pan I would be satisfied to find as my sole inheritance someday. In the meantime, I bake corn bread in a nine-inch round cast-iron skillet I grabbed up in a secondhand store because it already had a black, nasty crust on the outside and the proper sheen of seasoning within.

4 If you have to start with a pan fresh from the store, season it according to the instructions for cast iron, then fry bacon in it every morning for a month to add a little flavor. Pour the leftover bacon grease into an empty one-pound coffee can and refrigerate it. Wipe your pan clean with a paper towel and don't ever touch it with anything as destructive as soap and water. When the inside starts to turn black and shiny, you're ready to start making corn bread.

5 It's not enough to have the right pan, however; you also need to know how to heat it properly. Heating right is the most important facet of the art of making corn bread, because if you have your skillet and drippings just hot enough, you'll consistently turn out corn bread with a faultless brown and crispy crust.

6 "Just what are drippings?" you may ask here, thereby revealing that you have never been closer than a pig's eye to a country kitchen.

7 In my family, drippings were the bacon grease my mother saved every morning in coffee cans. If you've followed the directions for seasoning a new pan, you're in good shape here. But what if you've inherited a well-seasoned

pan and want to start baking corn bread before your next breakfast? Or what if you've never eaten bacon in your life? Don't despair. You will learn, as I did during a brief flirtation with vegetarianism, that while bacon drippings impart a distinctive taste to corn bread cooked with them, they aren't essential to baking great corn bread. You can improvise a lot with grease.

8   If you feel extravagant, you can use half a stick of butter, but if you need to conserve, you can use some not too flavorful oil with a teaspoon or two of butter for effect. If you like the taste, you can use peanut oil or the thick, golden corn oil sold in health food stores that tastes like Kansas in the heady throes of late August. But you can't use olive oil or sesame oil (too strong and foreign), and margarine won't heat right.

9   To heat the pan correctly, you must leave it in the oven until it and the drippings are really hot but not smoking. Knowing just how long that takes is a trick you'll learn with time. A good rule of thumb: Leave the pan in the oven while you mix the other ingredients, but don't stir too slowly. A good precaution, in the early stages of making corn bread, is to check the pan frequently.

10   A final secret on the art of heating: It does not work to heat the corn bread skillet on top of the stove. Doing so may save you from setting off the smoke alarm, but the burner will create circular hot spots in your skillet and when you flip it to get the corn bread out, the middle crust will stay behind, clinging to those spots.

11   You will need cornmeal, of course. You may want to invest in a sturdy little grinder and pulverize the kernels yourself at home. Or you may want to cultivate a dark and narrow little store somewhere that sells only stone-ground cornmeal in expensively priced brown paper bags. Either method is fine. Both will bake up just as nicely as the commercially ground white corn-meal you can find in bags on any supermarket shelf. That's what my mother always used, and years of sampling gourmet grinds have given me no reason to scotch her preference.

12   In my mother's kitchen, where I learned to make corn bread, there were two kinds of measurements: enough and not enough. If we owned anything as fancy as a measuring cup, I'm sure it was not taken down for an occurrence so everyday as the baking of dinner corn bread. I do know that we had a set of four measuring spoons in primary colors, because it made a dandy toy for visiting children, but I don't remember ever seeing it in my mother's hand as she sprinkled salt, baking powder, or soda into the corn bread mixing bowl. In the interest of science, however, and for those unable to visit my mother's kitchen, her instinctive art is converted here to teaspoons, tablespoons, and cups. What follows is a recipe for real corn bread, enough to accompany dinner for six:

13   Turn on your oven to 450 degrees.

14   In a nine-inch round cast-iron skillet or a reasonable facsimile thereof, place four tablespoons of the grease of your choice. Place the skillet in the oven and heat it until the grease pops and crackles when you wiggle the pan.

15   While the grease heats, mix together in a medium-sized bowl two cups of fairly finely ground white cornmeal with one teaspoon of salt, one-half tea-spoon of baking soda, and one-half teaspoon of baking powder. Use your fin-gers to blend them together well.

16   Crack one big egg or two little ones into the meal mixture.

17   Add one and a half cups of milk or buttermilk.

18   Stir until just blended.

19   Remove the skillet from the oven and swirl it carefully so the grease coats most of the inside edges of the pan but not your hand. Pour the grease into the corn bread mixture, and if everything is going right, it will crackle invit-ingly. Mix together well with a big wooden spoon, using about twenty-five strokes.

20   Pour the mixture back into the hot skillet and return it to the oven for twenty minutes. Run the pan under the broiler for a few seconds to get a light-brown top crust, then remove it from the oven and turn it upside down onto a large plate. If your skillet is seasoned right, the bread will slide out in a hot brown slab. If not, then just serve it straight from the pan. It will taste every bit as good. (This recipe can also be baked in a corn stick pan, but the baking time is cut in half.)

21   Serve the bread with fresh sweet butter, or crumble it in a bowl and cover with hot pinto beans, a green onion, and sweet pickle on the side. Now, that's real corn bread.

WHAT DID THE WRITER SAY AND WHAT DID YOU THINK?

1. What is Lundy's thesis?
2. How does this recipe differ from most recipes?
3. How does the author's use of personal background affect the essay?
4. Why does Lundy devote so much attention to the seasoned skillet?
5. Why does Lundy use the overworked "If God had meant . . ." in paragraph 1?

HOW DID THE WRITER SAY IT?

1. How do the essay title and paragraph 2 relate?
2. Are the obvious repetitions in paragraph 2 effective? Why or why not?
3. What is the overall tone of the essay? Is it unusual for a recipe? Explain.

4. Is Lundy's conclusion typical for a recipe? Why or why not?
5. Where does Lundy begin presenting the actual recipe? Why so late?

WHAT ABOUT **YOUR** WRITING?

Your instructors are captive audiences. They may often enjoy their captivity and be eager to read your work, but in fact they have no choice. In the mood or not, they have to read it. That's their job. Fret all you want about their grading—you'll never find such soft touches again. Your future, noncaptive audiences will be infinitely tougher. They don't use red ink, but they don't need any. All they need is a wastebasket. And every good writer respects and fears wastebaskets.

Like Ronni Lundy in "Corn Bread with Character," the professional writer of a magazine article or advertisement suffers from, and benefits tremendously from, one problem that more writers ought to feel. *How do I get my reader's attention?* Nobody starts to read a magazine wondering what Lundy or the Jones and Smith Company has to say that day. The author or the company has to make the reader stop turning the pages. The soft-touch instructor may sometimes comment, "This essay starts slowly but gets better as it goes along." The other folks out there just keep turning the pages.

Think about your readers. They're rooting strongly for you, if only because they want their own reading experience to be pleasurable, but they need your help. Here are three specific suggestions for making a good start.

First, try for a strong title. You don't normally personify food as Lundy does in her title, "Corn Bread with Character." But it is original and catchy, a title that can easily stimulate a reader's curiosity. (For a more detailed discussion of titles, see p. 244.)

Second, spare the reader such unpromising first sentences as "In this composition I will try to show . . ." or "My paper has as its thesis . . ." or "According to Webster's Dictionary . . ." You needn't go overboard—there's no virtue in being self-consciously cute or eccentric. (Lundy's opening sentence, for example, is mostly a simple, straightforward statement.) Still, a well-calculated touch of show biz now and then never hurt anyone and can sometimes work miracles. Consider these first sentences from three essays by George Orwell:

As I write, highly civilised human beings are flying overhead, trying to kill
  me.

Soon after I arrived at Crossgates (not immediately, but after a week or two, just when I seemed to be settling into the routine of school life) I began wetting my bed.

In Moulmein, in Lower Burma, I was hated by large numbers of people—the only time in my life that I have been important enough for this to happen to me.

Third, and most important, remember that there's a real person reading what you've written. Writing isn't just self-expression—it's communication. If self-expression were the whole story, you'd be better off doodling or singing in the shower or making funny noises while you run through the nearest meadow. Whenever you can—and that will be most of the time—give your reader an immediate reason for paying attention to you. In "Corn Bread with Character," the author employs the oldest, and still most effective, technique in the writer's trade: From the first sentence on, she appeals to the reader's self-interest. "Do what I tell you, and you will soon be enjoying the world's best corn bread." Not all of your writing will deal with life and death issues, but you can almost always give your reader a reason to care—even about family recipes.

A writer is at one end and a reader at the other, and unless the reader is your instructor, that reader has a wastebasket.

HOW TO TAKE A JOB INTERVIEW
Kirby W. Stanat

Author of *Job Hunting Secrets and Tactics* (1977) and one-time recruiter and placement officer for the University of Wisconsin—Milwaukee, Kirby W. Stanat writes with authority about job interviews. As you read, note the versatility of how-to-do-it writing. Instructions aren't always about straightforward physical activities like housecleaning (see p. 133) or making bread (see p. 136): they can also involve psychological complexities like making good impressions.

Words to check:

adamant (paragraph 35)

1 To succeed in campus job interviews, you have to know where that recruiter is coming from. The simple answer is that he is coming from corporate headquarters.

2   That may sound obvious, but it is a significant point that too many students do not consider. The recruiter is not a free spirit as he flies from Berkeley to New Haven, from Chapel Hill to Boulder. He's on an invisible leash to the office, and if he is worth his salary, he is mentally in corporate headquarters all the time he's on the road.

3   If you can fix that in your mind—that when you walk into that bare-walled cubicle in the placement center you are walking into a branch office of Sears, Bendix or General Motors—you can avoid a lot of little mistakes and maybe some big ones.

4   If, for example, you assume that because the interview is on campus the recruiter expects you to look and act like a student, you're in for a shock. A student is somebody who drinks beer, wears blue jeans and throws a Frisbee. No recruiter has jobs for student Frisbee whizzes.

5   A cool spring day in late March, Sam Davis, a good recruiter who has been on the college circuit for years, is on my campus talking to candidates. He comes out to the waiting area to meet the student who signed up for an 11 o'clock interview. I'm standing in the doorway of my office taking in the scene.

6   Sam calls the candidate: "Sidney Student." There sits Sidney. He's at a 45 degree angle, his feet are in the aisle, and he's almost lying down. He's wearing well-polished brown shoes, a tasteful pair of brown pants, a light brown shirt, and a good looking tie. Unfortunately, he tops off this well-coordinated outfit with his Joe's Tavern Class A Softball Championship jacket, which has a big woven emblem over the heart.

7   If that isn't bad enough, in his left hand is a cigarette and in his right hand is a half-eaten apple.

8   When Sam calls his name, the kid is caught off guard. He ditches the cigarette in an ashtray, struggles to his feet, and transfers the apple from the right to the left hand. Apple juice is everywhere, so Sid wipes his hand on the seat of his pants and shakes hands with Sam.

9   Sam, who by now is close to having a stroke, gives me that what-do-I-have-here look and has the young man follow him into the interviewing room.

10   The situation deteriorates even further—into pure Laurel and Hardy. The kid is stuck with the half-eaten apple, doesn't know what to do with it, and obviously is suffering some discomfort. He carries the apple into the interviewing room with him and places it in the ashtray on the desk—right on top of Sam's freshly lit cigarette.

11   The interview lasts five minutes. . . .

12   Let us move in for a closer look at how the campus recruiter operates.

13   Let's say you have a 10 o'clock appointment with the recruiter from the XYZ Corporation. The recruiter gets rid of the candidate in front of you at about 5 minutes to 10, jots down a few notes about what he is going to do

with him or her, then picks up your résumé or data sheet (which you have submitted in advance). . . .

14   Although the recruiter is still in the interview room and you are still in the lobby, your interview is under way. You're on. The recruiter will look over your sheet pretty carefully before he goes out to call you. He develops a mental picture of you.

15   He thinks, "I'm going to enjoy talking with this kid," or "This one's going to be a turkey." The recruiter has already begun to make a screening decision about you.

16   His first impression of you, from reading the sheet, could come from your grade point. It could come from misspelled words. It could come from poor erasures or from the fact that necessary information is missing. By the time the recruiter has finished reading your sheet, you've already hit the plus or minus column.

17   Let's assume the recruiter got a fairly good impression from your sheet.

18   Now the recruiter goes out to the lobby to meet you. He almost shuffles along, and his mind is somewhere else. Then he calls your name, and at that instant he visibly clicks into gear. He just went to work.

19   As he calls your name he looks quickly around the room, waiting for somebody to move. If you are sitting on the middle of your back, with a book open and a cigarette going, and if you have to rebuild yourself to stand up, the interest will run right out of the recruiter's face. You, not the recruiter, made the appointment for 10 o'clock, and the recruiter expects to see a young professional come popping out of that chair like today is a good day and you're anxious to meet him.

20   At this point, the recruiter does something rude. He doesn't walk across the room to meet you halfway. He waits for you to come to him. Something very important is happening. He wants to see you move. He wants to get an impression about your posture, your stride, and your briskness.

21   If you slouch over to him, sidewinderlike, he is not going to be impressed. He'll figure you would probably slouch your way through your workdays. He wants you to come at him with lots of good things going for you. If you watch the recruiter's eyes, you can see the inspection. He glances quickly at shoes, pants, coat, shirt; dress, blouse, hose—the whole works.

22   After introducing himself, the recruiter will probably say, "Okay, please follow me," and he'll lead you into his interviewing room.

23   When you get to the room, you may find that the recruiter will open the door and gesture you in—with him blocking part of the doorway. There's enough room for you to get past him, but it's a near thing.

24   As you scrape past, he gives you a closeup inspection. He looks at your hair; if it's greasy, that will bother him. He looks at your collar; if it's dirty,

that will bother him. He looks at your shoulders; if they're covered with dandruff, that will bother him. If you're a man, he looks at your chin. If you didn't get a close shave, that will irritate him. If you're a woman, he checks your makeup. If it's too heavy, he won't like it.

25   Then he smells you. An amazing number of people smell bad. Occasionally a recruiter meets a student who smells like a canal horse. That student can expect an interview of about four or five minutes.

26   Next the recruiter inspects the back side of you. He checks your hair (is it combed in front but not in back?), he checks your heels (are they run down?), your pants (are they baggy?), your slip (is it showing?), your stockings (do they have runs?).

27   Then he invites you to sit down.

28   At this point, I submit, the recruiter's decision on you is 75 to 80 percent made.

29   Think about it. The recruiter has read your résumé. He knows who you are and where you are from. He knows your marital status, your major and your grade point. And he knows what you have done with your summers. He has inspected you, exchanged greetings with you and smelled you. There is very little additional hard information that he must gather on you. From now on it's mostly body chemistry.

30   Many recruiters have argued strenuously with me that they don't make such hasty decisions. So I tried an experiment. I told several recruiters that I would hang around in the hall outside the interview room when they took candidates in.

31   I told them that as soon as they had definitely decided not to recommend (to department managers in their companies) the candidate they were interviewing, they should snap their fingers loud enough for me to hear. It went like this.

32   First candidate: 38 seconds after the candidate sat down: Snap!

33   Second candidate: 1 minute, 42 seconds: Snap!

34   Third candidate: 45 seconds: Snap!

35   One recruiter was particularly adamant, insisting that he didn't rush to judgment on candidates. I asked him to participate in the snapping experiment. He went out in the lobby, picked up his first candidate of the day, and headed for an interview room.

36   As he passed me in the hall, he glared at me. And his fingers went "Snap!"

WHAT DID THE WRITER SAY AND WHAT DID YOU THINK?

1. What is the thesis? When is it stated?
2. What point is established by the "snap" experiment?

3. What personal physical details will make an interviewer take an instant dislike to an applicant?
4. Does Stanat's advice apply to all job seekers, or only to those currently attending college? Why?
5. What is so important about a resume or data sheet?
6. Why would an interviewer want to watch an applicant walk?

HOW DID THE WRITER SAY IT?

1. What specific details about "Sidney Student" accent his unacceptability as a job applicant?
2. This essay concentrates almost entirely on what happens before the actual job interview. With this in mind, is the title really appropriate? Why or why not?
3. The essay has no normal concluding paragraph. Does it need one? Why or why not?

WHAT ABOUT <u>YOUR</u> WRITING?

Countless thousands of students have been told never to write *you*. They were misinformed. *You* is a tricky word, and it's easy enough to understand how some teachers, distraught at seeing the word so frequently mismanaged, might invent a rule that outlaws it—but no such rule exists in standard English.

The tricky part is that *you* is both a pronoun of direct address, aimed at a specific person or group, and an indefinite pronoun meaning something like *people* or *one* or *everybody*. When it's used in writing aimed at a general audience—like most freshman English writing—it can be taken in both ways and can often turn out to be unintentionally confusing, insulting, or funny. Imagine a casual reader coming across sentences like

When you catch syphilis you must consult your doctor immediately.

Your paranoid concern with what others think of you makes you a likely candidate for suicide.

The new night school program should give you fresh hope for overcoming your illiteracy.

Those sentences demand immediate revision:

Victims of syphilis must consult their doctors immediately.

Paranoid concern with what others think increases the likelihood of suicide.

The new night school program should give fresh hope for overcoming illiteracy.

To be fair to the inventors of imaginary rules, then, it's wise in most classroom writing to be extremely conservative with *you* as an indefinite pronoun. The assumed audience is a general one of mixed ages, sexes, backgrounds, and interests; using *you* for this audience is nearly always asking for trouble.

There is nothing wrong with *you*, however, in writing that does address itself to a specific audience: the purchaser of a bike who now has to put it together, the new employee who wants information on the pension plan and hospitalization program, the college student worried about a job interview, as in this reading selection by Kirby W. Stanat. This book addresses itself to college freshmen taking a course in English composition, each of whom receives similar reading and writing assignments every day. An audience can't get much more specific than that, and therefore this book feels free to make frequent use of *you*. You must have noticed.

See pages 182–183 for comments on the use of *I*.

TWELVE STEPS TO QUIT SMOKING
Robert Bezilla

Until his death in 1997, three years after this article was written, Robert Bezilla worked with the Princeton Religion Research Center and the Gallup organization in surveying religious attitudes, especially among the young. Bezilla uses irony (see pp. 310–311) to deliver a strong anti-smoking message. As you read, try to distinguish between what is said—or seems to be said—and what is meant.

Words to check:

CAT scan	thoracic (8)	lymph (11)
(paragraph 6)	pathologist (8)	pummeled (14)
sternum (8)	squamous (8)	oncologist (17)

1 It won't be long before cigarette smoking is banned in just about every public place in the country, giving smokers yet another incentive to quit.

2 So this seems a good time to reveal one of the most effective smoking-cessation programs ever devised.

3 I stopped smoking cigarettes eight years ago, cold turkey. Friends, especially envious smokers, remembering how I used to chain smoke two to three packs

a day, marvel at this deed. I did it through a special 12-step Stop Smoking Program developed for me by members of the Princeton Medical Group and their colleagues at the Medical Center of Princeton, N.J. Here's how it works.

Step 1: Realize You May Have a Problem

4   I was constantly tired, my work was deteriorating, my smoker's hack kept getting worse. My children began to argue about whose turn it was to sit downwind from Daddy at the dinner table, my colleagues were exasperated with my growing inefficiency, and my wife threatened to leave me if I didn't go to see a doctor. I realized I might have a problem.

Step 2: Examine the Problem

5   On the basis of lab tests, my internist told me I had the blood chemical profile of a starvation victim, the wind capacity of a parakeet, and not enough strength to beat a 6-year-old child at arm wrestling. Then his eyes widened as he described a grapefruit-sized shadow on the X-ray of my left lung. I was becoming more convinced that I might have a problem.

Step 3: Get a Second Opinion

6   Within a few hours I was introduced to modern medical technology by way of a CAT scan. It provided a three-dimensional view of my chest that showed the shadow on the X-ray really was a depiction of a collapsed lung—no wonder I had been feeling so tired. There were still some ominous shadows, and there seemed little doubt that I had a really big problem.

Step 4: Take a Deeper Look

7   The doctors wanted a closer look at my lungs and recommended a simple procedure of sticking a contraption on a flexible tube down my windpipe to enable them to examine and even sample parts of my lung. I agreed to the procedure and was scheduled for it within a week. I was advised to stop smoking because it would make the anesthesiologist's job easier.

8   The test was done, and when I woke up there was also a small scar over my sternum where my thoracic area had been examined further. The pathologist's report showed my lung had a tumor of large squamous cancer cells, commonly known as "smoker's cancer." My throat was very sore from the operation and my desire to smoke was decreasing rapidly.

Step 5: Prepare for Action

9   I was given an impressive battery of tests that demonstrated that I certainly had cancer, but that it did not seem to have spread beyond the primary

site yet. The Medical Center is a teaching hospital and my case was deemed sufficiently interesting for troops of student interns and nurses to come examine and interview me.

10   Invariably, they asked if I was a smoker and nodded knowingly when I described my smoking habits. I was advised not to smoke before my forthcoming operation—"it's better for the anesthesiology."

Step 6: Strike Boldly

11   My left lung was surgically removed. Some of the surrounding lymph tissue looked a bit suspicious to the surgeon and he removed it as well. Being unconscious, I of course could not smoke.

Step 7: Recover

12   In the recovery room I woke up with a respirator tube stuck down my throat. I was convinced I was going to choke to death. I had never done drugs but obviously I was high on pain killers and was having a bad trip. Who needed to smoke?

Step 8: Play It Safe

13   I spent about 36 hours in the Intensive Care Unit. I was pretty heavily sedated, but conscious enough to know there were tubes going in and out all over my body. I got the impression other people around me were dying. I didn't even think about smoking.

Step 9: Rest and Recuperate

14   Transferred to the main floor, I began the long, slow process of recovery. I wore an oxygen mask and was afraid to sleep at nights, thinking I would never wake up again. I caught up on my sleep during the day, but was interrupted constantly by nurses taking vital signs and jolly physical therapists who pummeled my back to encourage me to bring up phlegm even if the act of coughing was painful.

15   Instead of a cigarette I was given a device consisting of a Ping-Pong ball in a tube that I attempted to raise by blowing into an attached hose. I counted the minutes until I would be allowed to take another pain-killing pill. Because of the oxygen, no smoking was allowed in the room.

Step 10: Take a Giant Step Backward

16   I was released from the hospital but was back in two days after a respiratory infection invaded my weakened body. I fought it for nearly a month. I

was given increasing amounts of oxygen until I reached a point where I began to wonder what would happen to me when they could no longer turn the oxygen up any more. Fortunately, the infection went away. I was in no condition to smoke.

Step 11: Take Preventive Measures

17   Before I left the hospital my oncologist introduced me to the staff radiologist. Together they explained that the pathologist's report showed the cancer was beginning to spread slightly to the area where the lung used to be. I took the prescribed treatment of 29 radiation exposures over the next 10 weeks. Each succeeding exposure made me weaker and more nauseated and less attracted to cigarette smoking.

Step 12: Restructure Your Life

18   I survived and was no longer smoking. I learned to celebrate the gift of life I had regained with my friends and loved ones. My greatest joy was those who profited by my example and tried to quit smoking, with some actually succeeding.

19   While this 12-step program may seem daunting, there are four alternative courses for those who may want to take a short-cut.

20   The easy one-step program. Never start smoking. Stay away from those who do, to reduce your chances of being affected by their second-hand smoke.

21   The challenging one-step program. Stop smoking and you may never have to go through all the other steps. The medical evidence says that if you do this now, it will dramatically decrease your chances of getting cancer or other smoker's diseases. Fortunately, success in quitting seems highest among those who do it cold turkey.

22   The two-step program. Not everybody is lucky enough to be able to quit on the first try. Don't get discouraged, but keep trying until you succeed. Once you do, it immediately will decrease your chances of getting a smoker's fatal illness.

23   The zero-step program. Do none of the above, start or continue smoking, and the chances are overwhelmingly likely that you will some day be among the more than 400,000 people each year in this country who die prematurely because of smoking-related illnesses.

WHAT DID THE WRITER SAY AND WHAT DID YOU THINK?

1. At which step in the twelve-step process does Bezilla stop smoking?
2. Subsequent steps contain reminders that the writer has stopped smoking. What do these reminders have in common?

3. The essay is characterized by some extremely bitter humor. Who or what is the bitterness directed at?

HOW DID THE WRITER SAY IT?

1. Where does Bezilla drop the use of irony and make direct comments about smoking? Do these direct comments spoil the essay by breaking the mood?
2. Why is it important to devote so much attention to specific medical details?
3. Is this reading selection really a how-to-do-it essay? If not, what term might be more appropriate?

WHAT ABOUT <u>YOUR</u> WRITING?

"I had the blood chemical profile of a starvation victim, the wind capacity of a parakeet, and not enough strength to beat a 6-year-old at arm wrestling," writes Robert Bezilla in paragraph 6. The author is using *hyperbole*, deliberate exaggeration for dramatic or humorous impact. Bezilla's point is that his health was extremely poor, and both he and his readers are well aware that the references to a parakeet and a small child can't be taken literally. The hyperbole adds a helpful note of humor to a profoundly grim and depressing doctor's report.

Hyperbole has been around a long time. Shakespeare used it, for example, when Macbeth, after murdering the king of Scotland, expresses his horror and shame with these words:

> Will all great Neptune's ocean wash this blood
> Clean from my hand? No, this my hand will rather
> The multitudinous seas incarnadine [turn red, redden]
> Making the green one red.

Stylistically, hyperbole is showy and loud; it should not be used frequently. For *occasional* special effects, though, hyperbole might sometimes help liven up your writing:

Beware of Professor Reeves. That man eats students for breakfast and picks his teeth with their bones.

Cynthia was hungry enough for a lunch of fifty Big Macs and two dozen chocolate shakes.

Offer him a tax-free deal at a guaranteed 10-percent return, and he would gladly sell his mother and sister into lives of slavery.

————

THE SPIDER AND THE WASP

Alexander Petrunkevitch

Alexander Petrunkevitch (1875–1964) was one of the world's leading authorities on spiders. Born in Russia, he taught at various American universities. His wide range of skills and interests is suggested by his translation of English (to Russian) and Russian (to English) poetry and by such titles as *Index Catalogue of Spiders of North, Central, and South America* (1911), *Choice and Responsibility* (1947), and *Principles of Classification* (1952).

Words to check:

progeny (paragraph 1)	nectar (9)	secretion (13)
archenemy (1)	pungent (9)	olfactory (14)
unwittingly (1)	chitinous (9)	simulating (15)
tactile (8)	girth (11)	

1 In the feeding and safeguarding of their progeny insects and spiders exhibit some interesting analogies to reasoning and some crass examples of blind instinct. The case I propose to describe here is that of the tarantula spiders and their archenemy, the digger wasps of the genus Pepsis. It is a classic example of what looks like intelligence pitted against instinct—a strange situation in which the victim, though fully able to defend itself, submits unwittingly to its destruction.

2   Most tarantulas live in the tropics, but several species occur in the temperate zone and a few are common in the southern U.S. Some varieties are large and have powerful fangs with which they can inflict a deep wound. These formidable looking spiders do not, however, attack man; you can hold one in your hand, if you are gentle, without being bitten. Their bite is dangerous only to insects and small mammals such as mice; for a man it is no worse than a hornet's sting.

3   Tarantulas customarily live in deep cylindrical burrows, from which they emerge at dusk and into which they retire at dawn. Mature males wander about after dark in search of females and occasionally stray into houses. After mating, the male dies in a few weeks, but a female lives much longer and can

mate several years in succession. In a Paris museum is a tropical specimen which is said to have been living in captivity for 25 years.

4   A fertilized female tarantula lays from 200 to 400 eggs at a time; thus it is possible for a single tarantula to produce several thousand young. She takes no care of them beyond weaving a cocoon of silk to enclose the eggs. After they hatch, the young walk away, find convenient places in which to dig their burrows and spend the rest of their lives in solitude. The eyesight of tarantulas is poor, being limited to a sensing of change in the intensity of light and to the perception of moving objects. They apparently have little or no sense of hearing, for a hungry tarantula will pay no attention to a loudly chirping cricket placed in its cage unless the insect happens to touch one of its legs.

5   But all spiders, and especially hairy ones, have an extremely delicate sense of touch. Laboratory experiments prove that tarantulas can distinguish three types of touch: pressure against the body wall, stroking of the body hair, and riffling of certain very fine hairs on the legs called trichobothria. Pressure against the body, by the finger or the end of a pencil, causes the tarantula to move off slowly for a short distance. The touch excites no defensive response unless the approach is from above where the spider can see the motion, in which case it rises on its hind legs, lifts its front legs, opens its fangs and holds this threatening posture as long as the object continues to move.

6   The entire body of a tarantula, especially its legs, is thickly clothed with hair. Some of it is short and wooly, some long and stiff. Touching this body hair produces one of two distinct reactions. When the spider is hungry, it responds with an immediate and swift attack. At the touch of a cricket's antennae the tarantula seizes the insect so swiftly that a motion picture taken at the rate of 64 frames per second shows only the result and not the process of capture. But when the spider is not hungry, the stimulation of its hairs merely causes it to shake the touched limb. An insect can walk under its hairy belly unharmed.

7   The trichobothria, very fine hairs growing from disclike membranes on the legs, are sensitive only to air movement. A light breeze makes them vibrate slowly, without disturbing the common hair. When one blows gently on the trichobothria, the tarantula reacts with a quick jerk of its four front legs. If the front and hind legs are stimulated at the same time, the spider makes a sudden jump. This reaction is quite independent of the state of its appetite.

8   These three tactile responses—to pressure on the body wall, to moving of the common hair, and to flexing of the trichobothria—are so different from one another that there is no possibility of confusing them. They serve the tarantula adequately for most of its needs and enable it to avoid most annoyances and dangers. But they fail the spider completely when it meets its deadly enemy, the digger wasp Pepsis.

9   These solitary wasps are beautiful and formidable creatures. Most species are either a deep shiny blue all over, or deep blue with rusty wings. The largest have a wing span of about four inches. They live on nectar. When excited, they give off a pungent odor—a warning that they are ready to attack. The sting is much worse than that of a bee or common wasp, and the pain and swelling last longer. In the adult stage the wasp lives only a few months. The female produces but a few eggs, one at a time at intervals of two or three days. For each egg the mother must provide one adult tarantula, alive but paralyzed. The mother wasp attaches the egg to the paralyzed spider's abdomen. Upon hatching from the egg, the larva is many hundreds of times smaller than its living but helpless victim. It eats no other food and drinks no water. By the time it has finished its single Gargantuan meal and become ready for wasphood, nothing remains of the tarantula but its indigestible chitinous skeleton.

10   The mother wasp goes tarantula-hunting when the egg in her ovary is almost ready to be laid. Flying low over the ground late on a sunny afternoon, the wasp looks for its victim or for the mouth of a tarantula burrow, a round hole edged by a bit of silk. The sex of the spider makes no difference, but the mother is highly discriminating as to species. Each species of Pepsis requires a certain species of tarantula, and the wasp will not attack the wrong species. In a cage with a tarantula which is not its normal prey, the wasp avoids the spider and is usually killed by it in the night.

11   Yet when a wasp finds the correct species, it is the other way about. To identify the species the wasp apparently must explore the spider with her antennae. The tarantula shows an amazing tolerance to this exploration. The wasp crawls under it and walks over it without evoking any hostile response. The molestation is so great and so persistent that the tarantula often rises on all eight legs, as if it were on stilts. It may stand this way for several minutes. Meanwhile the wasp, having satisfied itself that the victim is of the right species, moves off a few inches to dig the spider's grave. Working vigorously with legs and jaws, it excavates a hole 8 to 10 inches deep with a diameter slightly larger than the spider's girth. Now and again the wasp pops out of the hole to make sure that the spider is still there.

12   When the grave is finished, the wasp returns to the tarantula to complete her ghastly enterprise. First she feels it all over once more with her antennae. Then her behavior becomes more aggressive. She bends her abdomen, protruding her sting, and searches for the soft membrane at the point where the spider's legs join its body—the only spot where she can penetrate the horny skeleton. From time to time, as the exasperated spider slowly shifts ground, the wasp turns on her back and slides along with the aid of her wings, trying to get under the tarantula for a shot at the vital spot. During all this maneuvering,

which can last for several minutes, the tarantula makes no move to save itself. Finally the wasp corners it against some obstruction and grasps one of its legs in her powerful jaws. Now at last the harassed spider tries a desperate but vain defense. The two contestants roll over and over on the ground. It is a terrifying sight and the outcome is always the same. The wasp finally manages to thrust her sting into the soft spot and holds it there for a few seconds while she pumps in the poison. Almost immediately the tarantula falls paralyzed on its back. Its legs stop twitching, its heart stops beating. Yet it is not dead, as is shown by the fact that if taken from the wasp it can be restored to some sensitivity by being kept in a moist chamber for several months.

13   After paralyzing the tarantula, the wasp cleans herself by dragging her body along the ground and rubbing her feet, sucks the drop of blood oozing from the wound in the spider's abdomen, then grabs a leg of the flabby, helpless animal in her jaws and drags it down to the bottom of the grave. She stays there for many minutes, sometimes for several hours, and what she does all that time in the dark we do not know. Eventually she lays her egg and attaches it to the side of the spider's abdomen with a sticky secretion. Then she emerges, fills the grave with soil carried bit by bit in her jaws, and finally tramples the ground all around to hide any trace of the grave from prowlers. Then she flies away, leaving her descendant safely started in life.

14   In all this the behavior of the wasp evidently is qualitatively different from that of the spider. The wasp acts like an intelligent animal. This is not to say that instinct plays no part or that she reasons as man does. But her actions are to the point; they are not automatic and can be modified to fit the situation. We do not know for certain how she identifies the tarantula—probably it is by some olfactory or chemo-tactile sense—but she does it purposefully and does not blindly tackle a wrong species.

15   On the other hand, the tarantula's behavior shows only confusion. Evidently the wasp's pawing gives it no pleasure, for it tries to move away. That the wasp is not simulating sexual stimulation is certain, because male and female tarantulas react in the same way to its advances. That the spider is not anesthetized by some odorless secretion is easily shown by blowing lightly at the tarantula and making it jump suddenly. What, then, makes the tarantula behave as stupidly as it does?

16   No clear, simple answer is available. Possibly the stimulation by the wasp's antennae is masked by a heavier pressure on the spider's body, so that it reacts as when prodded by a pencil. But the explanation may be much more complex. Initiative in attack is not in the nature of tarantulas; most species fight only when cornered so that escape is impossible. Their inherited patterns of behavior apparently prompt them to avoid problems rather than attack them. For example, spiders always weave their webs in three dimensions, and when

a spider finds that there is insufficient space to attach certain threads in the third dimension, it leaves the place and seeks another, instead of finishing the web in a single plane. This urge to escape seems to arise under all circumstances, in all phases of life, and to take the place of reasoning. For a spider to change the pattern of its web is as impossible as for an inexperienced man to build a bridge across a chasm obstructing his way.

17   In a way the instinctive urge to escape is not only easier but often more efficient than reasoning. The tarantula does exactly what is most efficient in all cases except in an encounter with a ruthless and determined attacker dependent for the existence of her own species on killing as many tarantulas as she can lay eggs. Perhaps in this case the spider follows its usual pattern of trying to escape, instead of seizing and killing the wasp, because it is not aware of its danger. In any case, the survival of the tarantula species as a whole is protected by the fact that the spider is much more fertile than the wasp.

WHAT DID THE WRITER SAY AND WHAT DID YOU THINK?

1. A primary thesis tells why the process is worth discussing. What is the thesis, and where does it appear?
2. A secondary thesis tries to explain why the process happens as it does. What is the thesis, and where does it appear?
3. Does the author acknowledge alternate explanations?
4. What makes the behavior of the spider so puzzling?
5. Where does the author suggest his own emotional reaction to the process?
6. Is the reader meant to take sides, to root for the spider or wasp?
7. People who think they are totally indifferent to nature and science often become deeply involved in "The Spider and the Wasp." Can you suggest why?
8. Can you think of certain types of human beings whose behavior corresponds to the spider's? The wasp's?

HOW DID THE WRITER SAY IT?

1. Who is the intended audience for this selection?
2. The description of the process does not begin until paragraph 10, though paragraph 9 presents a summary of the process. What has the author been doing until then?
3. Are all obscure scientific terms defined?
4. Consult the table of contents. What patterns of writing are in this selection in addition to *process*?

5. Does the author gather the many separate steps into groups? If so, into how many?
6. "The mother wasp goes tarantula-hunting. . . ." Does this phrase seem too informal, almost slangy, for a scientific article? Are there other unusually informal words or phrases? Are they justified?

WHAT ABOUT <u>YOUR</u> WRITING?

Nobody reads "The Spider and the Wasp" as an interesting little essay on the strange behavior of some strange little creatures. Most readers respond because the essay reaches them at a deep emotional level, because it appeals dramatically to some permanent human concerns: in this case, life and death, care of progeny, survival of the fittest, and so on.

As you read at the start of this selection that Petrunkevitch was "one of the world's leading authorities on spiders." Do you have an esoteric specialty that you can relate to universal human concerns? If you're an enthusiastic player of video games, you have a beautiful piece on man versus machine that's waiting to be written. If you own tropical fish and have seen adult fish eating their own young, you have the potential for a powerful cruelty-of-nature essay that takes a different approach from Petrunkevitch's. In a sense, you're a specialist on anything that has ever hit you hard. If you waited week after week as a child for a "free offer" after you sent in a box top, aren't you "one of the world's leading authorities" on what waiting can do to the soul? Don't shy away from specialties because you're afraid that people won't be interested. Show how the specialty is related to a universal issue, and make them interested.

Comparison and Contrast

A comparison-and-contrast paper is one of the most common kinds of writing assignments because it reflects one of the most common kinds of thinking, the kind of thinking on which most practical decisions are based. Comparison and contrast often dominate thought in choosing a college, a major field, a career, a job. We compare and contrast doctors and dentists; husbands and wives (actual and potential) and children; homes, neighborhoods, and cities; breakfast foods, pizza joints, and brands of soda pop. The comparison-and-contrast assignment on an essay exam or composition in an English class is not a remote intellectual exercise but a natural extension of the role played by comparison and contrast in human life.

Just as comparison-and-contrast thinking aims at a decision or judgment—the school I attend, the job offer I accept, the horse I bet on, the toothpaste I buy—so comparison-and-contrast writing must add up to something. Without a thesis, comparison-and-contrast writing is a pointless game in a never-never land where the only activity people engage in is devising elaborate lists of similarities and differences or advantages and disadvantages. The comparison-and-contrast paper must commit itself firmly to the persuasive principle.

Late novels by Dickens express a far more pessimistic view of life than early novels by Dickens.

Boston is a more exciting city than San Francisco.

The community college can sometimes offer a number of benefits unknown at the four-year college.

The dream and the reality of owning a car are seldom the same.

Sexual discrimination is harder to fight than racial discrimination.

There is no logical way of determining whether Babe Ruth or Henry Aaron was the better home-run hitter.

Three quick pointers:

1. As a matter of common sense and convenience, stick to two units for comparison and contrast. No regulation prohibits three or more units, but two are far easier to manage.
2. Avoid vague, what-else-is-new theses like "There are many similarities between Smith and Jones." The same statement could be made of any two human beings and is therefore worthless.
3. Don't feel that you need to pay equal attention to comparisons and contrasts. In practice, most papers give much greater weight to similarities (comparisons) *or* to differences (contrasts). Some papers may deal entirely with one or the other; their whole point may be that two seemingly similar items are, in fact, very different or that two seemingly different items are very similar. Check with your instructor whether an all-contrast or all-comparison paper is acceptable. In any event, theses like "Despite obvious differences, drug addiction and alcoholism present strikingly similar psychological problems" are both common and workable. In a paper with that thesis, the "obvious differences" could be taken care of in the introduction, and the rest of the paper would deal solely with the similarities.

Patterns

Comparison-and-contrast papers can use one of two patterns, both highly structured. A long paper can sometimes shift patterns from one distinct division of the paper to another, but most papers should stick to one pattern.

Block Pattern

In the first pattern, the writer discusses one unit in its entirety before going on to the other.

Thesis Statement: Boston is a more exciting city than San Francisco.

I. Boston
   A. Cultural opportunities
   B. Recreational opportunities
   C. Sense of history
   D. Physical beauty

II. San Francisco
    A. Cultural opportunities
    B. Recreational opportunities
    C. Sense of history
    D. Physical beauty

Thesis Statement: The community college can sometimes offer a number of benefits unknown at the four-year college.

I. Community college
    A. Cost
    B. Convenience
    C. Instructors
    D. Training for a vocation

II. Four-year college
    A. Cost
    B. Convenience
    C. Instructors
    D. Lack of training for a vocation

Notice that in these sample outlines we could easily reverse the order of the major topics. Rather than concluding with negative comments about San Francisco or four-year colleges, some writers may want to stress the positive by ending with praise of Boston or community colleges. Which comes first is up to the writer.

The danger built into the block pattern is that the writer can end up with two separate essays instead of one unified comparison-and-contrast essay. To ensure unity, take note of the following guidelines:

Each Subtopic in Part I Must Also Be Discussed in Part II: Bring up Boston's cultural opportunities only if you have something to say about San Francisco's cultural opportunities or lack of them. Boston's cultural opportunities must be compared with or contrasted to something; in comparison-and-contrast writing, they are not significant in themselves.

Subtopics Should Be Discussed in the Same Order in Both Parts: If cost and convenience are the first two subtopics you consider for community colleges, they should be the first two subtopics when you turn to four-year colleges.

Paragraphing Should Be Similar in Both Parts: A paper with only one or two sentences for each subtopic under Boston will probably gather the subtopics together into one good-sized Boston paragraph. A paper with a lot to say on each Boston subtopic will probably give a separate paragraph to each. Whatever paragraph arrangement is appropriate for Boston should usually be maintained for San Francisco.

Subtopics in Part II Should Generally Include Reminders of the Point Made about the Same Subtopic in Part I: Since in the block pattern you consider the first unit (Boston, community colleges) before moving on to the second (San Francisco, four-year colleges), your readers may experience some memory lapses by the time they finally reach Part II. Their memories need refreshing. Above all, they should not be allowed to forget that they are reading a single comparison-and-contrast paper rather than two separate essays. In the paragraph outlines that follow, note the italicized reminders:

¶ 1—Presentation of thesis: Boston is a more exciting city than San Francisco.

Start of ¶ 2—Boston's cultural opportunities are unrivaled anywhere in the country . . .

Start of ¶ 3—Recreational opportunities in Boston are every bit as impressive . . .

Start of ¶ 4—The sense of a rich, still vital past adds to the excitement of Boston . . .

Start of ¶ 5—Finally, Boston is a surprising delight to the eye . . .

Start of ¶ 6—When we look at San Francisco, we find a cultural scene that, *in sharp contrast to Boston's* . . .

Start of ¶ 7—San Francisco's recreational opportunities, though plentiful, also *suffer when placed against the something-for-everyone of Boston* . . .

Start of ¶ 8—The sense of a living history in San Francisco *seems bland and shallow when we think of Boston* . . .

Start of ¶ 9—Even in its overwhelming physical beauty, San Francisco *fails to surpass the breathtaking charm of Boston* . . .

¶ 1—Presentation of thesis: The community college can sometimes offer a number of benefits unknown at the four-year college.

Start of ¶ 2—First, community colleges are cheap . . .

Start of ¶ 3—Second, they are incredibly convenient . . .

Start of ¶ 4—Third, most instructors are likely to be experienced and readily available . . .

Start of ¶ 5—Last, community colleges offer the practical education most students want . . .

Start of ¶ 6—At many four-year colleges, the cost of attending is so *much greater than at community colleges* that . . .

Start of ¶ 7—*Contrasting dramatically to the convenience of a community college*, a four-year college . . .

Start of ¶ 8—*Instead of meeting full-time, professional teachers*, the beginning student at a four-year college will more probably . . .

Start of ¶ 9—Finally, many four-year colleges are still fighting against *the vocational trends in education that the community colleges have welcomed* . . .

Alternating Pattern

This pattern can be thought of as a seesaw. It swings back and forth between its two subjects.

Thesis Statement: Boston is a more exciting city than San Francisco.

I. Cultural opportunities
   A. Boston
   B. San Francisco

II. Recreational opportunities
   A. Boston
   B. San Francisco

III. Sense of history
   A. Boston
   B. San Francisco

IV. Physical beauty
   A. Boston
   B. San Francisco

Thesis Statement: The community college can sometimes offer a number of benefits unknown at the four-year college.

I. Cost
   A. Community college
   B. Four-year college

II. Convenience
    A. Community college
    B. Four-year college

III. Instructors
    A. Community college
    B. Four-year college

IV. Training for a vocation
    A. Community college
    B. Four-year college

Most of the principles applicable to the block pattern still hold. You still say something about both subjects for each issue considered; you still use a consistent order (observe how "Boston" and "Community college" always come first); you still make a consistent arrangement of paragraphs. The major difference is that reminders are not nearly as important as in the block pattern. Instead of getting to San Francisco's cultural opportunities one or two pages after dealing with Boston's cultural opportunities, you'll be getting to them in the very next sentences.

Which Pattern?

Both patterns enable you to write what you want. Both patterns cover the same territory, though in different order. In many cases, you can probably do a good job with either pattern, so your decision may be more a matter of taste than anything else. It is possible, however, to make some distinctions between patterns, and for whatever the distinctions are worth, here are a couple to keep in mind:

- *The block pattern tends to work better for short papers, alternating for long papers.* In short papers, alternating can sometimes bounce back and forth between subjects too frequently to let anything settle in the reader's mind. In long papers, the block pattern can put too much of a burden on the reader's memory: the reader should not have to wonder on page 7 what it was that you said on page 2, and you may be forced to spend a disproportionate amount of time and words on reminders.
- *The block pattern tends to work better with few subtopics, alternating with many.* With only a few subtopics, the reader should have no difficulty keeping track of them. You can safely make your four points about Boston and then go on to San Francisco. The seesaw, back-and-forth movement of alternating could be somewhat distracting. With many

subtopics, alternating is probably safest; if you had a dozen or more elements to consider about Boston and San Francisco, for example, discussing each city one after the other within each element would make the comparison-and-contrast relationship immediately clear. The block pattern could again put a fierce strain on the reader's memory and patience.

WRITING SUGGESTIONS FOR
COMPARISON-AND-CONTRAST THEMES

Comparison-and-contrast writing offers almost endless variation in choice of subject. The subjects listed here may be less valuable for themselves than for bringing other subjects to your mind. In any event, don't forget the necessity for a thesis and for sticking to one of the two patterns of organization.

1. Two household chores.
2. Life in a city vs. life in a suburb; life in two cities or two suburbs.
3. Two commercial products: razor blades, hair sprays, tires, breakfast foods.
4. Two department stores or discount stores.
5. Contrasting fates of two married couples.
6. Two sports or two athletes: baseball vs. football, football vs. soccer, Venus Williams vs. Martina Hingis, and so on.
7. Two clergymen or two churches.
8. Two movies or television programs (should be of same basic type: Science fiction, horror movies, situation comedies).
9. Two politicians.
10. Two musicians or singers.
11. Conflicting viewpoints on controversial subjects: capital punishment, abortions, and so on.
12. Two character traits or emotions that can be confused: courage and recklessness, love and infatuation.
13. Two high schools or two colleges; high school versus college.
14. Two teachers with contrasting educational philosophies.
15. Dogs versus cats.
16. Attitude you had as a child versus attitude you have now toward parents, religion, sex, and so on.
17. Contrast between advertising claims and reality.
18. Two "dates."
19. Two tourist attractions.
20. Two employers.

Block Pattern

COMING IN LAST
Annette P. Grossman (student)

Thesis: The huge contrast between the runners at the beginning and end of the Chicago Marathon taught me a lot about what it means to be a sports hero.

    I. Runners at the head of the marathon
      A. Look like runners
      B. Dress like runners
      C. Focus intensely

    II. Runners at the back of the marathon
      A. Don't look like runners
      B. Don't dress like runners
      C. Have poor focus, but more fun

Conclusion: The real sports heroes are the second set, who look nothing like real runners, but who run marathons anyway.

I am not an athlete. So when a couple of my more active friends asked me to get up at 7 A.M. with them and go cheer for the runners in this year's Chicago Marathon I almost refused. I'm still not sure what convinced me to go, but I went. I stood on the sidewalk for about six hours, passing out cups of water, or banging on a pot with a wooden spoon, or just yelling my head off to cheer on complete strangers. In between the cheering and the banging and the jumping about, though, I had a chance to do something I'd never done before: Watch a marathon. It was fascinating. I'd always thought that all runners were pretty much the same, but as I watched the 29,000 people who ran this year, I realized that there are huge differences between the runners at the beginning of the race and the runners at the end. This contrast even taught me a little bit about what it means to be a sports hero.

The runners at the head of the pack in a marathon look like *runners*. Their bodies are built for running and little else. These are people who have carefully trained for peak performance. They're lean, with corded muscles in places that I never knew could have muscles. Their legs are long and hard with strength enough to run more than 26 miles in a day but not slow them down with extra bulk.

The runners at the front of the marathon dress like runners too. They wear t-shirts they've gotten for participating in previous marathons. They wear clothes made from materials invented for the space program—materials with names like Neotex and Gorprene. They wear really short shorts, and really tight tights. These frontrunners carry impressive accessories as well. They start with gloves and hats and extra layers, but they shed them as the race heats up and their bodies get warm. By the end of the race, their only accessories are watches, sports goo, and shoes. The watches are marvels of modern sports technology that let them track their heart rate and their pace for every quarter mile as well as letting them figure a projected finish time, all of this while running, of course. The goo is contained in small foil packets of a jelly-like mess that's all carbohydrates and caffeine. They suck on these packets for energy as the race wears on. They wear shoes that cost half a month's rent. Everything about their running gear is serious.

The runners at the front of the pack have one more special quality: focus. They run with an intensity that blocks out everything. When we passed these people cups of water they didn't speak, smile, or glance our way. They didn't even slow down. The cups just went from our hands to theirs, mid-stride. These runners don't seem to hear the cheering or see the signs and people lining the streets. Their running takes them away from the outside world to someplace deep inside themselves that's made of work, determination, strength, and will. They don't need cheering to help them along.

Back at the end of the race, trailing about five hours behind the people at the front are the other runners. These people don't look like runners. They look like lawyers, and plumbers, and administrative assistants, and people who never pass up a dessert or a french fry. They look as if running is an extremely rare activity for them, as if they'd feel much more natural in a recliner, watching a football game. They limp a lot.

The runners at the end of the race don't dress like runners either. They wear old gym shorts and baggy t-shirts with funny sayings on them. They carry signs that say things like, "59 years old, first marathon. Cheer for me!" and "I'm running in memory of my mother." They wear clown wigs and pigs' noses and antennae with stars on them. They don't wear watches because they're don't really care how much time this is taking. They carry sports goo, too, but they want a ham sandwich. They wear expensive shoes, like the runners at the front of the race, but you can tell that their feet hurt anyway.

The real difference, though, is that the runners at the back don't have the focus that the others do. They need the music and the pot banging and the enthusiastic cheering more than the real runners because they're doing something that's hard for them. It's hard for everyone, of course, but it simply has to be harder for an overweight accountant to finish his first marathon than it is for a dedicated runner to finish her tenth, even with a personal best time. These runners at the end of the race need the cheering sections, and they show their appreciation. They wave back and give exhausted "thumbs up" signs. Once in a while, one will slow down for long enough to say "Thanks," and one man who must have been at least 75 actually stopped to dance with me for a minute or two before he turned and ran off to finish the final stretch of the course. These runners have at least as much determination as the runners at the front of the race, but they need to know that somebody cares about them, too, and not just about the people who can run the marathon in under three hours.

Everyone I saw that day impressed me, all 29,000 complete lunatics who finished the race. The athletic skill of the front runners, their devotion to their sport, was humbling. Even more humbling was hearing that the winner of the race set a world's record, running the marathon in 2:05. The newspapers called him a sports hero. For me, though, the real sports heroes were the people at the end of the race, the ones who didn't look or dress or act a thing like "real runners," but who ran anyway. I cheered for them the loudest.

Alternating Pattern

CHICK MOVIES AND GUY MOVIES
Edith Renaldo (student)

Thesis: Chick movies and guy movies are different in almost all respects.

  I. Settings
    A. Chick movies
    B. Guy movies

  II. Lead characters
    A. Chick movies
    B. Guy movies

  III. Plots
    A. Chick movies
    B. Guy movies

Conclusion: Men and women keep coming closer together in the real world, but their tastes in movies will probably stay far apart.

Ever since that wonderful scene in *Sleepless in Seattle* when a group of male and female friends discuss the movie *An Affair to Remember,* everyone has known that there are only two kinds of movies: guy movies and chick movies. While many of us may object to the sexist terminology of this statement, we know that the distinction in the movie choices of men and women still exists. In addition to my longstanding addiction to movies, a recent heat wave and a stifling city apartment caused me to spend big chunks of time at the local movie theater and made me something of an expert on the wild differences in the settings, lead characters, and plots of these two kinds of movies.

Consider, first of all, where the movies are likely to take place. Chick movies are set in small town beauty parlors, in the English countryside, or anywhere that looks like a postcard of someplace you'd like to go on vacation. Everything except beauty parlor scenes, crying scenes, and sex scenes happens outside on beautiful sunny days. Guy movies, on the other hand, take place in prisons, big cities, spaceships, or anywhere that's filthy, sweaty, and filled with machinery. Nothing ever happens outside unless it involves a car chase.

Every movie requires a lead character to fill up the setting. In a chick movie, the lead character is always a woman. She is named something like Kat—short for Katherine—or Emerald, or Sparkle. Sometimes she is just an office worker, but usually she does something glamorous, but not too glamorous, like photography or radio announcing or freelance writing. She is always beautiful, but her last boyfriend left because he was married, or insensitive, or unable to appreciate her intelligence. In a guy movie, the lead character is always a man. He is named Mike or Spike, Chance or Lucky, or is simply nameless and mysterious. He is probably a cop or used to be one. If not, he's a soldier, a spy, a private detective, or an ordinary guy who just happens to know seven languages and sixteen ways to kill people with a socket wrench. He is always ruggedly handsome and muscular, but his girlfriend died in the last movie, right after she turned out to be working for the other side.

Then, of course, something must happen to the main character. The plot of a chick movie involves four women seeking meaningful relationships with their mothers, their sisters, their lovers, their husbands, or their cats. The final scene is a soft focus on a wedding or at least a passionate kiss. The plot of a guy movie centers on one man seeking violent revenge on the bad guys who got him fired, killed his girl, killed his buddy, stole a nuclear warhead, or shot his dog. The final scene is a tight close-up of our sweaty hero smiling as he contemplates a building he has just blown up.

While everyone knows that men and women are daily coming closer in real life, our tastes in movie fantasy are as far apart as ever and will probably stay that way. That's fine with me. As long as none of the men I know expect me to watch the *Die Hard* series with them, I won't ask them to watch any movie based on Jane Austen novels.

LASSIE NEVER CHASES RABBITS
Kevin Cowherd

Kevin Cowherd is a columnist for the *Baltimore Sun*. As you read this good-natured, seemingly freewheeling set of humorous complaints, notice how carefully the author follows one of the formal comparison-contrast patterns outlined in this chapter.

Words to check:

Grizzled (paragraph 28)

1 Look, I am the last person in the world who would rip Lassie or speak unkindly about a dog that has accomplished so much over the years, rescued so many terrified children from swollen rapids, fought off so many enraged coyotes, etc.

2 But my kids just dragged me to see the new "Lassie" movie. And it occurred to me that many of the things that bugged me about Lassie 30 years ago still bug me today.

3 For instance, how did everyone around Lassie always know what she was saying when she barked?

4 When I was a kid, it seemed like every "Lassie" episode on TV had a scene like this:

5 Lassie: "Woof, woof!"

6 Mr. Martin: "What's that, girl? You say Timmy's down by the power plant?"

7 Lassie: "Woof, woof!"

8 Mr. Martin: "And he's clinging to a vine while trapped in 30 feet of oozing quicksand?"

9 Lassie: "Woof, woof!"

10 Mr. Martin: "And the bad guys who pulled that bank job are heading north out of town?"

11 Lassie: "Woof, woof!"

12 Now, I have a dog myself. And my dog barks at me all the time.

13 But whenever my dog barks at me, my first reaction is: What the heck is he saying?

14 In fact, most of our conversations (if you want to call them that) go something like this:

15 My dog: "Woof, woof!"

16 Me: "What? You wanna go out?"

17 (I open the screen door. The dog just sits there.)

18 My dog: "Woof, woof!"

19 Me: "What?! Food? I gave you food!"

20 My dog: "Woof, woof!"

21 Me: "What, a dog biscuit?"

22 (I hold out a dog biscuit. The dog doesn't move. The dog looks at me like I'm holding a fistful of sand.)—The point is, all I get out of that "woof, woof!" stuff is, well, woof, woof.

23 When my dog barks at me, it never occurs to me to say: "What's that? You say a bolt of lightning from the electrical storm just hit the garage? You say

we better get out of here pronto before the whole place goes up in flames?" Because if anybody heard me say that, they'd be hustling me into an ambulance and shooting me up with 250 milligrams of Thorazine.

24   You know another thing that irritates me about Lassie? She never, ever makes a mistake.

25   Just once I'd like to see Lassie mess up big-time. Instead of jumping into a raging river to rescue a 5-year-old, I'd like to see her, I don't know, start chasing a rabbit or something.

26   Or instead of leading the grizzled old-timer out of the collapsed, mine shaft, I'd like to see Lassie start digging for bones.

27   Understand, it's not that I want to see anyone get hurt.

28   But it would be neat to have someone else rescue the kid in the river or the old-timer in the mine for a change.

29   Then everyone could turn to Lassie and say: "Where the heck were you? You're vastly overrated, you know that?" I guess what I'm saying is: I'd like to see Lassie act more like a real dog.

30   Let's put it this way: If I were clinging to a vine while trapped in 30 feet of oozing quicksand, you know what my dog would do? I'll tell you what he'd do: nothing. My dog would find a nice comfortable place under the nearest tree and fall asleep. Because that's all my dog ever does: sleep.

31   Believe me, it would be a total waste of time to scream: "Pudgie, go get help!"

32   In fact, my dog would be so mad at me for waking him up that he'd start chewing the vine. Just so I'd sink into the quicksand faster and shut up. Lassie, of course, is far too busy to sleep. Everything is always go, go, go.

33   In the course of this new movie, she leads her sullen 13-year-old master to his late mom's long-lost diary, rescues a kid in the familiar raging river, battles a coyote in a cave, herds sheep, gently helps the 13-year-old adapt to his new surroundings, hooks him up with a babe and does everything else but join O.J. Simpson's defense team. For my dog, a big day is moving from one side of the couch to the other.

34   Believe me, if I ever fell into a raging river, my dog would never even know it—unless someone moved the couch down to the river.

35   Even then his philosophy would be: Hey, it's nap time. You're on your own, pal.

36   He's not exactly a go-getter, if you catch my drift.

WHAT DID THE WRITER SAY AND WHAT DID YOU THINK?

1. Which does the author emphasize more—his own dog's worthlessness or the unrealistic glorification of Lassie?

2. To what extent could this essay be considered a humorous treatment of the issue dealt with seriously in Eco's "How to Speak of Animals," (p. 108)?

HOW DID THE WRITER SAY IT?

1. Where is the thesis stated most directly?
2. Which comparison-contrast pattern does the author use?
3. The title may strike some readers as needing improvement. Why is it misleading in some ways? Any suggestions for better titles?

WHAT ABOUT <u>YOUR</u> WRITING?

"Lassie Never Chases Rabbits" ends with a body paragraph, a comment on the laziness of the author's dog. Many readers and instructors may feel that the essay should have had an additional paragraph, a normal concluding paragraph designed in one way or another to remind readers of the main point of the whole essay.

Ordinarily, your paper needs a concluding paragraph. Without one, your paper usually ends with the last small detail of supporting evidence, and your reader is all too likely to forget about or neglect your main point—in this case, the absurdity of Hollywood's fantasy of a perfect dog.

Your conclusion must be related to, must grow out of, what has come before. It is your last chance to remind your reader of your thesis and to drive home its importance. It is not the place to introduce irrelevant or trivial new topics. It is not the place to worry about being under or over any assigned number of words. The words of your conclusion are the last ones your reader will see, and they ought to be good words.

Beyond these observations, unfortunately, there are no tidy rules governing the writing of conclusions. Too many different kinds of conclusions exist to be wrapped into one neat package. Your best bet for writing a good conclusion is to keep the various choices in mind so they'll be available when you need them—and then to trust your instincts and common sense.

The following list suggests a few of the most useful kinds of conclusions:

Summary We can see, then, that for many people divorce has become the preferred method of settling marital problems. Liberalized grounds for divorce, the increased social acceptance of those who have been divorced, and the loosening of religious taboos have all contributed to the dramatic increase in the divorce rate.

Note: Summaries run the risk of dullness. If your conclusion is a summary, try not to make it a word-for-word repetition of language used earlier in the paper. Summaries work best in long papers. The shorter the paper, the more you should consider another kind of conclusion.

Call for Action As this paper has shown, the divorced man gets sympathy and attention and lots of dinner invitations. The divorced woman generally just gets propositioned. It's time she got some sympathy, too. She's not asking for special favors, but it's time to stop treating her like a social outcast.

Prediction And so it goes. Divorce becomes more common every day. Eventually it may become so common that it will stop mattering much. Then, perhaps, we will find people boasting about their former marriages the way our quaint old grandparents used to boast about shipping on a tramp steamer, or winning first prize for apple pie at the county fair, or with voices soft with pride and joy and love, staying happily married for forty or fifty years.

Question The increasing divorce rate is not merely a colorful statistic. It raises disturbing questions. How great is the damage done to children? Does divorce solve a problem or only run away from it? Is marriage itself a dying institution? Can a society of broken homes be a healthy society? These and other questions will trouble this nation for years to come.

Quotation All in all, there seems little any one person or group can do about the increasing number of broken marriages except to start taking seriously the century-old wisecrack of *Punch* magazine: "Advice to those about to marry: Don't."

Anecdote Yes, everybody's doing it. The tragedy has gone from divorce. It's now an official part of the natural cycle. Last week one of the churches in my town had a divorce service. It was a big dress-up occasion. Friends and relatives got invited. Music. Prayers. Lots of lofty sentiments about change and growth and stages. It was just like getting married. It was just like dying.

Restatement of Importance of the Topic At a time when newsmagazines and television specials go into weekly panics about gas mileage and electric bills, about the balance of payments and inflation, about deficits and dictatorships, it may seem almost frivolous to start brooding about how many people are getting divorced. In an age of revolution, it may seem almost irresponsible to create a new panic by studying statistics at the county courthouse. In the long run, however, nothing may be less frivolous or more thoroughly revolutionary for American civilization than the frightening basic truths revealed by the divorce figures of our turbulent society.

SPEAKING OF WRITING

William Zinsser

A distinguished newspaper editor and critic, teacher, and author of many books, William Zinsser is perhaps best known for his writing about writing. The following selection is from *On Writing Well*, an established classic now in its fifth edition.

Words to check:

vocation (paragraph 1)   arduous (3)
avocation (1)   gusto (15)
bohemian (2)

1   About ten years ago a school in Connecticut held "a day devoted to the arts," and I was asked if I would come and talk about writing as a vocation. When I arrived I found that a second speaker had been invited—Dr. Brock (as I'll call him), a surgeon who had recently begun to write and had sold some stories to national magazines. He was going to talk about writing as an avocation. That made us a panel, and we sat down to face a crowd of student newspaper editors, English teachers and parents, all eager to learn the secrets of our glamorous work.

2   Dr. Brock was dressed in a bright red jacket, looking vaguely bohemian, as authors are supposed to look, and the first question went to him. What was it like to be a writer?

3   He said it was tremendous fun. Coming home from an arduous day at the hospital, he would go straight to his yellow pad and write his tensions away. The words just flowed. It was easy.

4.   I then said that writing wasn't easy and it wasn't fun. It was hard and lonely, and the words seldom just flowed.

5   Next Dr. Brock was asked if it was important to rewrite. Absolutely not, he said. "Let it all hang out," and whatever form the sentences take will reflect the writer at his most natural.

6   I then said that rewriting is the essence of writing. I pointed out that professional writers rewrite their sentences repeatedly and then rewrite what they have rewritten. I mentioned that E. B. White and James Thurber rewrote their pieces eight or nine times.

7   "What do you do on days when it isn't going well?" Dr. Brock was asked. He said he just stopped writing and put the work aside for a day when it would go better.

8   I then said that the professional writer must establish a daily schedule and stick to it. I said that writing is a craft, not an art, and that the man who runs away from his craft because he lacks inspiration is fooling himself. He is also going broke.

9   "What if you're feeling depressed or unhappy?" a student asked. "Won't that affect your writing?"

10   Probably it will, Dr. Brock replied. Go fishing. Take a walk.

11   Probably it won't, I said. If your job is to write every day, you learn to do it like any other job.

12   A student asked if we found it useful to circulate in the literary world. Dr. Brock said that he was greatly enjoying his new life as a man of letters, and he told several stories of being taken to lunch by his publisher and his agent at chic Manhattan restaurants where writers and editors gather. I said that professional writers are solitary drudges who seldom see other writers.

13   "Do you put symbolism in your writing?" a student asked me.

14   "Not if I can help it," I replied. I have an unbroken record of missing the deeper meaning in any story, play or movie, and as for dance and mime, I have never had even a remote notion of what is being conveyed.

15   "I *love* symbols!" Dr. Brock exclaimed, and he described with gusto the joys of weaving them through his work.

16   So the morning went, and it was a revelation to all of us. At the end Dr. Brock told me he was enormously interested in my answers—it had never occurred to him that writing could be hard. I told him I was just as interested in *his* answers—it had never occurred to me that writing could be easy. (Maybe I should take up surgery on the side.)

17   As for the students, anyone might think we left them bewildered. But in fact we probably gave them a broader glimpse of the writing process than if only one of us had talked. For of course there isn't any "right" way to do such intensely personal work. There are all kinds of writers and all kinds of methods, and any method that helps people to say what they want to say is the right method for them.

WHAT DID THE WRITER SAY AND WHAT DID YOU THINK?

1. What is the thesis? Where is it stated?
2. Summarize in your own words the main difference between the two men's approach to writing.
3. Apply the approaches to writing of Zinsser and Dr. Brock to areas such as cooking, sports, and driving an automobile. Do you agree that the proper approach is really up to the individual?

HOW DID THE WRITER SAY IT?

1. Which comparison-contrast approach does Zinsser use—alternating or block?
2. Why are we given details about Dr. Brock's clothing?
3. Is Zinsser's quip, "Maybe I should take up surgery on the side," a harmless wisecrack or does it make a serious point beneath the humor?

WHAT ABOUT <u>YOUR</u> WRITING?

Just because writers of short essays usually present their theses by the end of their first paragraphs doesn't mean they always do. Or always should. William Zinsser lets us wait until the last paragraph before directly presenting his thesis that any approach to writing is valid as long as it works for the writer. Had he presented the thesis in the first paragraph, some of the humor of the contradictory statements might have been lost as the story became too much like a sermon. If the formula that usually works doesn't turn out to work this time, it's too bad for the formula.

THAT LEAN AND HUNGRY LOOK[1]

Suzanne Britt

First published in *Newsweek* in 1978, "That Lean and Hungry Look" has become something of a humorous classic. The author has taught college and written for newspapers. In addition to collections of her essays, she has published an English textbook, *A Writer's Rhetoric* (1988).

Words to check:

metabolism (paragraph 3)	nebulous (5)	pat (10)
inert (3)	fiscal (7)	prognose (11)
wizened (4)	cerebral (10)	convivial (12)
	machinations (10)	

---

[1] The title alludes to the words from Act I, Scene ii of Shakespeare's *Julius Caesar* spoken by the title character:

> Let me have men about me that are fat;
> Sleek-headed men and such as sleep o' nights;
> Yond' Cassius has a lean and hungry look;
> He thinks too much: such men are dangerous.

1 Caesar was right. Thin people need watching. I've been watching them for most of my adult life, and I don't like what I see. When these narrow fellows[2] spring at me, I quiver to my toes. Thin people come in all personalities, most of them menacing. You've got your "together" thin person, your mechanical thin person, your condescending thin person, your tsk-tsk thin person, your efficiency-expert thin person. All of them are dangerous.

2 In the first place, thin people aren't fun. They don't know how to goof off, at least in the best, fat sense of the word. They've always got to be adoing. Give them a coffee break, and they'll jog around the block. Supply them with a quiet evening at home, and they'll fix the screen door and lick S&H green stamps. They say things like "there aren't enough hours in the day." Fat people never say that. Fat people think the day is too damn long already.

3 Thin people make me tired. They've got speedy little metabolisms that cause them to bustle briskly. They're forever rubbing their bony hands together and eyeing new problems to "tackle." I like to surround myself with sluggish, inert, easygoing fat people, the kind who believe that if you clean it up today, it'll just get dirty again tomorrow.

4 Some people say the business about the jolly fat person is a myth, that all of us chubbies are neurotic, sick, sad people. I disagree. Fat people may not be chortling all day long, but they're a hell of a lot nicer than the wizened and shriveled. Thin people turn surly, mean and hard at a young age because they never learn the value of a hot-fudge sundae for easing tension. Thin people don't like gooey soft things because they themselves are neither gooey nor soft. They are crunchy and dull, like carrots. They go straight to the heart of the matter while fat people let things stay all blurry and hazy and vague, the way things actually are. Thin people want to face the truth. Fat people know there is no truth. One of my thin friends is always staring at complex, unsolvable problems and saying, "The key thing is . . ." Fat people never say that. They know there isn't any such thing as the key thing about anything.

5 Thin people believe in logic. Fat people see all sides. The sides fat people see are rounded blobs, usually gray, always nebulous and truly not worth worrying about. But the thin person persists. "If you consume more calories than you burn," says one of my thin friends, "you will gain weight. It's that simple." Fat people always grin when they hear statements like that. They know better.

6 Fat people realize that life is illogical and unfair. They know very well that God is not in his heaven and all is not right with the world. If God was up there, fat people could have two doughnuts and a big orange drink anytime they wanted it.

---

[2] "A narrow Fellow in the Grass" is the first line of an Emily Dickinson poem about snakes.

7   Thin people have a long list of logical things they are always spouting off to me. They hold up one finger at a time as they reel off these things, so I won't lose track. They speak slowly as if to a young child. The list is long and full of holes. It contains tidbits like "get a grip on yourself," "cigarettes kill," "cholesterol clogs," "fit as a fiddle," "ducks in a row," "organize" and "sound fiscal management." Phrases like that.

8   They think these 2,000-point plans lead to happiness. Fat people know happiness is elusive at best and even if they could get the kind thin people talk about, they wouldn't want it. Wisely, fat people see that such programs are too dull, too hard, too off the mark. They are never better than a whole cheesecake.

9   Fat people know all about the mystery of life. They are the ones acquainted with the night, with luck, with fate, with playing it by ear. One thin person I know once suggested that we arrange all the parts of a jigsaw puzzle into groups according to size, shape and color. He figured this would cut the time needed to complete the puzzle at least by 50 per cent. I said I wouldn't do it. One, I like to muddle through. Two, what good would it do to finish early? Three, the jigsaw puzzle isn't the important thing. The important thing is the fun of four people (one thin person included) sitting around a card table, working a jigsaw puzzle. My thin friend had no use for my list. Instead of joining us, he went outside and mulched the boxwoods. The three remaining fat people finished the puzzle and made chocolate, double-fudged brownies to celebrate.

10   The main problem with thin people is they oppress. Their good intentions, bony torsos, tight ships, neat corners, cerebral machinations and pat solutions loom like dark clouds over the loose, comfortable, spread-out, soft world of the fat. Long after fat people have removed their coats and shoes and put their feet up on the coffee table, thin people are still sitting on the edge of the sofa, looking neat as a pin, discussing rutabagas. Fat people are heavily into fits of laughter, slapping their thighs and whooping it up, while thin people are still politely waiting for the punch line.

11   Thin people are downers. They like math and morality and reasoned evaluation of the limitations of human beings. They have their skinny little acts together. They expound, prognose, probe and prick.

12   Fat people are convivial. They will like you even if you're irregular and have acne. They will come up with a good reason why you never wrote the great American novel. They will cry in your beer with you. They will put your name in the pot. They will let you off the hook. Fat people will gab, giggle, guffaw, gallumph, gyrate and gossip. They are generous, giving and gallant. They are gluttonous and goodly and great. What you want when you're down is soft and jiggly, not muscled and stable. Fat people know this. Fat people have plenty of room. Fat people will take you in.

WHAT DID THE WRITER SAY AND WHAT DID YOU THINK?

1. How accurate do you feel the comments are about fat and skinny people in general? To what extent do you feel the author is contrasting two different temperaments rather than two different body types?
2. On a more serious level, do you think that illnesses such as anorexia and bulimia help confirm any of the comments about skinny people?
3. How can we be reasonably sure that the observations in paragraph 6 are not intended to express Britt's serious thoughts on the existence of God?

HOW DID THE WRITER SAY IT?

1. Britt mixes the alternating and block patterns. Which pattern dominates?
2. Why is the jigsaw puzzle story worth telling?
3. Do you feel the heavy use of alliteration in the last paragraph is effective or overdone?

WHAT ABOUT <u>YOUR</u> WRITING?

Skinny people "are crunchy and dull, like carrots," Suzanne Britt writes. The comparison works well in a number of ways. It connects the abstract idea of skinny people in general with the everyday specific reality of a actual item in the reader's refrigerator. It communicates the author's attitude toward skinny people by calling to mind the distant respect and utter lack of interest that most members of the public feel for carrots. Finally, skinny people and carrots go together because carrots are a standard dreary diet food, so different from cheesecakes and chocolates.

Comparisons can sometimes add a spark to your own writing. Instead of settling for "I was embarrassed," for example, you might try to finish off the thought with a comparison:

I was as embarrassed as a poolroom hustler hitting the cue ball off the table.

I hadn't been so embarrassed since I was six and my mother caught me playing doctor with Jimmy Fisher next door.

I was so embarrassed it was like having a simultaneous attack of dandruff, noisy stomach, and underarm perspiration.

The two most common kinds of comparisons are similes and metaphors. *Similes* make the comparison explicit by using *like* or *as*. A few words by George Orwell describe a man trampled by an elephant:

> The friction of the great beast's foot had stripped the skin from his back as
> neatly as one skins a rabbit.

Metaphors are sometimes defined as similes without the *like* or *as*. The simile,
"The moon was like a silver dollar," becomes a metaphor when expressed,
"The moon was a silver dollar." A metaphor can be more sophisticated than
that, however, and the term is best defined as a word or phrase ordinarily
associated with one context that is transferred to another. Some metaphors
have become part of the language—so much so that they are either hopelessly trite or barely recognizable as metaphors:

Life is a rat race.

He ought to come down from his ivory tower.

Keep your paws off me.

She has a good nose for news.

. . . branches of knowledge

. . . key to the problem

. . . legs of a table

. . . hit below the belt

Other metaphors are waiting to be created to add impact, originality, and
excitement to your writing:

Cautiously, the psychiatrist started to enter the haunted castle of his
    patient's mind.

It was the same thing all over again. My whole life had turned into a
    summer rerun.

Don't ever let your dreams of scaling Mount Everest some day keep you
    from facing the practicalities of daily life here in Death Valley.

Two cautions are necessary. First, use comparisons in moderation; otherwise, your style, instead of becoming enlivened, will become bogged down by
excess baggage. Second, don't be tempted into using the ready-made trite
comparisons that fill the language: "as easy as pie," "so hungry I could eat a
horse," "like taking candy from a baby," "like a bolt out of the blue," and so on.
Trite phrases, by definition, are dead, and good comparisons are intended to
be life-giving.

CONVERSATIONAL BALLGAMES

Nancy Masterson Sakamoto

This frequently anthologized selection from Nancy Sakamoto's textbook *Polite Fictions* (1982) draws on tennis, bowling, and volleyball to explain elusive and difficult cultural differences between Japan and the West. Sakamoto, coauthor of *Mutual Understanding of Different Cultures* (1981) is professor of American Studies at Shitennoji Gakuen University.

1   After I was married and had lived in Japan for a while, my Japanese gradually improved to the point where I could take part in simple conversations with my husband and his friends and family. And I began to notice that often, when I joined in, the others would look startled, and the conversational topic would come to a halt. After this happened several times, it became clear to me that I was doing something wrong. But for a long time, I didn't know what it was.

2   Finally, after listening carefully to many Japanese conversations, I discovered what my problem was. Even though I was speaking Japanese, I was handling the conversation in a western way.

3   Japanese-style conversations develop quite differently from western-style conversations. And the difference isn't only in the languages. I realized that just as I kept trying to hold western-style conversations even when I was speaking Japanese, so my English students kept trying to hold Japanese-style conversations even when they were speaking English. We were unconsciously playing entirely different conversational ballgames.

4   A western-style conversation between two people is like a game of tennis. If I introduce a topic, a conversational ball, I expect you to hit it back. If you agree with me, I don't expect you simply to agree and do nothing more. I expect you to add something—a reason for agreeing, another example, or an elaboration to carry the idea further. But I don't expect you always to agree. I am just as happy if you question me, or challenge me, or completely disagree with me. Whether you agree or disagree, your response will return the ball to me.

5   And then it is my turn again. I don't serve a new ball from my original starting line. I hit your ball back again from where it has bounced. I carry your idea further, or answer your questions or objections, or challenge or question you. And so the ball goes back and forth, with each of us doing our best to give it a new twist, an original spin, or a powerful smash.

6   And the more vigorous the action, the more interesting and exciting the game. Of course, if one of us gets angry, it spoils the conversation, just as it spoils a tennis game. But getting excited is not at all the same as getting angry.

After all, we are not trying to hit each other. We are trying to hit the ball. So long as we attack only each other's opinions, and do not attack each other personally, we don't expect anyone to get hurt. A good conversation is supposed to be interesting and exciting.

7   If there are more than two people in the conversation, then it is like doubles in tennis, or like volleyball. There's no waiting in line. Whoever is nearest and quickest hits the ball, and if you step back, someone else will hit it. No one stops the game to give you a turn. You're responsible for taking your own turn.

8   But whether it's two players or a group, everyone does his best to keep the ball going, and no one person has the ball for very long.

9   A Japanese-style conversation, however, is not at all like tennis or volleyball. It's like bowling. You wait for your turn. And you always know your place in line. It depends on such things as whether you are older or younger, a close friend or a relative stranger to the previous speaker, in a senior or junior position, and so on.

10   When your turn comes, you step up to the starting line with your bowling ball, and carefully bowl it. Everyone else stands back and watches politely, murmuring encouragement. Everyone waits until the ball has reached the end of the alley, and watches to see if it knocks down all the pins, or only some of them, or none of them. There is a pause, while everyone registers your score.

11   Then, after everyone is sure that you have completely finished your turn, the next person in line steps up to the same starting line, with a different ball. He doesn't return your ball, and he does not begin from where your ball stopped. There is no back and forth at all. All the balls run parallel. And there is always a suitable pause between turns. There is no rush, no excitement, no scramble for the ball.

12   No wonder everyone looked startled when I took part in Japanese conversations. I paid no attention to whose turn it was, and kept snatching the ball halfway down the alley and throwing it back at the bowler. Of course the conversation died. I was playing the wrong game.

13   This explains why it is almost impossible to get a western-style conversation or discussion going with English students in Japan. I used to think that the problem was their lack of English language ability. But I finally came to realize that the biggest problem is that they, too, are playing the wrong game.

14   Whenever I serve a volleyball, everyone just stands back and watches it fall, with occasional murmurs of encouragement. No one hits it back. Everyone waits until I call on someone to take a turn. And when that person speaks, he doesn't hit my ball back. He serves a new ball. Again, everyone just watches it fall.

15   So I call on someone else. This person does not refer to what the previous speaker has said. He also serves a new ball. Nobody seems to have paid any attention to what anyone else has said. Everyone begins again from the same starting line, and all the balls run parallel. There is never any back and forth. Everyone is trying to bowl with a volleyball.

16   And if I try a simpler conversation, with only two of us, then the other person tries to bowl with my tennis ball. No wonder foreign English teachers in Japan get discouraged.

17   Now that you know about the difference in the conversational ballgames, you may think that all your troubles are over. But if you have been trained all your life to play one game, it is no simple matter to switch to another, even if you know the rules. Knowing the rules is not at all the same thing as playing the game.

18   Even now, during a conversation in Japanese I will notice a startled reaction, and belatedly realize that once again I have rudely interrupted by instinctively trying to hit back the other person's bowling ball. It is no easier for me to "just listen" during a conversation, than it is for my Japanese students to "just relax" when speaking with foreigners. Now I can truly sympathize with how hard they must find it to try to carry on a western-style conversation.

19   If I have not yet learned to do conversational bowling in Japanese, at least I have figured out one thing that puzzled me for a long time. After his first trip to America, my husband complained that Americans asked him so many questions and made him talk so much at the dinner table that he never had a chance to eat. When I asked him why he couldn't talk and eat at the same time, he said that Japanese do not customarily think that dinner, especially on fairly formal occasions, is a suitable time for extended conversation.

20   Since westerners think that conversation is an indispensable part of dining, and indeed would consider it impolite not to converse with one's dinner partner, I found this Japanese custom rather strange. Still, I could accept it as a cultural difference even though I didn't really understand it. But when my husband added, in explanation, that Japanese consider it extremely rude to talk with one's mouth full, I got confused. Talking with one's mouth full is certainly not an American custom. We think it very rude, too. Yet we still manage to talk a lot and eat at the same time. How do we do it?

21   For a long time, I couldn't explain it, and it bothered me. But after I discovered the conversational ballgames, I finally found the answer. Of course! In a western-style conversation, you hit the ball, and while someone else is hitting it back, you take a bite, chew, and swallow. Then you hit the ball again, and then eat some more. The more people there are in the conversation, the more chances you have to eat. But even with only two of you talking, you still have plenty of chances to eat.

22   Maybe that's why polite conversation at the dinner table has never been a traditional part of Japanese etiquette. Your turn to talk would last so long without interruption that you'd never get a chance to eat.

WHAT DID THE WRITER SAY AND WHAT DID YOU THINK?

1. What is the thesis?
2. What are the sports to which conversations are compared?
3. What specifically makes class discussions so difficult for an English-speaking teacher in Japan?
4. What determines a person's "place in line" in a Japanese conversation?
5. Why does Sakamoto describe her husband's difficulty with dinner-table conversation? How well does this section of the essay fit with the rest?
6. Does the author prefer one form of conversation to another? How can you tell?

HOW DID THE WRITER SAY IT?

1. In which pattern is the essay written? Is more than one pattern used?
2. Do the sports analogies make the author's points more interesting? Easier to understand?
3. How do humorous touches contribute to the success of this essay?
4. Is the thesis ever stated specifically? If so, where?

WHAT ABOUT <u>YOUR</u> WRITING?

At one time or another, nearly every English teacher starts chatting with a student about writing, and more often than seems possible, this kind of scene takes place.

"You write well enough," says the teacher. "But I wonder if you can't try for a little more life in your writing. Don't be so stiff, so formal. Drop in a personal touch now and then."

"A personal touch?" asks the student.

"Well, yes. If you're writing about raising children or something like that, don't just come on like a professional sociologist. Start out with an argument you once had with your parents. Then get into the sociology, if you have to."

"You mean I can use I if I want to?"

"?"

"We were never allowed to use I."

"?"

It seems that a lot of students had high school teachers who understandably got upset with weasel sentences like "I think that Abraham Lincoln was an important figure in American history" and personal letters like "I remember last week you said in class that Hemingway started his writing career as a newspaper reporter, and I wonder what you think of this idea I came up with." So the teacher made up a rule that prohibited the use of *I*. It's possible to sympathize with the teacher, but the rule has nothing to do with the realities of writing.

Sakamoto's essay successfully breaks the ice by using the "I" approach. The author has some serious discussion of complex social and cultural differences in store for her audience, and it makes good sense to do what she can to create a reader-friendly atmosphere. Using *I* in your writing is neither good nor bad in itself, but when *I* works, go ahead.

You're allowed.

THE PRISONER'S DILEMMA

Stephen Chapman

Stephen Chapman is a columnist and editorial writer for the *Chicago Tribune*. His twice-weekly syndicated column on national and international affairs appears in some sixty papers across the country. In "The Prisoner's Dilemma," he contrasts the legendary cruelty of Moslem forms of legal punishment to presumably humane American forms. "Legendary" and "presumably" seem accurate words because Chapman reaches some disturbing conclusions. As you read, note how the contrasts are always used to establish or support a point, never just to concoct a long list of differences.

Words to check:

punitive (epigraph)	squeamish (2)	regimen (6)
occidental (epigraph)	brazen (3)	sociopaths (8)
fervor (paragraph 1)	superfluous (3)	impede (10)
stipulated (2)	flourish (3)	incarceration (12)
penological (2)	macabre (4)	recidivism (13)
malefactors (2)	decapitated (4)	

If the punitive laws of Islam were applied for only one year, all the devastating injustices would be uprooted. Misdeeds must be punished by the law of retaliation: cut off the hands of the thief; kill the murderers; flog the adulterous woman or man. Your concerns, your "humanitarian" scruples are more childish than reasonable. Under the terms of Koranic law, any judge fulfilling the seven requirements (that he have reached puberty, be a believer, know the Koranic laws perfectly, be just, and not be affected by amnesia, or be a bastard, or be of the female sex) is qualified to be a judge in any type of case. He can thus judge and dispose of twenty trials in a single day, whereas the Occidental justice might take years to argue them out.

—From *Sayings of the Ayatollah Khomeini*
(New York: Bantam Books, 1980)

1 One of the amusements of life in the modern West is the opportunity to observe the barbaric rituals of countries that are attached to the customs of the dark ages. Take Pakistan, for example, our newest ally and client state in Asia. Last October President Zia, in harmony with the Islamic fervor that is sweeping his part of the world, revived the traditional Moslem practice of flogging lawbreakers in public. In Pakistan, this qualified as mass entertainment, and no fewer than 10,000 law-abiding Pakistanis turned out to see justice done to 26 convicts. To Western sensibilities the spectacle seemed barbaric—both in the sense of cruel and in the sense of pre-civilized. In keeping with Islamic custom each of the unfortunates—who had been caught in prostitution raids the previous night and summarily convicted and sentenced—was stripped down to a pair of white shorts, which were painted with a red stripe across the buttocks (the target). Then he was shackled against an easel, with pads thoughtfully placed over the kidneys to prevent injury. The floggers were muscular, fierce-looking sorts—convicted murderers, as it happens—who paraded around the flogging platform in colorful loincloths. When the time for the ceremony began, one of the floggers took a running start and brought a five-foot stave down across the first victim's buttocks, eliciting screams from the convict and murmurs from the audience. Each of the 26 received from five to 15 lashes. One had to be carried from the stage unconscious.

2 Flogging is one of the punishments stipulated by Koranic law, which has made it a popular penological device in several Moslem countries, including Pakistan, Saudi Arabia, and, most recently, the ayatollah's Iran. Flogging, or *ta'zir,* is the general punishment prescribed for offenses that don't carry an explicit Koranic penalty. Some crimes carry automatic *hadd* punishments—stoning or scourging (a severe whipping) for illicit sex, scourging for drinking alcoholic beverages, amputation of the hands for theft. Other crimes—as varied as murder and abandoning Islam—carry the death penalty (usually carried out in public). Colorful practices like these have given the Islamic world an image in the West, as described by historian G. H. Jansen, "of blood dripping from the stumps of amputated hands and from the striped backs of malefactors, and piles of stones barely concealing the battered bodies of

adulterous couples." Jansen, whose book *Militant Islam* is generally effusive in its praise of Islamic practices, grows squeamish when considering devices like flogging, amputation, and stoning. But they are given enthusiastic endorsement by the Koran itself.

3   Such traditions, we all must agree, are no sign of an advanced civilization. In the West, we have replaced these various punishments (including the death penalty in most cases) with a single device. Our custom is to confine criminals in prison for varying lengths of time. In Illinois, a reasonably typical state, grand theft carries a punishment of three to five years; armed robbery can get you from six to 30. The lowest form of felony theft is punishable by one to three years in prison. Most states impose longer sentences on habitual offenders. In Kentucky, for example, habitual offenders can be sentenced to life in prison. Other states are less brazen, preferring the more genteel sounding "indeterminate sentence," which allows parole boards to keep inmates locked up for as long as life. It was under an indeterminate sentence of one to 14 years that George Jackson served 12 years in California prisons for committing a $70 armed robbery. Under a Texas law imposing an automatic life sentence for a third felony conviction, a man was sent to jail for life last year because of three thefts adding up to less than $300 in property value. Texas also is famous for occasionally imposing extravagantly long sentences, often running into hundreds or thousands of years. This gives Texas a leg up on Maryland, which used to sentence some criminals to life plus a day—a distinctive if superfluous flourish.

4   The punishment *intended* by Western societies in sending their criminals to prison is the loss of freedom. But, as everyone knows, the actual punishment in most American prisons is of a wholly different order. The February 2 [1980] riot at New Mexico's state prison in Santa Fe, one of several bloody prison riots in the nine years since the Attica bloodbath, once again dramatized the conditions of life in an American prison. Four hundred prisoners seized control of the prison before dawn. By sunset the next day 33 inmates had died at the hands of other convicts and another 40 people (including five guards) had been seriously hurt. Macabre stories came out of prisoners being hanged, murdered with blowtorches, decapitated, tortured, and mutilated in a variety of gruesome ways by drug-crazed rioters.

5   The Santa Fe penitentiary was typical of most maximum-security facilities, with prisoners subject to overcrowding, filthy conditions, and routine violence. It also housed first-time, non-violent offenders, like check forgers and drug dealers, with murderers serving life sentences. In a recent lawsuit, the American Civil Liberties Union called the prison "totally unfit for human habitation." But the ACLU says New Mexico's penitentiary is far from the nation's worst.

6   That American prisons are a disgrace is taken for granted by experts of every ideological stripe. Conservative James Q. Wilson has criticized our "[c]rowded, antiquated prisons that require men and women to live in fear of one another and to suffer not only deprivation of liberty but a brutalizing regimen." Leftist Jessica Mitford has called our prisons "the ultimate expression of injustice and inhumanity." In 1973 a national commission concluded that "the American correctional system today appears to offer minimum protection to the public and maximum harm to the offender." Federal courts have ruled that confinement in prisons in 16 different states violates the constitutional ban on "cruel and unusual punishment."

7   What are the advantages of being a convicted criminal in an advanced culture? First there is the overcrowding in prisons. One Tennessee prison, for example, has a capacity of 806, according to accepted space standards, but it houses 2,300 inmates. One Louisiana facility has confined four and five prisoners in a single six-foot-by-six-foot cell. Then there is the disease caused by overcrowding, unsanitary conditions, and poor or inadequate medical care. A federal appeals court noted that the Tennessee prison had suffered frequent outbreaks of infectious diseases like hepatitis and tuberculosis. But the most distinctive element of American prison life is its constant violence. In his book *Criminal Violence, Criminal Justice*, Charles Silberman noted that in one Louisiana prison, there were 211 stabbings in only three years, 11 of them fatal. There were 15 slayings in a prison in Massachusetts between 1972 and 1975. According to a federal court, in Alabama's penitentiaries (as in many others), "robbery, rape, extortion, theft and assault are everyday occurrences."

8   At least in regard to cruelty, it's not at all clear that the system of punishment that has evolved in the West is less barbaric than the grotesque practices of Islam. Skeptical? Ask yourself: would you rather be subjected to a few minutes of intense pain and considerable public humiliation, or be locked away for two or three years in a prison cell crowded with ill-tempered sociopaths? Would you rather lose a hand or spend 10 years or more in a typical state prison? I have taken my own survey on this matter. I have found no one who does not find the Islamic system hideous. And I have found no one who *given the choices* mentioned above, would not prefer its penalties to our own. . . .

9   Imprisonment is now the universal method of punishing criminals in the United States. It is thought to perform five functions, each of which has been given a label by criminologists. First, there is simple *retribution*: punishing the lawbreaker to serve society's sense of justice and to satisfy the victims' desire for revenge. Second, there is *specific deterrence*: discouraging the offender from misbehaving in the future. Third, *general deterrence*: using the offender as an example to discourage others from turning to crime. Fourth, *prevention*:

at least during the time he is kept off the streets, the criminal cannot victimize other members of society. Finally, and most important, there is *rehabilitation:* reforming the criminal so that when he returns to society he will be inclined to obey the laws and able to make an honest living.

10   How satisfactorily do American prisons perform by these criteria? Well, of course, they do punish. But on the other scores they don't do so well. Their effect in discouraging future criminality by the prisoner or others is the subject of much debate, but the soaring rates of the last 20 years suggest that prisons are not a dramatically effective deterrent to criminal behavior. Prisons do isolate convicted criminals, but only to divert crime from ordinary citizens to prison guards and fellow inmates. Almost no one contends any more that prisons rehabilitate their inmates. If anything, they probably impede rehabilitation by forcing inmates into prolonged and almost exclusive association with other criminals. And prisons cost a lot of money. Housing a typical prisoner in a typical prison costs far more than a stint at a top university. This cost would be justified if prisons did the job they were intended for. But it is clear to all that prisons fail on the very grounds—humanity and hope of rehabilitation—that caused them to replace earlier, cheaper forms of punishment.

11   The universal acknowledgment that prisons do not rehabilitate criminals has produced two responses. The first is to retain the hope of rehabilitation but do away with imprisonment as much as possible and replace it with various forms of "alternative treatment," such as psychotherapy, supervised probation, and vocational training. Psychiatrist Karl Menninger, one of the principal critics of American penology, has suggested even more unconventional approaches, such as "a new job opportunity or a vacation trip, a course of reducing exercises, a cosmetic surgical operation or a herniotomy, some night school courses, a wedding in the family (even one for the patient!), an inspiring sermon." This starry-eyed approach naturally has produced a backlash from critics on the right, who think that it's time to abandon the goal of rehabilitation. They argue that prisons perform an important service just by keeping criminals off the streets, and thus should be used with that purpose alone in mind.

12   So the debate continues to rage in all the same old ruts. No one, of course, would think of copying the medieval practices of Islamic nations and experimenting with punishments such as flogging and amputation. But let us consider them anyway. How do they compare with our American prison system in achieving the ostensible objectives of punishment? First, do they punish? Obviously they do, and in a uniquely painful and memorable way. Of course any sensible person, given the choice, would prefer suffering these punishments to years of incarceration in a typical American prison. But presumably no Western penologist would criticize Islamic punishments on the grounds

that they are not barbaric enough. Do they deter crime? Yes, and probably more effectively than sending convicts off to prison. Now we read about a prison sentence in the newspaper, then think no more about the criminal's payment for his crimes until, perhaps, years later we read a small item reporting his release. By contrast, one can easily imagine the vivid impression it would leave to be wandering through a local shopping center and to stumble onto the scene of some poor wretch being lustily flogged. And the occasional sight of an habitual offender walking around with a bloody stump at the end of his arm no doubt also would serve as a forceful reminder that crime does not pay.

13   Do flogging and amputation discourage recidivism? No one knows whether the scars on his back would dissuade a criminal from risking another crime, but it is hard to imagine that corporal measures could stimulate a higher rate of recidivism than already exists. Islamic forms of punishment do not serve the favorite new right goal of simply isolating criminals from the rest of society, but they may achieve the same purpose of making further crimes impossible. In the movie *Bonnie and Clyde*, Warren Beatty successfully robs a bank with his arm in a sling, but this must be dismissed as artistic license. It must be extraordinarily difficult, at the very least, to perform much violent crime with only one hand.

14   Do these medieval forms of punishment rehabilitate the criminal? Plainly not. But long prison terms do not rehabilitate either. And it is just as plain that typical Islamic punishments are no crueler to the convict than incarceration in the typical American state prison.

15   Of course there are other reasons besides its bizarre forms of punishment that the Islamic system of justice seems uncivilized to the Western mind. One is the absence of due process. Another is the long list of offenses—such as drinking, adultery, blasphemy, "profiteering," and so on—that can bring on conviction and punishment. A third is all the ritualistic mumbo-jumbo in pronouncements of Islamic law (like that talk about puberty and amnesia in the ayatollah's quotation at the beginning of this article). Even in these matters, however, a little cultural modesty is called for. The vast majority of American criminals are convicted and sentenced as a result of plea bargaining, in which due process plays almost no role. It has been only half a century since a wave of religious fundamentalism stirred this country to outlaw the consumption of alcoholic beverages. Most states also still have laws imposing austere constraints on sexual conduct. Only two weeks ago the *Washington Post* reported that the FBI had spent two and a half years and untold amounts of money to break up a nationwide pornography ring. Flogging the clients of prostitutes, as the Pakistanis did, does seem silly. But only a few months ago Mayor Koch of New York was proposing that clients caught in his own city

have their names broadcast by radio stations. We are not so far advanced on such matters as we often like to think. Finally, my lawyer friends assure me that the rules of jurisdiction for American courts contain plenty of petty requirements and bizarre distinctions that would sound silly enough to foreign ears.

16   Perhaps it sounds barbaric to talk of flogging and amputation, and perhaps it is. But our system of punishment also is barbaric, and probably more so. Only cultural smugness about their system and willful ignorance about our own make it easy to regard the one as cruel and the other as civilized. We inflict our cruelties away from public view, while nations like Pakistan stage them in front of 10,000 onlookers. Their outrages are visible; ours are not. Most Americans can live their lives for years without having their peace of mind disturbed by the knowledge of what goes on in our prisons. To choose imprisonment over flogging and amputation is not to choose human kindness over cruelty, but merely to prefer that our cruelties be kept out of sight, and out of mind.

17   Public flogging and amputation may be more barbaric forms of punishment than imprisonment, even if they are not more cruel. Society may pay a higher price for them, even if the particular criminal does not. Revulsion against officially sanctioned violence and infliction of pain derives from something deeply ingrained in the Western conscience, and clearly it is something admirable. Grotesque displays of the sort that occur in Islamic countries probably breed a greater tolerance for physical cruelty, for example, which prisons do not do precisely because they conceal their cruelties. In fact it is our admirable intolerance for calculated violence that makes it necessary for us to conceal what we have not been able to do away with. In a way this is a good thing, since it holds out the hope that we may eventually find a way to do away with it. But in another way it is a bad thing, since it permits us to congratulate ourselves on our civilized humanitarianism while violating its norms in this one area of our national life.

WHAT DID THE WRITER SAY AND WHAT DID YOU THINK?

1. What are the methods of punishment used in Moslem countries?
2. What is the one method used in "the West"? Why does the author feel the West is more cruel?
3. Does the author approve of Moslem methods?
4. Why is the author skeptical about prison reform?
5. Is the Western system equal or superior to the Moslem system in any respects, according to the author? Can anything be said in favor of Western methods? Does the author present only one side of the case?

6. What is the main reason that most Westerners think their system is less cruel?

7. Do the attacks on American prisons seem well substantiated, or are they merely unsupported outbursts?

HOW DID THE WRITER SAY IT?

1. Is the thesis of the whole essay ever stated directly? If so, where? If not, does it need to be?

2. Paragraphs 1–8 contrast the cruelty of the two systems. Paragraphs 9–17 contrast how well or poorly each system performs the five functions of imprisonment. Which comparison-contrast pattern is used in both sections? Which section more closely follows the instructions for comparison-contrast writing on pages 158–162?

3. In paragraph 8, the author addresses his readers directly. "Ask yourself: would you rather be subjected to a few minutes of intense pain and considerable public humiliation, or be locked away for two or three years in a prison cell crowded with ill-tempered sociopaths? Would you rather lose a hand or spend 10 years or more in a typical state prison?" Do you consider these sentences a clinching argument to establish the author's point or a cheap emotional appeal?

WHAT ABOUT <u>YOUR</u> WRITING?

Even people who boast about their ignorance of grammar think they know at least one rule: *Never end a sentence with a preposition.* In paragraph 17 of Chapman's "The Prisoner's Dilemma," these people tremble with joy when they see the following sentence: "In fact it is our admirable intolerance for calculated violence that makes it necessary for us to conceal what we have not been able to do away with." Here's a professional writer who seems to know even less about grammar than they.

The truth is that for centuries good and great writers have been ending their sentences with prepositions. And the sentences have ended that way not through carelessness or lack of knowledge but through a sense of good style. Would anyone seriously propose that Chapman reword his sentence to read, "In fact it is our admirable intolerance for calculated violence that makes it necessary for us to conceal that with which we have not been able to do away"? Compared to the original, the revised sentence is stiff, wordy, awkward, and ugly.

For most practical purposes, the rule against ending a sentence with a preposition doesn't exist today. It's doubtful if it ever existed in any rigid way outside the heads of a few deranged schoolmasters and schoolmistresses. Extremely formal English, when given a choice, probably still leans toward avoiding the preposition at the end of a sentence when possible, but won't hesitate to use it if it improves the style. Less formal English generally does what comes naturally. Certainly, the issue is one of style, not of some imaginary, unbreakable rule of grammar.

As always, be careful of excess. The story is told of a father accustomed to read bedtime stories to his young son. One evening the child was sick in bed. The father took a book, brought it upstairs to the bedroom, and the child said, "What did you bring the book I didn't want to be read to out of up for?"

Cause and Effect

The school board of a suburban town near Denver has decided to ask the voters to approve a large increase in property tax assessments to construct a new high school. The board knows that, at best, its request will be unwelcome. It launches a vigorous campaign to make the voters more favorably inclined. Part of the campaign is a pamphlet setting forth the board's case. The pamphlet, of necessity, presents a study of cause-and-effect relationships.

The board first states the *causes* for its request. Student enrollment has more than doubled. Three years ago, the board had tried to cope with this problem by going to two sessions, but the classrooms are still too crowded for basic physical comfort as well as for optimum learning conditions. Moreover, the situation is not temporary; current enrollment in the junior high and elementary schools assures continued increases in the student population. Finally, the building is in poor physical condition: The roof leaks, the basement floods, the boiler is on its last legs. The board has investigated the possibility of remodeling and expanding the old building and has found that costs for that project would mean an average of only $35 a year less in taxes per family than if a completely new school were built.

Next, the board discusses the results, or *effects*, of voter approval. The town's leading eyesore will be replaced by a beautiful new structure in which everyone can take pride. New facilities for the most modern teaching devices will improve the quality of education. Experienced teachers will be more inclined to stay than to seek new employment. The strength of the town's educational system will be a selling point for new residents and consequently will increase property values.

The school board's pamphlet, in short, presents a thesis—the proposal for a new high school should be approved—and supports it with cause-and-effect writing.

It's worth noting here that cause-and-effect relationships can sometimes shift. In the first part of the pamphlet, for example, the proposal to build a new school is the effect that was caused by overcrowding and a decaying building. In the second part of the pamphlet, however, the approved proposal becomes the cause of such beneficial effects as beauty and improved education. A cause creates an effect, but that effect, in turn, can become the cause of another effect. No problems are likely to arise as long as the writer keeps any shifting relationships clearly in mind.

Many classroom papers are not lengthy enough to give equal weight to cause and effect and will emphasize one over the other. "Cause" papers might have theses like these:

The rioting at last week's rock concert was mostly the fault of the police.

The growth of interest in coin collecting is attributable to practical financial considerations.

Government policies penalize savers and reward borrowers.

Iago plots against Othello because of an accumulation of petty resentments.

The introduction of the cause paper will usually contain a brief description of the *effect*—the rioting that resulted from police actions, the decrease in bank deposits that resulted from government policies—and then the entire body of the paper will analyze the causes, giving a paragraph, perhaps, to each cause.

Effect papers might have theses like these:

Passage of a national health insurance program would result in heavy burdens on doctors.

Fear of germs made me a nervous wreck as a child.

The invention of the cotton gin helped perpetuate slavery in the South.

Rigid enforcement of holding penalties in professional football has made the sport less exciting than it used to be.

The introduction to an effect paper will naturally reverse the procedure of a cause paper. It will briefly describe or discuss the *cause*—the health insurance program, the cotton gin, and so on—and the rest of the paper will then be devoted to the effects.

As you plan your paper, try to remember a few logical requirements.

Do Not Oversimplify Causes

Most subjects worth writing about have more than one cause. Sometimes particular combinations of causes have to be present at the same time and in certain proportions to bring about a particular result. Attributing a young man's delinquency solely to the poverty of his family oversimplifies what everyone knows about life. Poverty may have been a contributing cause, but there had to be others; plenty of poor children do not become delinquents, and plenty of rich ones do.

Beware especially of the *post hoc ergo propter hoc* fallacy: "after this, therefore because of this." After Herbert Hoover was elected president, America had a depression; therefore, America had a depression because Herbert Hoover was elected. An argument like this depends purely on an accident of time; the writer must point out, if possible, actual policies of the Hoover administration that brought about the depression. Otherwise, the argument has no more logical validity than "I lost my job after a black cat crossed my path; therefore, I lost my job because a black cat crossed my path."

Do Not Oversimplify Effects

Uncontrolled enthusiasm is probably the biggest danger here. A writer may be able to present a strong case that an ill-conceived national health insurance program might have adverse effects on medical care; if the writer predicts that millions of people will die of neglect in waiting lines in the doctor's office, however, the writer's case—and common sense—is sure to be viewed skeptically. The school board's pamphlet said that a new high school would be an additional selling point to attract new residents; if it had said that property values would triple within five years, it would have oversimplified the effects in an irresponsible and hysterical fashion.

Distinguish Between Direct and Indirect Causes and Effects

Don't treat all causes and effects equally. Some are more remote than others, and the distinctions need to be made clear.

Bad design and incompetent management were direct causes of the nuclear disaster at Chernobyl in 1986. The centuries-old desire for cheap sources of energy was an indirect cause. Though indirect causes and effects can sometimes be important, you need to set limits on how many of them you can deal with, or nearly every cause-and-effect essay will turn into a history of the world.

Distinguish Between Major and Minor Causes and Effects

The Confederacy's firing on Fort Sumter was a direct cause of the Civil War, but not nearly as important as the issues of secession and slavery. Although acknowledging minor causes and effects, a paper should naturally spend most of its time on major ones.

Do Not Omit Links in a Chain of Causes and Effects

As previously noted, you may not always be faced with a set of separate causes for a particular effect or separate effects from a particular cause. One cause leads to another, the second to a third, and so on—and only then is the given effect brought about. Unless you carefully discuss each part of the sequence, your reader may get lost. One effect of television, for example, may be a growing number of discipline problems in elementary and high school classrooms, but before you can persuade your reader of that point, you will have to examine many intermediate effects.

Play Fair

Give some attention, where appropriate, to causes and effects that opponents of your thesis may point to. You may justifiably want to pin the rioting at the rock concert on the police, but your case will be strengthened, not weakened, if you concede that the promoters' selling of more tickets than there were seats and the attempt of a few fans to rush the stage and tear the clothes off the performers' backs also contributed to the disaster. You don't need to make a lavish production of these arguments on the other side; just show that you're aware of them and have given them serious consideration.

WRITING SUGGESTIONS FOR CAUSE-AND-EFFECT PAPERS

All of the listed subjects offer good opportunities for a cause-and-effect, cause-only, or effect-only paper. Explore each cause and effect thoroughly; don't just write a list:

1. A personal, unreasonable fear (your own or someone else's)
2. A personal, unreasonable irritation (your own or someone else's)
3. A personal habit or mannerism (your own or someone else's)
4. Outlawing of prayers in public schools
5. Violence on children's television programs
6. A personal experience with racial or religious discrimination
7. Your first romantic attachment

8. The quality of food at the school cafeteria
9. The popularity or decline in popularity of a hairstyle or clothing style
10. High school graduates who still can't read
11. Your like or dislike of a particular book, writer, movie, painter, musician, television program
12. Children's lack of respect for parents
13. Sexual harassment in high school or college
14. A minor invention (Scotch tape, electric toothbrushes, Post-It notes, parking meters)
15. Your interest or lack of interest in a sport
16. Your passionate like or dislike of a food
17. Your decision to continue your education
18. Being overweight or underweight
19. Swearing
20. Gossip

A FEW SHORT WORDS
Matthew Monroe (student)

Thesis: My height seems to bring out the worst in everyone.

    I. Stupid jokes
       A. When accepting an award
       B. From my girlfriend's dad

   II. Rudeness
       A. When trying to buy a suit
       B. When shopping for cars
       C. From total strangers

  III. Being overlooked
       A. In bars
       B. For sports
       C. By women

Conclusion: Although people assume I don't mind the abuse I take because of my height, it really does make me angry.

I am short. How short? Suffice it to say that for a man of almost twenty-two years of age, I am very short indeed. Now, I am comfortable with my height. I've lived with it for years, and it just doesn't bother me anymore. It is the effect that my height has on other people that I just can't stand. My height seems to bring out the worst in everyone.

People seem to see my height as an excellent excuse to try to be funny. Stupid jokes follow me wherever I go. When I had to accept an award for perfect high-school attendance, some jerk at the back of the room waited until I was about to say a gracious thank you, and then he hollered, "Stand up, pal. We can't see you!" There was, of course, much laughter, just as there was when my girlfriend's dad told her to "Throw the boy back. He's too small to keep!"

The jokes, though, are easier to handle than outright rudeness. There was the time I was trying to buy a suit and was told that not even the "very best" cut could disguise my height. There was the car salesman who refused to show me anything but sub-compacts, insisting that anything else would be far too big for such a little fellow. And then, I cannot forget the random strangers who feel compelled to walk up to me and say "Wow! You're really short." Thanks guys, I hadn't noticed.

The worst part, though, is being overlooked because of my height. I'm the last to get served at any bar, because the bartender can't see me. I'm never chosen for any pick-up sports teams, even though being short doesn't mean I can't run as fast or throw as straight as any other guy. Women look right past me and right into the eyes of the six-foot-tall idiot at the other end of the room. Sometimes they pat me on the head as they pass by.

People assume that my height makes me nothing more than a target for their dumb wisecracks, their insensitive rudenesses, or their complete disregard. They assume that because I can laugh it off, I just don't care. One day I will surprise them by taking a stand, making a statement, walking right up to them, and punching them in the kneecaps.

FALLING INTO PLACE

Jaime O'Neill

Jaime O'Neill is the author of *We're History!: The 20th-Century Survivor's Final Exam* (1998). In this cause-and-effect essay, O'Neill presents a personal history of his spectacular teenage foolishness and reflects on the ongoing foolishness of relationships between men and women.

Words to check:

palmetto (paragraph 1)	smitten (11)	gonadal (18)
mangrove (1)	psyche (11)	plummet (22)
backhoes (3)	feign (15)	imploded (22)
tenacious (3)	superseded (18)	raspily (22)

1 It is 1957 and I am up a tree. Though afraid of heights, I have taken to climbing the trees in the palmetto and mangrove swamp that spreads out from the little clearing where our house sits.

2   I cannot now remember what compelled me to climb trees when I was 13 years old, why I both liked and hated the twinge of fear as I scaled my way higher and higher, or what satisfactions might have settled over me when I found a niche between the branches where I could nest, more secure, and survey the swamp from that height. All that returns to me now is the way the breeze blew up there, stirring the leaves, not at all like the breeze on the ground.

3   The tree I am in towers over a hole, a gash in the sandy Florida soil, six or eight feet deep, packed hard, damp at the bottom. The swamp is slowly being cleared for development; the backhoes and the big Cats have been scraping away the tenacious vegetation, making way for homes. Soon we will have neighbors.

4   I am thinking about girls. If I thought of other things when I was 13, I can no longer imagine what those things might have been. It is, then, no wonder that I notice two girls who pass under my tree on that warm and humid afternoon, two girls from my class taking a shortcut home through the swamp.

5   I hear them before I see them; I see them before I know who they are. They are talking and keeping their eyes tight on the ground for fear of snakes, and they don't notice me. As they draw nearer, I know the pleasure of the spy, the Indian scout, the unseen watcher in hidden places. Perhaps I will overhear them saying wonderful things—"this cute boy in class, he just drives me wild"—and it will turn out to be me they are talking about.

6   No such luck. Still, it is good that they come by. Courage is much better when it has a female audience, and it has taken some courage for me to have climbed so high.

7   Had I been another kind of boy, I might have let them pass, but the "look at me" impulse is insistent, and one of the girls is exquisite, sporting breasts already, like cupcakes under her thin cotton blouse. Perhaps if she sees me up in this tree, a strange and solitary boy, friend of trees, neighbor of sky, mysterious creature of the swamps, she will love me at these heights—love me, and invite me to climb down.

8   "Hi," I call out. The two of them stop in their tracks, uncertain of where the voice is coming from. I like it that they have to search the trees to find me.

9   "What are you," asks the one who is not cute, "some kind of monkey?"

10   "Tarzan, more like," I say, and I stand upright on my branch and beat my chest with one hand while holding tight to a limb with my other.

11   "You're going to fall and hurt yourself," the cute girl says. I am further smitten by her concern for me. Smitten and imperiled. What is it in the male psyche that takes such words as encouragement toward further reckless self-endangerment?

12   "Nah," I say, and I step carelessly to another branch, "there's nothing to this." I release my steadying grip on the limb and stand barehanded. "See."

13   What I hope they can't see is that my knees are going a little wobbly with fear.

14   The not-cute girl shades her eyes, peering up at me. "Well," she says, "why don't you jump if you're so brave?"

15   I feign interest in her suggestion, survey the depression in the earth below, gauge the distance.

16   "You think I'm crazy," I say. "It's probably 100 feet down from here." Though this is surely a gross exaggeration, the actual distance is very great.

17   "Well, what are you, anyway," the girl said back to me, "some kind of chicken?"

18   Today, some 35 years later, I am an English teacher, one who routinely tries to convince students of the power of words. There are few words more powerful to an adolescent boy than the word "chicken." For all practical purposes, brain function ceases, superseded by gonadal override.

19   Still, the chicken side of me, the side I wanted to keep secret, might have protected me from harm if the word had come from the not-cute girl alone. If she wanted to think me chicken, I could live with that.

20   What I could not live with was when the cute girl echoed the challenge.

21   "Yeah," she says, "what are you, chicken?"

22   And so I jump. I cover my eyes with one hand, step purposefully off the branch and plummet like a spear to the hard-packed sand and dirt at the bottom of the Catscratched hole. I strike on my heels, fold up like an imploded building. It is as though every molecule of oxygen has been driven out my ears, out my nose, out the very pores of my scalp. In the pit, I cannot move. I gasp raspily, like an old man. The sound scares me; I have never made such a noise before.

23   Do the girls rush down into the pit, tend to me, beg me to forgive them for their thoughtless challenge? In your dreams, they do. Mine, too.

24   What they do is laugh and leave. A life lesson.

25   I will live to know this experience again—the laughing and the leaving—because I am not, as I first suspect, killed.

26   What I am is unable to move. Faintly, from our house, I can hear the radio playing. I try to call out, but the sound that escapes me is unintelligible and weak, no match for the radio.

27   Around dusk, I hear my Mom calling me for supper. Then, a while later, I hear movement in the brush and my brother's voice. I groan. He finds me, helps me up.

28   We hide it all from Mom, of course. My heels are bruised, and for a few days it hurts to stand straight.

29   Did I learn the life lesson, a lesson gained in pain and humiliation?

30   Hardly.
31   What man ever really does?

WHAT DID THE WRITER SAY AND WHAT DID YOU THINK?

1. What caused the author to climb the tree?
2. What caused the author to jump from the tree? Was it merely being called "some kind of chicken?"
3. What were the short-term effects of the jump? Long-term effects?
4. What is the "life lesson" the author still has not learned?
5. What do you think caused the girls to urge the author to jump? To laugh and walk away after the jump?

HOW DID THE WRITER SAY IT?

1. Why does the author describe events of thirty-five years ago almost entirely in the present tense?
2. One girl is described as "exquisite," one as "not cute." Are they individualized in any other way? If not, why not?
3. Where does the author come closest to stating the thesis directly?

WHAT ABOUT YOUR WRITING?

The title "Falling into Place" is a pun or play on words. Jaime O'Neill takes a standard expression for "making sense" or "coming together in an orderly way" and gives it a new twist by calling attention to the rarely used literal meaning—the actual physical act of falling, in this case from a tree. An everyday phrase has been reworked to make a special point, to fit in with a particular purpose, to acquire extra density. Opinions may differ, of course, on how successful this device is. Some people, too, probably still accept un-thinkingly the tired old cliché that puns and word plays are the lowest form of literature. In fact, however, writers as diverse as Shakespeare and Thoreau have been entranced by the exciting stylistic possibilities of word plays.

E.E. Cummings, the American poet, once wrote that poetry should do to you what the old burlesque gag does:

Question: Would you hit a woman with a baby?

Answer: No, I'd hit her with a brick.

Cummings' view is that poetry should fool around with words, should try to astonish and delight the reader by revealing previously unnoticed possibilities of language. Although prose is ordinarily more sedate than poetry, it too can profit from the touch of originality, the fresh slant, the new twist that fooling around with words can sometimes contribute.

Most frequently, word plays provide a welcome note of humor. "The orchestra played Beethoven last night. Beethoven lost." A *Time* magazine movie review once described a wagon train surrounded by Indians as being "in the Siouxp."

Word plays lend themselves to satire, too. In Shakespeare's *Henry IV, Part I*, Glendower, a braggart with mystical inclinations, is talking to Hotspur, an honest, downright soldier:

Glendower: I can call spirits from the vasty deep.

Hotspur: Why, so can I . . . But will they come when you do call for them?

Other word plays can be entirely serious. In *Walden*, Thoreau simply treats a common figurative expression with unexpected literalness:

If you have built castles in the air, your work need not be lost; that is where they should be. Now put the foundations under them.

There's no compulsion to experiment with word plays. They're risky. Unsuccessful word plays are always damaging because they call attention to themselves. They should generally be used in moderation; the writer wants to give an impression of being clever, but not of being a show-off. If you have neither the temperament nor the knack for word plays, you should avoid them completely. With all these cautions, however, a distinctive style helps capture your reader's attention, and skillful fooling around with words can help create a distinctive style.

WHY WE CRAVE HORROR MOVIES
Stephen King

It's a reasonable guess that if asked to "name a writer" most average citizens would name Stephen King. In 1996, King achieved the unprecedented feat of having five books on the best seller list at the same time. With total sales comfortably above 20 million, King's horror tales seem to have achieved a popularity unrestricted by education or social class. Among his books are *Carrie* (1974), *Salem's Lot* (1975), *The Shining* (1977), *The Dead Zone* (1979),

Firestarter (1980), *Christine* (1983), *Pet Semetary* (1983), *The Tommyknockers* (1988), *The Girl Who Loved Tom Gordon* (1999), and *Hearts in Atlantis* (1999). Many of these titles, as well as others, have been made into films, and King can write with considerable authority on the subject of horror movies.

Words to check:

grimaces (paragraph 1)	voyeur (6)	sanctions (10)
depleted (3)	penchant (7)	remonstrance (10)
innately (4)	status quo (9)	anarchistic (11)

1   I think that we're all mentally ill; those of us outside the asylums only hide it a little better—and maybe not all that much better, after all. We've all known people who talk to themselves, people who sometimes squinch their faces into horrible grimaces when they believe no one is watching, people who have some hysterical fear—of snakes, the dark, the tight place, the long drop . . . and, of course, those final worms and grubs that are waiting so patiently underground.

2   When we pay our four or five bucks and seat ourselves at tenth-row center in a theater showing a horror movie, we are daring the nightmare.

3   Why? Some of the reasons are simple and obvious. To show that we can, that we are not afraid, that we can ride this roller coaster. Which is not to say that a really good horror movie may not surprise a scream out of us at some point, the way we may scream when the roller coaster twists through a complete 360 or plows through a lake at the bottom of the drop. And horror movies, like roller coasters, have always been the special province of the young; by the time one turns 40 or 50, one's appetite for double twists or 360-degree loops may be considerably depleted.

4   We also go to re-establish our feelings of essential normality; the horror movie is innately conservative, even reactionary. Freda Jackson as the horrible melting woman in *Die, Monster, Die!* confirms for us that no matter how far we may be removed from the beauty of a Robert Redford or a Diana Ross, we are still light-years from true ugliness.

5   And we go to have fun.

6   Ah, but this is where the ground starts to slope away, isn't it? Because this is a very peculiar sort of fun, indeed. The fun comes from seeing others menaced—sometimes killed. One critic has suggested that if pro football has become the voyeur's version of combat, then the horror film has become the modern version of the public lynching.

7   It is true that the mythic, "fairy-tale" horror film intends to take away the shades of gray. . . . It urges us to put away our more civilized and adult penchant for analysis and to become children again, seeing things in pure blacks

and whites. It may be that horror movies provide psychic relief on this level because this invitation to lapse into simplicity, irrationality and even outright madness is extended so rarely. We are told we may allow our emotions a free rein . . . or no rein at all.

8   If we are all insane, then sanity becomes a matter of degree. If your insanity leads you to carve up women like Jack the Ripper or the Cleveland Torso Murderer, we clap you away in the funny farm (but neither of those two amateur-night surgeons was ever caught, heh-heh-heh); if, on the other hand, your insanity leads you only to talk to yourself when you're under stress or to pick your nose on your morning bus, then you are left alone to go about your business . . . though it is doubtful that you will ever be invited to the best parties.

9   The potential lyncher is in almost all of us (excluding saints, past and present; but then, most saints have been crazy in their own ways), and every now and then, he has to be let loose to scream and roll around in the grass. Our emotions and our fears form their own body, and we recognize that it demands its own exercise to maintain proper muscle tone. Certain of these emotional muscles are accepted—even exalted—in civilized society; they are, of course, the emotions that tend to maintain the status quo of civilization itself. Love, friendship, loyalty, kindness—these are all the emotions that we applaud, emotions that have been immortalized in the couplets of Hallmark cards and in the verses (I don't dare call it poetry) of Leonard Nimoy.

10   When we exhibit these emotions, society showers us with positive reinforcement; we learn this even before we get out of diapers. When, as children, we hug our rotten little puke of a sister and give her a kiss, all the aunts and uncles smile and twit and cry, "Isn't he the sweetest little thing?" Such coveted treats as chocolate-covered graham crackers often follow. But if we deliberately slam the rotten little puke of a sister's fingers in the door, sanctions follow—angry remonstrance from parents, aunts and uncles; instead of a chocolate-covered graham cracker, a spanking.

11   But anticivilization emotions don't go away, and they demand periodic exercise. We have such "sick" jokes as, "What's the difference between a truckload of bowling balls and a truckload of dead babies?" (You can't unload a truckload of bowling balls with a pitchfork . . . a joke, by the way, that I heard originally from a ten-year-old). Such a joke may surprise a laugh or a grin out of us even as we recoil, a possibility that confirms the thesis: If we share a brotherhood of man, then we also share an insanity of man. None of which is intended as a defense of either the sick joke or insanity but merely as an explanation of why the best horror films, like the best fairy tales, manage to be reactionary, anarchistic, and revolutionary all at the same time.

12   The mythic horror movie, like the sick joke, has a dirty job to do. It deliberately appeals to all that is worst in us. It is morbidity unchained, our most base instincts let free, our nastiest fantasies realized . . . and it all happens, fittingly enough, in the dark. For those reasons, good liberals often shy away from horror films. For myself, I like to see the most aggressive of them— *Dawn of the Dead*, for instance—as lifting a trap door in the civilized forebrain and throwing a basket of raw meat to the hungry alligators swimming around in that subterranean river beneath.

13   Why bother? Because it keeps them from getting out, man. It keeps them down there and me up here. It was Lennon and McCartney who said that all you need is love, and I would agree with that.

14   As long as you keep the gators fed.

WHAT DID THE WRITER SAY AND WHAT DID YOU THINK?

1. What is the thesis?
2. What are the main reasons why people like horror movies?
3. In what ways other than horror movies do we exercise our "anti-civilization emotions"?
4. What is the purpose of mentioning the "sick joke" in paragraph 11?
5. Explain the last sentence.

HOW DID THE WRITER SAY IT?

1. In paragraph 1, why is "I think we're all mentally ill" better than "I think people are all mentally ill?"
2. In paragraph 10, why is "rotten little puke of a sister" better than "irritating little sister?"
3. The author claims that horror movies urge us to "become children again." Where does the writing make use of some of the language of childhood?
4. Explain the meaning of "heh-heh-heh" in paragraph 8.

WHAT ABOUT <u>YOUR</u> WRITING?

In paragraph 9, Stephen King writes, "The potential lyncher is in almost all of us . . . and every now and then, he has to be let loose to scream and roll around in the grass." Most American publishers would strongly urge the author to rewrite this sentence—and some publishers would insist. The "potential lyncher" could just as easily be a woman as a man, after all. In fact, the sex of the person is totally irrelevant to the meaning of the sentence.

Isn't the use of *he* both illogical and unfair (even though few people actually want to be a lyncher)? In a technical sense, the wording in King's sentence is grammatical, but isn't there a way of being correct without the risk of offending some readers?

Many feminists have charged that our language echoes the sexual discrimination of society as a whole. The ease with which jokes, sometimes good ones, can be manufactured at the expense of the feminist movement probably tends to make it too easy for some to shrug off legitimate complaints. One may feel entitled to laugh at the insanely enlightened captain of a sinking ship who yells "Person the lifeboats" instead of "Man the lifeboats." One should be more hesitant, however, about laughing at the female employee of the post office who has spent an exhausting day trudging through the snow and who resents being known as a "mailman" instead of a "mail carrier." In any event, feminists have singled out for special attack the use of *he, his, him,* and *himself* when sex is unknown, mixed, or immaterial.

Whatever your personal preferences may be, publishers of books, magazines, and newspapers have responded positively to the complaints. The *he, his, him, himself* usage has all but disappeared from print. A sentence like *A driver needs to know how his car works* is already beginning to sound as outdated as words like *icebox* and *Victrola*.

The best and easiest way to solve the *he* problem without damaging your style is to rephrase into plural forms whenever possible:

Original	Rephrased
A good student turns in his assignments on time.	Good students turn in their assignments on time.
Nobody wants his friends to take him for granted.	People do not want their friends to take them for granted.
Everyone at the banquet rose from his seat to give the senator an ovation.	All the guests at the banquet rose from their seats to give the senator an ovation.

(*Note: Nobody* and *everyone*, in the original sentences, always take a singular verb and pronoun in standard written English. Use of *they, them, their* in those sentences would be incorrect.)

The word *one* can also be helpful at times, though it often creates an excessively formal tone. The plural approach is generally more satisfactory:

Original	Rephrased
A person must concentrate on his own happiness first.	One must concentrate on one's own happiness first.
Anybody can break his bad habits if he only tries.	One can break one's bad habits if one only tries.

If you find yourself, for some reason, locked into a singular form, repetition or substantial revisions may be necessary. In King's complete sentence, for example, he mentions *saints* as well as the *lyncher.* Changing *lyncher* to *lynchers* would create confusion because the nonsexist *they* could then refer to two different groups of people. When the plural form won't work, look for other possibilities:

Original	Rephrased
The potential lyncher is in all of us (excluding saints, past and present; but then, most saints have been crazy in their own ways), and every now and then, he has to be let loose to scream and roll around in the grass.	The potential lyncher is in all of us (excluding saints, past and present; but then, most saints have been crazy in their own ways), and every now and then, the lyncher has to be let loose to scream and roll around in the grass.
The reader will need to use all his attention to understand the plot.	The reader will need to be extremely attentive to understand the plot.
The best policy for someone who has been arrested is to keep his mouth shut.	The best policy for someone who has been arrested is to say as little as possible.

Now for two warnings. First, do what you can to avoid habitual reliance on the phrases *he or she, his or hers, him or her, himself or herself.* These expressions belong more to legal contracts than to ordinary writing, and when they are used repeatedly, the result is often absurd:

Poor	Better
A writer always should remember that he or she is writing for his or her audience, not just for himself or herself.	Writers always should remember that they are writing for their audience, not just for themselves.

Second, avoid artificial constructions like *s/he* or *he/she*. Many readers, and most English teachers, will view them as strained efforts to show off the writer's devotion to equal rights. The devotion may deserve praise, but straining and showing off have almost never resulted in good writing.

THE BEST YEARS OF MY LIFE
Betty Rollin

Betty Rollin has been editor for *Vogue* and *Look* magazines and a news correspondent for NBC and ABC. Her best-selling book *First, You Cry* (1976) describes her operation for breast cancer. Among her other books are *Am I Getting Paid for This?* (1982), and *Last Wish* (1985). "The Best Years of My Life" analyzes the effects of her operation—and survival.

Words to check:

intrinsically (paragraph 1)	hypochondriac (7)	hedonism (10)
chemotherapy (2)	gynecologist (8)	masochism (11)
harrowing (2)	orthopedist (8)	voracious (11)
	parsimonious (9)	

1   I am about to celebrate an anniversary. Not that there will be a party with funny hats. Nor do I expect any greetings in the mail. Hallmark, with its infinite variety of occasions about which to fashion a 50-cent card, has skipped this one. This, you see, is my cancer anniversary. Five years ago tomorrow, at Beth Israel Hospital in New York City, a malignant tumor was removed from my left breast and, along with the tumor, my left breast. To be alive five years later means something in cancer circles. There is nothing intrinsically magical about the figure five, but the numbers show that if you have survived that many years after cancer has been diagnosed, you have an 80 percent shot at living out a normal life span.

2   Still, you probably think Hallmark is right not to sell a card, and that it's weird to "celebrate" such a terrible thing as cancer. It's even weirder than you imagine. Because not only do I feel good about (probably) having escaped a recurrence of cancer, I also feel good about having gotten cancer in the first place. Here is the paradox: Although cancer was the worst thing that ever happened to me, it was also the best. Cancer (the kind I had, with no spread and no need of chemotherapy, with its often harrowing side effects) enriched my life, made me wiser, made me happier. Another paradox: although I would do everything possible to avoid getting cancer again, I am glad I had it.

3   There is a theory about people who have had a life-and-death scare that goes something like this: for about six months after surviving the scare, you feel shaken and grateful. Armed with a keen sense of what was almost The End, you begin to live your life differently. You pause during the race to notice the foliage, you pay more attention to the people you love—maybe you even move to Vermont. You have gained, as they say, a "new perspective." But then, according to this theory, when the six months are over, the "new perspective" fades, you sell the house in Vermont and go back to the same craziness that was your life before the car crash or whatever it was. What has happened is that you've stopped feeling afraid. The crash is in the past. The it-can't-happen-to-me feelings that were dashed by the accident re-emerge, after six months, as it-can't-happen-to-me-*again*.

4   It's different for people whose crash is cancer. You can stay off the freeways, but you can't do much about preventing whatever went wrong in your own body from going wrong again. Unless your head is buried deep in the sand, you know damn well it *can* happen again. Even though, in my case, the doctors say it isn't likely, the possibility of recurrence is very real to me. Passing the five-year mark is reassuring, but I know I will be a little bit afraid for the rest of my life. But—ready for another paradox?—certain poisons are medicinal in small doses. To be a little bit afraid of dying can do wonders for your life. It has done wonders for mine. That's because, unlike the way most people feel, my sense of death is not an intellectual concept. It's a lively presence in my gut. It affects me daily—for the better.

5   First, when you're even slightly afraid of death, you're less afraid of other things—e.g., bosses, spouses, plumbers, rape, bankruptcy, failure, not being liked, the flu, aging. Next to the Grim Reaper, how ferocious can even the most ferocious boss be? How dire the direst household calamity? In my own professional life, I have lost not only some big fears, but most of the small ones. I used to be nervous in front of television cameras. That kind of nervousness was a fear of not being thought attractive, smart and winning. It still pleases me greatly if someone besides my husband and mother thinks I'm attractive, smart and winning; but I am no longer afraid that someone won't. Cancer made me less worried about what people think of me, both professionally and socially. I am less concerned about where my career is going. I don't know where it's going. I don't think about that. I think about where I am and what I'm doing and whether I like it. The result is that these days I continually seem to be doing what I like. And probably I'm more successful than when I aimed to please.

6   My book *First, You Cry*, which has given me more pleasure than anything else in my professional life, is a good example of this. As a career move, leaving television for six months to write a book about a cancer operation seemed

less than sensible. But as soon as I got cancer, I stopped being "sensible." I wanted to write the book. And, just in case I croaked, I wanted to write it the way that was right for me, not necessarily for the market. So I turned down the publisher who wanted it to be a "how-to" book. I like to think I would have done that, cancer or not, but had it not been for cancer, I probably wouldn't have written a book at all, because I would have been too afraid to drop out of television even for six months. And if I had written a book, I doubt that I would have been so open about my life and honest about my less-than-heroic feelings. But, as I wrote, I remember thinking, "I might die, so what does it matter what anyone thinks of me?" A lot of people write honestly and openly without having had a disease, but I don't think I would have. I hadn't done it before.

7   A touch of cancer turns you into a hypochondriac. You get a sore throat and you think you've got cancer of the throat; you get a corn from a pair of shoes that are too tight and you're sure it's a malignant tumor. But—here's the bright side—cancer hypochondria is so compelling it never occurs to you that you could get anything *else*. And, when you do, you're so glad it's not cancer that you feel like celebrating. "Goody, it's the flu!" I heard myself say to myself a couple of weeks ago.

8   Some physicians are more sensitive than others to cancer anxiety. My gynecologist prattled on once about some menstrual irregularity without noticing that, as he spoke, I had turned to stone. "Is it cancer?" I finally whispered. He looked dumbfounded and said, "Of course not!" As if to say, "How could you think such a thing?" But an orthopedist I saw about a knee problem took an X-ray and, before saying a word about what it was (a torn cartilage), told me what it wasn't. I limped home joyously.

9   I never went to Vermont because I can't stand that much fresh air; but in my own fashion, I sop up pleasure where and when I can, sometimes at the risk of professional advancement and sometimes at the risk of bankruptcy. An exaggeration, perhaps, but there's no question about it: Since cancer, I spend more money than I used to. (True, I have more to spend, but that's mostly because of the book, which is also thanks to cancer.) I had always been parsimonious—some would say cheap—and I'm not anymore. The thinking is, "Just in case I do get a recurrence, won't I feel like a fool for having flown coach to Seattle?" (I like to think I'm more generous with others as well. It seems to me that, since having cancer, I give better presents.)

10   Cancer kills guilt. You not only take a vacation now because next year you might be dead, but you take a *better* vacation because, even if you don't die soon, after what you've been through, you feel you deserve it. In my own case, I wouldn't have expected that feeling to survive six months because,

once those months passed, I realized that, compared to some people, I had not been through much at all. But my hedonism continues to flourish. Maybe it was just a question of changing a habit.

11   My girlish masochism didn't resurface, either. Most women I know go through at least a phase of needing punishment from men. Not physical punishment, just all the rest: indifference, harshness, coldness, rudeness or some neat combination. In the past, my own appetite for this sort of treatment was voracious. Conversely, if I happened to connect with a man who was nice to me, I felt like that song: "This can't be love because I feel so well." The difference was that, in the song, it really *was* love, and with me, it really *wasn't*. Only when I was miserable did I know I really cared.

12   The minute I got cancer, my taste in men improved. It's not that my first husband was a beast. I'm fond of him, but even he would admit he was very hard on me. Maybe I asked for it. Well, once you've been deftly kicked in the pants by God (or whoever distributes cancer), you stop wanting kicks from mortals. Everyone who knows the man I married a year ago thinks I'm lucky—even my mother!—and I do, too. But I know it wasn't only luck. It was that cancer made me want someone wonderful. I wasn't ready for him before. I was so struck by this apparent change in me that I checked it out with a psychoanalyst, who assured me that I was not imagining things—that the damage to my body had, indeed, done wonders for my head.

13   Happiness is probably something that shouldn't be talked about too much, but I can't help it. Anyway, I find the more I carry on about it, the better it gets. A big part of happiness is noticing it. It's trite to say, but if you've never been ill, you don't notice—or enjoy—not being ill. I even notice my husband's good health. (He doesn't, but how could he?)

14   I haven't mentioned losing that breast, have I? That's because, in spite of the fuss I made about it five years ago, that loss now seems almost not worth mentioning. Five years ago, I felt sorry for myself that I could no longer keep a strapless dress up. Today I feel that losing a breast saved my life, and wasn't I lucky. And when I think of all the other good things that have come from that loss, I just look at that flat place on my body and think: small price.

15   Most of my friends who are past 40 shudder on their birthdays. Not me. They feel a year closer to death, I suppose. I feel a year further from it.

16   O.K., what if I get a recurrence? I'm not so jolly all the time that I haven't given this some serious thought. If it happens, I'm sure I won't be a good sport about it—especially if my life is cut short. But even if it is, I will look back at the years since the surgery and know I got the best from them. And I will be forced to admit that the disease that is ending my life is the very thing that made it so good.

WHAT DID THE WRITER SAY AND WHAT DID YOU THINK?

1. What is Rollin's thesis?
2. Does the essay strike you as convincing and realistic or as too overwhelmingly cheerful?
3. Does the author deal with any unpleasant effects? What are they?
4. Do you think the author wants the essay to come through as purely personal comments or as a piece with a message that people in general can apply to their own lives?
5. Explain in your own words the change in Rollin's "taste in men."
6. How much attention does Rollin pay to the often traumatic physical and emotional effects of losing a breast (rather than surviving an operation for cancer)? What is her current attitude toward the loss?
7. Explain these lines: "Most of my friends who are past 40 shudder on their birthdays. Not me. They feel a year closer to death, I suppose. I feel a year further from it."

HOW DID THE WRITER SAY IT?

1. Point out some instances of the author's use of humor. Is the humor appropriate for the subject?
2. The writing is frequently informal, even slangy—"you know damn well," "just in case I croaked," and so on. Is this tone appropriate for the subject?
3. In paragraph 2, the author mentions the "paradox" that cancer was the worst and best thing that ever happened to her. Are there other paradoxes in the reading selection, either direct or implied?

WHAT ABOUT <u>YOUR</u> WRITING?

In paragraph 3, the author writes, "You pause during the race to notice the foliage, you pay more attention to the people you love. . . ." Two sentences later, she writes, ". . . the 'new perspective' fades, you sell the house in Vermont . . ."

Betty Rollin is an experienced, professional writer who has written a moving and inspirational essay, but the chances are at least fair that your instructor would have used some red ink on those sentences. (The chances are even better that your instructor would have complained about the many sentence fragments, such as the second sentence in paragraph 1, but that's another matter. See p. 233.) The red ink would have underlined or circled the commas in both sentences, and then above those commas or out in the margin would be the letters CS, meaning *comma splice.*

The comma splice is one of the most frequent errors in punctuation. From the point of view of many instructors, it's also more serious than most punctuation errors because it suggests that the writer not only doesn't know about commas but also doesn't know what a sentence is. In your own writing, you need to avoid comma splices and know how to get rid of them if they do pop up. You need to know, too, about those special occasions when, like Betty Rollin, you may be able to use a comma splice deliberately—and get away with it.

A comma splice results when the writer forgets this simple rule: *a comma all by itself cannot join independent clauses.* (An independent clause is a group of words with a subject and verb that can stand alone as a separate sentence.)

Let's look first at an old-fashioned *fused-sentence,* sometimes called a run-on sentence:

I took an aspirin and went straight to bed I had a headache.

Few writers are likely to make this gross an error. The sentence contains two independent clauses—*I took an aspirin and went straight to bed* and *I had a headache*—with no punctuation of any kind between them.

The comma splice occurs when the writer sees that something is wrong with the fused sentence, knows precisely where it's wrong, and tries to fix the sentence like this:

I took an aspirin and went straight to bed, I had a headache.

Remember the rule: *A comma all by itself cannot join independent clauses.* The writer has created a comma splice, a kind of sophisticated fused sentence. It's a slight improvement, probably, but it's still wrong.

A comma splice can be eliminated in a variety of ways:

1. Replace the comma with a period.

   I took an aspirin and went straight to bed. I had a headache.

2. Replace the comma with a semicolon.

   I took an aspirin and went straight to bed; I had a headache.

3. Add one of the following coordinating conjunctions *after* the comma: *and, but, or, nor, for, yet, so.* Which word you choose will depend on the logical relationship between clauses:

   I took an aspirin and went straight to bed, for I had a headache.

4. Change one of the independent clauses to a dependent clause:

Because I had a headache, I took an aspirin and went straight to bed.

I took an aspirin and went straight to bed because I had a headache.

All four of these techniques result in correctly punctuated sentences. Which one you choose often depends on subtle issues of style, and sometimes any of the four can work well. Nevertheless, it's not always a pure matter of taste. If you've just written a string of short sentences, for example, you'd want to break the monotony with a longer sentence—and thus avoid replacing the comma with a period. Conversely, with a string of long sentences, the period would probably be your first choice.

Now what about those sentences by Betty Rollin? Why was an experienced writer guilty of comma splices? Why did this discussion begin by saying that the chances of your instructor's objecting to the comma splices were only "fair"? The answer is that rules almost always have exceptions. When the clauses are short and express activities going on at the same time or an unbroken sequence of activities, comma splices can sometimes be acceptable:

I came, I saw, I conquered.

Add the eggs, beat the mixture, pour it in the pan.

The wedding was an emotional explosion. We laughed, we cried, we danced, we hugged, we kissed.

. . . the "new perspective" fades, you sell the house in Vermont . . .

If you're tempted to use a comma splice deliberately, make certain that the writing assignment does not call for a highly formal tone, as in a scholarly research paper. If in doubt, check with your instructor.

ONLY DAUGHTER

Sandra Cisneros

Sandra Cisneros is the author of *The House on Mango Street* (1983), *My Wicked Wicked Ways* (1987), *Woman Hollering Creek* (1992), and *Loose Woman* (1994). In "Only Daughter," Cisneros explores the reasons she feels she became a successful writer.

Words to check:

philandering (paragraph 7)   mortar (7)   woo (8)

1 Once, several years ago, when I was just starting out my writing career, I was asked to write my own contributor's note for an anthology I was part of. I wrote: "I am the only daughter of a family of six sons. *That* explains everything."

2 Well, I've thought about that ever since, and yes, it explains a lot to me, but for the reader's sake I should have written: "I am the only daughter in a *Mexican* family of six sons." Or even: "I am the only daughter of a Mexican father and a Mexican-American mother." Or: "I am the only daughter of a working-class family of nine." All of these had everything to do with who I am today.

3 I was/am the only daughter and *only* a daughter. Being an only daughter in a family of six sons forced me by circumstance to spend a lot of time by myself because my brothers felt it beneath them to play with a *girl* in public. But that aloneness, that loneliness, was good for a would-be writer—it allowed me time to think and think, to imagine, to read and prepare myself.

4 Being only a daughter for my father meant my destiny would lead me to become someone's wife. That's what he believed. But when I was in the fifth grade and shared my plans for college with him, I was sure he understood. I remember my father saying, *"Qué bueno, mi'ja,* that's good." That meant a lot to me, especially since my brothers thought the idea hilarious. What I didn't realize was that my father thought college was good for girls—good for finding a husband. After four years in college and two more in graduate school, and still no husband, my father shakes his head even now and says I wasted all that education.

5 In retrospect, I'm lucky my father believed daughters were meant for husbands. It meant it didn't matter if I majored in something silly like English. After all, I'd find a nice professional eventually, right? This allowed me the liberty to putter about embroidering my little poems and stories without my father interrupting with so much as a "What's that you're writing?"

6 But the truth is, I wanted him to interrupt. I wanted my father to understand what it was I was scribbling, to introduce me as "My only daughter, the writer." Not as "This is only my daughter. She teaches." *Es maestra*—teacher. Not even *profesora.*

7 In a sense, everything I have ever written has been for him, to win his approval even though I know my father can't read English words, even though my father's only reading includes the brown-ink *Esto* sports magazines from Mexico City and the bloody *¡Alarma!* magazines that feature yet another sighting of *La Virgen de Guadalupe* on a tortilla or a wife's revenge on her philandering husband by bashing his skull in with a *molcajete* (a kitchen mortar made of volcanic rock). Or the *fotonovelas*, the little picture paperbacks with tragedy and trauma erupting from the characters' mouths in bubbles.

8   My father represents, then, the public majority. A public who is uninterested in reading, and yet one whom I am writing about and for, and privately trying to woo.

9   When we were growing up in Chicago, we moved a lot because of my father. He suffered bouts of nostalgia. Then we'd have to let go our flat, store the furniture with mother's relatives, load the station wagon with baggage and bologna sandwiches and head south. To Mexico City.

10   We came back, of course. To yet another Chicago flat, another Chicago neighborhood, another Catholic school. Each time, my father would seek out the parish priest in order to get a tuition break, and complain or boast: "I have seven sons."

11   He meant *siete hijos*, seven children, but he translated it as "sons." "I have seven sons." To anyone who would listen. The Sears Roebuck employee who sold us the washing machine. The short-order cook where my father ate his ham-and-eggs breakfasts. "I have seven sons." As if he deserved a medal from the state.

12   My papa. He didn't mean anything by that mistranslation, I'm sure. But somehow I could feel myself being erased. I'd tug my father's sleeve and whisper: "Not seven sons. Six! and *one daughter.*"

13   When my oldest brother graduated from medical school, he fulfilled my father's dream that we study hard and use this—our heads, instead of this—our hands. Even now my father's hands are thick and yellow, stubbed by a history of hammer and nails and twine and coils and springs. "Use this," my father said, tapping his head, "and not this," showing us those hands. He always looked tired when he said it.

14   Wasn't college an investment? And hadn't I spent all those years in college? And if I didn't marry, what was it all for? Why would anyone go to college and then choose to be poor? Especially someone who had always been poor.

15   Last year, after ten years of writing professionally, the financial rewards started to trickle in. My second National Endowment for the Arts Fellowship. A guest professorship at the University of California, Berkeley. My book, which sold to a major New York publishing house.

16   At Christmas, I flew home to Chicago. The house was throbbing, same as always; hot *tamales* and sweet *tamales* hissing in my mother's pressure cooker, and everybody—my mother, six brothers, wives, babies, aunts, cousins—talking too loud and at the same time, like in a Fellini film, because that's just how we are.

17   I went upstairs to my father's room. One of my stories had just been translated into Spanish and published in an anthology of Chicano writing,

and I wanted to show it to him. Ever since he recovered from a stroke two years ago, my father likes to spend his leisure hours horizontally. And that's how I found him, watching a Pedro Infante movie on Galavisión and eating rice pudding.

18   There was a glass filmed with milk on the bedside table. There were several vials of pills and balled Kleenex. And on the floor, one black sock and a plastic urinal that I didn't want to look at but looked at anyway. Pedro Infante was about to burst into song, and my father was laughing.

19   I'm not sure if it was because my story was translated into Spanish, or because it was published in Mexico, or perhaps because the story dealt with Tepeyac, the *colonia* my father was raised in and the house he grew up in, but at any rate, my father punched the mute button on his remote control and read my story.

20   I sat on the bed next to my father and waited. He read it very slowly. As if he were reading each line over and over. He laughed at all the right places and read lines he liked out loud. He pointed and asked questions: "Is this So-and-so?" "Yes," I said. He kept reading.

21   When he was finally finished, after what seemed like hours, my father looked up and asked: "Where can we get more copies of this for the relatives?"

22   Of all the wonderful things that happened to me last year, that was the most wonderful.

WHAT DID THE WRITER SAY AND WHAT DID YOU THINK?

1. What is the difference in meaning between being the "only daughter" and "only a daughter?"
2. In paragraph 2, Cisneros states that all three versions of a sentence about her upbringing "had everything to do with who I am today." Which one of the three do you think most accurately anticipates the rest of the essay? Is the thesis expressed in this paragraph?
3. What caused Cisneros to spend so much time alone as a child? How did this loneliness benefit her?
4. What caused Cisneros' father to encourage her to go to college?
5. What caused Cisneros' father to allow her to major in presumably impractical subjects?
6. Explain Cisneros' observation of her father that "everything I have written has been for him, to win his approval."
7. The father could have complimented his daughter by saying, "I enjoyed reading your story. It was very good." Why are his actual words in paragraph 21 a more meaningful comment?

HOW DID THE WRITER SAY IT?

1. In paragraph 15, does the list of the author's accomplishments serve any important purpose, or is it mostly a form of bragging?
2. Why does Cisneros devote special attention to the state of her father's health?
3. Are all Spanish words and titles adequately translated for the reader unfamiliar with the language?

WHAT ABOUT <u>YOUR</u> WRITING?

Sandra Cisneros draws all of the material in "Only Daughter" from her own life, particularly her family life. Tolstoy began his great novel *Anna Karenina* with the comment that "All happy families resemble one another, but each unhappy family is unhappy in its own way." Both Cisneros and Tolstoy know that writers can get unbeatable material for a one-page essay or a one thousand page novel without ever going farther than their own homes.

When you use your own family as the subject of an essay, you start with several advantages. You are already an expert on the subject. You know these people and their good and bad sides better than anyone else. You know how your parents look at one another when they talk about their first date. You know the nicest things your brothers and sisters have ever done for you. You've suffered through your mother's overcooked pot roasts, your father's embarrassingly bad jokes, your sister's operatic temper tantrums, your brother's patented torture techniques, and your Aunt Tilda's ghastly birthday presents. You know your material, and that can make essay writing far easier. Single-parent families or so-called broken homes need not disqualify you from writing, either—they just make you an expert on additional subject matter.

You also care about your material. Family is family, after all. Though they may drive you mad sometimes, you love them anyway. Expressing that frustration and love, as Cisneros does, can capture a reader and make your essay far more effective. If right now you happen to be closer to hating your family than to loving them, that's no problem. From a writer's point of view, hate is at least as strong and usable an emotion as love.

Last, your audience will have related experiences. You aren't trying to describe an ocean to people who have never seen a rain puddle. Maybe your reader never tasted your mother's pot roast, but her uncle always bought the cheapest charcoal for the grill and could never keep the fire lit. Maybe your reader's father didn't tell embarrassing jokes, but he scratched himself in funny places. Your readers will, from their own experiences, be able to understand and sympathize with yours.

You get the idea. Everyone's family is wonderful, irritating, funny, and sad. Everyone's family is good material for writing.

———

THINKING LIKE A MOUNTAIN
Aldo Leopold

Best known for his book *A Sand County Almanac* (1949), Aldo Leopold (1886–1948) wrote extensively on nature and the environment. He is often credited with being among the first to apply scientific knowledge rather than emotional rhetoric to conservation and ecology.

Words to check:

rimrock (paragraph 1)	tyro (3)	anaemic (7)
gleanings (2)	fording (4)	desuetude (7)
decipher (3)	melee (4)	defoliated (7)
implicit (3)	extirpate (7)	dictum (10)

1 A deep chesty bawl echoes from rimrock to rimrock, rolls down the mountain, and fades into the far blackness of the night. It is an outburst of wild defiant sorrow, and of contempt for all the adversities of the world.

2   Every living thing (and perhaps many a dead one as well) pays heed to that call. To the deer it is a reminder of the way of all flesh, to the pine a forecast of midnight scuffles and of blood upon the snow, to the coyote a promise of gleanings to come, to the cowman a threat of red ink at the bank, to the hunter a challenge of fang against bullet. Yet behind these obvious and immediate hopes and fears there lies a deeper meaning, known only to the mountain itself. Only the mountain has lived long enough to listen objectively to the howl of a wolf.

3   Those unable to decipher the hidden meaning know nevertheless that it is there, for it is felt in all wolf country, and distinguishes that country from all other land. It tingles in the spine of all who hear wolves by night, or who scan their tracks by day. Even without sight or sound of wolf, it is implicit in a hundred small events: the midnight whinny of a pack horse, the rattle of rolling rocks, the bound of a fleeing deer, the way shadows lie under the spruces. Only the ineducable tyro can fail to sense the presence or absence of wolves, or the fact that mountains have a secret opinion about them.

4   My own conviction on this score dates from the day I saw a wolf die. We were eating lunch on a high rimrock, at the foot of which a turbulent river elbowed its way. We saw what we thought was a doe fording the torrent, her breast awash in white water. When she climbed the bank toward us and shook out her tail, we realized our error: it was a wolf. A half-dozen others, evidently grown pups, sprang from the willows and all joined in a welcoming mêlée of wagging tails and playful maulings. What was literally a pile of wolves writhed and tumbled in the center of an open flat at the foot of our rimrock.

5   In those days we had never heard of passing up a chance to kill a wolf. In a second we were pumping lead into the pack, but with more excitement than accuracy: how to aim a steep downhill shot is always confusing. When our rifles were empty, the old wolf was down, and a pup was dragging a leg into impassable slide-rocks.

6   We reached the old wolf in time to watch a fierce green fire dying in her eyes. I realized then, and have known ever since, that there was something new to me in those eyes—something known only to her and to the mountain. I was young then, and full of trigger-itch; I thought that because fewer wolves meant more deer, that no wolves would mean hunters' paradise. But after seeing the green fire die, I sensed that neither the wolf nor the mountain agreed with such a view.

7   Since then I have lived to see state after state extirpate its wolves. I have watched the face of many a newly wolfless mountain, and seen the south-facing slopes wrinkle with a maze of new deer trails. I have seen every edible bush and seedling browsed, first to anaemic desuetude, and then to death. I have seen every edible tree defoliated to the height of a saddlehorn. Such a mountain looks as if someone had given God a new pruning shears, and forbidden Him all other exercise. In the end the starved bones of the hoped-for deer herd, dead of its own too-much, bleach with the bones of the dead sage, or molder under the high-lined junipers.

8   I now suspect that just as a deer herd lives in mortal fear of its wolves, so does a mountain live in mortal fear of its deer. And perhaps with better cause, for while a buck pulled down by wolves can be replaced in two or three years, a range pulled down by too many deer may fail of replacement in as many decades.

9   So also with cows. The cowman who cleans his range of wolves does not realize that he is taking over the wolf's job of trimming the herd to fit the range. He has not learned to think like a mountain. Hence we have dust-bowls, and rivers washing the future into the sea.

10   We all strive for safety, prosperity, comfort, long life, and dullness. The deer strives with his supple legs, the cowman with trap and poison, the statesman

with pen, the most of us with machines, votes, and dollars, but it all comes to the same thing: peace in our time. A measure of success in this is all well enough, and perhaps is a requisite to objective thinking, but too much safety seems to yield only danger in the long run. Perhaps this is behind Thoreau's dictum: In wildness is the salvation of the world. Perhaps this is the hidden meaning in the howl of the wolf, long known among mountains, but seldom perceived among men.

WHAT DID THE WRITER SAY AND WHAT DID YOU THINK?

1. What is the thesis?
2. Why are wolves so important to the "life" of a mountain?
3. What does it mean to "think like a mountain?"
4. How have Leopold's feelings about wolves changed over the years?
5. What does the howl of a wolf signify to a deer? to a pine? to a coyote? to a cowman?
6. Why is the mountain afraid of deer?
7. Why does Leopold consider wildness a salvation?

HOW DID THE WRITER SAY IT?

1. What image does Leopold use to describe an overgrazed mountain? Comment on the effectiveness of this image.
2. What is the intended audience for this essay? Are the style and vocabulary appropriate?
3. What is the purpose of the hunting story in paragraphs 4–6?

WHAT ABOUT YOUR WRITING?

Leopold makes frequent use of words that belong far more to formal English than to the everyday English more familiar to most people. He writes *tyro* instead of *beginner, extirpate* instead of *wipe out, desuetude* instead of *lack of use.* Isn't this language too fancy? Is fancy writing good English?

The best reply to those questions is that they need to be rethought. It's like asking if a tuxedo or an evening gown is good dress. It's good dress for formal dances, but it's bad dress for mowing the lawn. Shorts and a T-shirt are good dress for mowing the lawn, but bad dress for a formal dance. There's no one kind of good dress. A good dresser is someone who knows what kind of clothes to wear for different occasions.

There's no one kind of good English, either. It varies. It's what's appropriate to the subject, situation, and audience. As these elements change, the nature of what's appropriate will change. Tuxedo English is appropriate for ceremonial occasions, serious studies of specialized subjects, and so on. Lincoln's Gettysburg Address is written in formal English. If it had been written in a chatty, conversational style with folksy anecdotes about Lincoln's childhood, it would have been written in bad English and bad taste. On the other hand, shorts-and-T-shirt English is good English for much conversation and the dialogue of certain characters in works of fiction. A quarterback in a huddle says, "Play 32. Left tackle. Let's get the bums"—or something like that. It would be bad English for him to say, "Let us, my teammates, utilize Play 32 to assault the left tackle position of our adversaries."

Most Freshman English papers should probably be written at the coat-and-tie or skirt-and-sweater level. A tuxedo is absurd. Even a business suit might sometimes be a bit stiff for the subject, situation, and audience. But shorts and a T-shirt are also out of place. Grammar still counts. Organization still counts. There aren't as many rules to worry about as in tuxedo English, but there are still plenty of rules.

In "Thinking Like a Mountain," Leopold is probably writing what could be called business-suit English. The subject is a serious one on life and death issues, and the author feels it needs to be treated with gravity and dignity. He doesn't write everyday English because he's not dealing with an everyday subject. Good English changes all the time—and it doesn't have much to do with avoiding words like *ain't* or *desuetude.*

Division and Classification

Some topics are difficult or impossible to attack head on. Such topics are often best approached through analysis: studying a complex subject by breaking it down into smaller units. Analysis itself calls for analysis and can be broken down into division and classification.

Division

What are the moving parts of a rotary engine? What are the major characteristics of realism in literature? What are the three major divisions of the federal government? The United States of America is divided into fifty states. Can you name them all? Your own state is divided into counties or parishes. How many of them can you name?

In *division* (also known as *partition*) a subject commonly thought of as a single unit is reduced to its separate parts. Potential renters of an apartment rarely begin by thinking of the apartment as a whole. They mentally divide it into living room, bedroom, kitchen, and bathroom. If they think it worthwhile, they may go on to subdivisions of each room: walls, ceiling, floor, for example. At any rate, they study each division separately before reaching any useful conclusion about the entire apartment. Soldiers use division to study a rifle; chemists use division to find out the ingredients of a compound; doctors use division in a physical checkup to examine a patient—heart, lungs, blood, and so forth.

Division is a natural, logical, and necessary form of thought. For writing purposes, however, it often tends to be more cut-and-dried than classification, and most English teachers generally prefer classification assignments.

223

Besides, any students who have written a process paper (see Chapter 5) have already used a form of division to break the process into its separate steps. For these reasons, the rest of this chapter concentrates on classification.

Classification

Are you an introvert or an extrovert? Are you lower class, middle class, or upper class? Are you a Democrat, Republican, or Independent? Are you a Protestant, Catholic, Jew, Muslim, Hindu, Buddhist, Sikh, atheist, agnostic, or "other"? Are you heterosexual, homosexual, or bisexual? Are you left-handed, right-handed, or ambidextrous? Are you a nondrinker, light drinker, normal drinker, heavy drinker, or alcoholic?

No answers are necessary. The questions aren't intended to snoop. They're intended to demonstrate the universality of classification.

In *classification* we analyze a subject like apartments, not *an* apartment; engines, not *an* engine. We analyze the subject by arranging it into groups or categories rather than separate parts. We divide an apartment into rooms, but we classify apartments into high rises, garden apartments, tenements, and so on. We classify when we make out a shopping list to deal with the thousands of articles in a supermarket: dairy, meat, produce, paper goods. A business manager classifies: complaints I can ignore, complaints I have to do something about. A college catalog classifies: required courses, elective courses.

Without classification, certain kinds of systematic thought would be impossible. Biologists, for example, classify to make basic sense of the world, to be able to function at all. They classify living things into Plants and Animals. They classify animals into Vertebrates and Invertebrates. They classify Vertebrates into Mammals, Birds, Reptiles, Amphibians, and Fish. Each class has its distinct characteristics, so when biologists meet some wriggly little item they haven't seen before, they have some way of at least beginning to cope with it. As another example, political leaders in presidential elections undoubtedly classify the states. Which states are Sure for Us? Which states are Sure for Them? Which states are Toss-ups? Classification here is not a parlor game or intellectual exercise. It's the only way of determining where the time and money should go.

Classification can sometimes be a game, however, and it can lead to excellent humorous papers. Members of a bad football team could be classified as Hopeless Bums, Hopeless Mediocrities, and Hopeless Physical Wrecks. Household chores could be classified as Chores I Can Put Off for a Week,

Chores I Can Put Off for a Month, and Chores I Can Put Off Forever. A student once classified teachers as Fascist Pigs, Middle-of-the-Road Sheep, and Mad Dog Radicals.

The pattern of a classification—or division—paper is straightforward and pretty much self-evident. Each class or division generally represents a major section of the paper. Each is defined and described, with as many examples as are needed for clarity. Each is carefully differentiated from the others when any possibility of confusion occurs.

In writing a classification paper, keep the following elementary principles of logic in mind:

Use Only One Principle of Classification

Different classifications can apply at different times to the same subject, depending on one's interests and insights. The essential requirement is that only one basis of classification be used at a time. Cars, for instance, can be classified by size. They can also be classified by manufacturer, price, body style, country of origin, and so on. Choose the principle of classification suitable to your purpose. Something is obviously cockeyed in this arrangement of cars: subcompact, compact, intermediate, Fords, full-size.

Exercise

What are the errors in the following classification outlines?

Schools

   I. Elementary schools

  II. Junior high schools

 III. Parochial schools

 IV. High schools

  V. Colleges and universities

Students

   I. Bright

  II. Average

 III. Hardworking

 IV. Dull

Teachers

   I. Hard graders

  II. Friendly

 III. Easy graders

Crimes

   I. Violent

  II. Non-violent

 III. Fraud

Sections of America	Politicians
I. East	I. Good
II. South	II. Bad
III. Midwest	III. Mediocre
IV. Slums	IV. Honest
V. Far West	

Be Consistent

Once you have determined a principle of classification, stick with it throughout the paper. Mixing principles invariably creates illogical overlapping of classes.

Make the Classifications as Complete as Possible

All individual units within your subject should be able to fit into one of the classes you have devised. Classifying politicians as only good or bad doesn't take care of the many who are neither all one nor all the other; you need another category. When you face the prospect of an endless number of classes, it's generally better to revise the subject a bit than to add a catch-all class like "Miscellaneous" or "Others." A paper classifying religions, for example, could go on forever, whereas a paper classifying "Major Religions in America" would have a much simpler task.

Exercise

Point out incompleteness in the following classification outlines.

Academic Degrees	Career Opportunities
I. B.A.	I. Business
II. B.S.	II. Government
III. M.A.	
IV. Ph.D.	

Television Programs	Where to Live in America
I. Comedies	I. Cities
II. Dramas	II. Suburbs
III. Sports	
IV. Quiz shows	

Acknowledge Any Complications

Classification is logical and essential, but it's also arbitrary and artificial. It pins labels on materials that weren't born with them. It may be helpful at times to classify people as introverts or extroverts, but a good paper points out that introverts can sometimes be outgoing among close friends, and extroverts can sometimes be shy in unfamiliar or threatening circumstances. Similarly, labels like liberal and conservative can be valuable, but a good paper will mention that few people are entirely liberal or conservative about everything.

Follow the Persuasive Principle

Finally, what of the persuasive principle? A classification paper classifies. What does it have to persuade anyone about?

In a fussy, technical sense, every classification paper has a thesis whether the writer wants one or not. The writer asserts that there are three classes of teachers or four classes of mental illness or five classes of surgeons. By the end of the paper, sure enough, there are the three, four, or five classes, logically consistent and complete.

And there, sure enough, if that's all the writer does, is a distortion of the persuasive principle.

A good classification paper can utilize the persuasive principle in far more effective ways. To the logic and order of classification it can add the power and bite of a forceful point of view. In some papers, the naming of classes in itself can express the writer's attitude. An introductory paragraph stating that the three kinds of teachers are Fascist Pigs, Middle-of-the-Road Sheep, and Mad Dog Radicals probably doesn't need an explicit thesis statement that all three classes are obnoxious. A paper with less dramatic labels can declare a thesis by expressing a strong preference for one class over the others. It can express scorn for all classes. It can ridicule traditional classifications. Almost all the subjects for classification brought up in this chapter invite a thesis:

Each different kind of car has serious drawbacks.

Good politicians in this country are vastly outnumbered by the bad and mediocre.

Every major religion in America has a similar concept of God.

The distinctions among normal drinkers, heavy drinkers, and alcoholics are dangerously vague.

Only one kind of television program makes any appeal to the viewer's intelligence.

It's not hard to see the extra interest such approaches can give a paper. Don't just classify, then. Convince.

WRITING SUGGESTIONS FOR CLASSIFICATION THEMES

Use classification to analyze one of the following subjects. Narrow down any of the subjects as necessary, and remember the importance of working a thesis into your paper. With slight changes, some topics may also lend themselves to analysis by division.

1. Television doctors
2. Snobbishness
3. Drug users
4. People at a concert or sporting event
5. Methods of making excuses
6. Cashiers in supermarkets
7. Clothing
8. Parents
9. Love
10. Hate
11. Laziness
12. News programs or commentators
13. Freshman English students
14. Managers or coaches of athletic teams
15. Ambition
16. Summer jobs
17. Pessimists or optimists
18. Attitudes toward Christmas
19. Attitudes toward money
20. Attitudes toward sex

GIVE THEM A LITTLE CREDIT
Harry Pritchard (student)

Thesis: Only one way of dealing with credit cards will keep college students out of trouble.

   I. Carpe Diem
      A. Spend credit limit quickly
      B. Think of credit as "free money"
      C. Always have a card, can never use it

  II. Accumulators
      A. Spend their whole credit limit at once
      B. Get more cards to get more credit

 III. Deniers
      A. Never even look at their bills
      B. Ignore threatening letters and phone calls

 IV. Responsible
      A. Consider credit card a convenience, not a license to spend
      B. Occasionally splurge, but mostly wait for emergencies
      C. Pay bills off in full nearly every month
      D. Know the only sane way to manage a credit card

Conclusion: Learning to manage the powerful, but dangerous tool of a credit
              card will make your life easier.

I'm not through with *David Copperfield* yet, but I love it. Even though I know Dickens wasn't thinking about college students and their credit troubles I could think of nothing else when I read the lines, "Annual income twenty pounds, annual expenditure nineteen nineteen six, result, happiness. Annual income twenty pounds, annual expenditure twenty pounds ought and six, result misery."

Nearly every college student gets invited daily to spend more money than he or she has. Nearly every college student has a mailbox bursting with offers for free credit cards, pre-approved, and with special, low, one-time-only interest rates. Nearly every college student takes up the offers of at least one of these advertisements, and nearly every student has his or her own way of dealing with the inevitable bills. Be careful, though, because nearly every one of these ways will leave you in worse financial shape than if you'd just tossed all your money out of the nearest window.

First we have the Carpe Diem crowd. For these credit card users, "seize the day" means "reach your credit limit in a day, if possible." For them, a $10,000 limit doesn't mean a nice safety net to have their car repaired or cover an extra tuition payment; it means $10,000 of free money. Large-screen televisions, new mountain bikes, "essential" computer equipment—all the big ticket items are suddenly within their reach, and they've got to have them and have them now. The fun doesn't last much more than a day, however. The credit runs out almost immediately, but the bills can keep coming until long after graduation.

Some students are smart enough to realize that the Carpe Diem crowd is on their way to destruction. Unfortunately they're not much smarter than that. They figure they can beat the system by becoming Accumulators. Realizing that it would be unwise to use up a credit limit in a matter of days, they ingeniously accumulate more cards, transfer balances, and keep on shopping. Why worry about a maxed-out credit card when you can get more of them by just asking? The problem, of course, is that owing $50,000 to five companies is at least five times as bad as owing $10,000 to one.

The Deniers seem to come from another planet entirely. Firmly believing that if you can't see something it doesn't exist, these folks never actually open their bills. They just toss them away. They dodge the phone calls from the credit card companies and then dodge the calls from the collection agencies. They're brave souls, these deniers. Stern looking envelopes with lots of red print and capital letters don't sway them. Nasty phone calls from early in the morning to late at night don't bother them at all. They stand firm. If you hide from a problem, how can the problem find you? This works just beautifully until the guy who serves subpoenas finds them.

None of these people, of course, are dealing reasonably with credit cards. It's for the few, the proud, the Responsible users to show us how to do that. These bright folks realize that a credit card is a convenience, not a license to spend beyond their means. They use them occasionally, to cover a big ticket item, or at times when they just don't have cash on them, or when it's just quicker and more convenient to use a credit card. They pay their bills. In full. Every month. Well, almost. They're students, after all, and sometimes money gets a little tight. They're bright enough to know that carrying a small balance for a month or two won't do too much harm, but clearing up the card is always their first priority.

Credit cards are a powerful tool. They can make your life easier, make financial transactions a lot faster, and make it possible to pay for some of the more expensive things that you need. But college students who are just learning to use them need to learn to be careful. Don't be a Carpe Diem user, an Accumulator, or a Denier. Don't dig that kind of a financial hole for yourself. Be a responsible user, and make your life easier. And, check out *David Copperfield* some time.

HOW FIT ARE YOU?

Kenneth H. Cooper

Kenneth Cooper is called "the father of aerobics" and is the founder of The Cooper Aerobics Center as well as a much-published author. His book *Aerobics*, based on his experience as a doctor in the U.S. Air Force, presents a physical fitness program designed to increase the oxygen capacity of the body through exercises like swimming, jogging, walking, and cycling. This selection is an excerpt from the second chapter of the book.

Words to check:

physiological (paragraph 2)   calisthenics (13)
candidly (3)   skeletal (19)
isometrics (5)   cardiovascular (21)
treadmill (12)

1   I was visiting a colleague who was testing volunteers for a special project that would require men in the best possible condition. I passed three of the volunteers in the hall. Two had normal builds, but the third was definitely muscular.

2   "Which of the three do you think will get our recommendation?" my friend asked, tossing their medical records across the desk. I skimmed over the physiological data until I came to the slot where it asked, "Regular exercise?"

3   One wrote, candidly, "None."

4   The second, "Nothing regular. Just ride my bike to the base and back every day. About three miles one way."

5   The third, "Isometrics and weight lifting, one hour a day, five days a week." The muscular one!

6   I glanced back over each of the records. All pilots, all in their early 30s, none with any history of illness.

7   "Well?" asked my friend.

8   "I'd bet on the cyclist."

9   "Not the weight lifter?"

10   "Not if that's all he does."

11   My friend smiled. "I think you're right."

12   Next day he proved it. The three came back for their treadmill tests and the nonexerciser and the weight lifter were completely fatigued within the first five minutes. The cyclist was still going strong 10 minutes later, running uphill at a 6½ mph clip. He was recommended for the project. The other two weren't.

13   This story, when I use it in my lectures, always surprises people. The nonexerciser they can believe. The cyclist, maybe. But the weight lifter, or anyone who does strictly isometrics or calisthenics, they all *look* in such good condition!

14   In my business, looks are deceitful. Some exceptionally physically fit men tested in our laboratory were middle-aged types with slight builds, including an occasional one with a paunch. Some of the most unfit we've ever seen were husky young men with cardiac conditions.

15   If this shatters any illusions about slim waistlines and large biceps being the key to good health, I'm sorry. They're not a deterrent, but they're no guarantee either. They're mostly a byproduct. The real key is elsewhere.

16   Take those three volunteers. By ordinary standards, all three should have been accepted. None of them had any physical defects, or ever had any. Why the discrimination?

17   For special projects, the military services can afford to be discriminate. They can afford to classify the physically fit into their three classic categories and choose only the most fit.

18   The nonexerciser represents passive fitness. There's nothing wrong with him—not yet anyway—but there's nothing really right with him either. If he's lucky, he can coast like that for years. But, without any activity, his body is essentially deteriorating.

19   The weight lifter, or those who emphasize isometrics or calisthenics, represent muscular fitness. These types, who have the right motives but the wrong approach, are struck with the myth that muscular strength or agility means physical fitness. This is one of the great misconceptions in the field of exercise. The muscles that show—the skeletal muscles—are just one system in the body, and by no means the most important. If your exercise program is directed only at the skeletal muscles, you'll never achieve real physical fitness.

20   The cyclist, whether he knew it or not, had found one of the most basic means to overall fitness. . . . By riding three miles to work, six miles round trip, he was earning more than enough points to answer the question, "How much exercise?"[1] and he proved it on the treadmill.

21   The cyclist represents the third, and best, kind of fitness, overall fitness. We call it endurance fitness, or working capacity, the ability to do prolonged work without undue fatigue. It assumes the absence of any ailment, and it has little to do with pure muscular strength or agility. It has very much to do with the body's *overall* health, the health of the heart, the lungs, the entire cardiovascular system and the other organs, *as well as* the muscles.

WHAT DID THE WRITER SAY AND WHAT DID YOU THINK?

1. What group does Cooper classify?
2. Is there a thesis? If so, what is it?
3. What is the main advantage of cycling over weight lifting and calisthenics?
4. Does the writer maintain that anything is wrong with weight lifting and calisthenics in themselves?

---

[1] Cooper had devised a point system for measuring physical fitness.

HOW DID THE WRITER SAY IT?

1. What purposes are served by starting with a story rather than with the system of classification?
2. Does the writer merely describe each class, or does he also provide convenient labels for each?
3. Does the writer recognize the possibility that the second and third classes can overlap?

WHAT ABOUT <u>YOUR</u> WRITING?

"The cyclist, maybe." Isn't that a sentence fragment? "Why the discrimination?" Isn't that another sentence fragment? Aren't sentence fragments illegal? The answers to these questions are *yes, yes,* and *sort of.*

Look at it this way: There's a sensible speed limit on the road. One night you're driving well over the limit. A police officer who is worth anything would stop you to give you a ticket. This night an officer stops you and finds that you're speeding in order to get a pregnant woman to the hospital on time or a badly beaten man to the emergency ward. If the officer is worth anything now, you get a siren escort that enables you to break the law more safely and efficiently.

Your instructor, in some respects, is the police officer. By and large, sentence fragments are not standard written English, and your instructor rightly gives you a ticket for them. Every once in a while, a situation turns up when a fragment can be justified. You want a special dramatic effect, a sudden note of breeziness or informality, perhaps, that a grammatically complete sentence could not achieve as well. In that case, your instructor usually tries to be cooperative.

You don't speed to the emergency ward often, however, and sentence fragments, too, should be saved for special occasions. The burden of proof is on you: The officer wants to see the pregnant woman or beaten man, and the instructor wants to be convinced that the sentence fragment was justified by the demands of your paper. Finally, just as the officer wants assurance that you knew you were speeding and were in constant control, the instructor wants assurance that your sentence fragment was a deliberate stylistic device, not a simple grammatical error.

MOTHER-IN-LAW

Charlotte Latvala

Charlotte Latvala, a free-lance writer and a correspondent for the *Beaver County Times*, has fun in this essay analyzing the many different kinds of bad mothers-in-law and longing for the one good kind.

Words to check:

nirvana (paragraph 3)	uterus (10)	impromptu (20)
adversary (5)	precocious (15)	maxims (32)
guises (5)	harpies (16)	decadence (34)
fallopian tubes (10)	vipers (16)	liposuction (37)

1 You're in heaven. You've found a man who adores you, who makes you laugh and keeps you sane. For the first time in your life, you're thinking about a long-term commitment; in fact, you're discussing *the* long-term commitment, the June bride, till-death-do-us-part one.

2   Everything's going well; you've worked out a plan for careers, children, where you'll live, etc. Your bliss knows no bounds; your world is a sunny, positive place where birds chirp from dawn to dusk and all the movies have happy endings.

3   Sooner or later, however, you must leave nirvana for a few moments and face the one very real obstacle that women throughout the centuries have faced: You must meet his mother.

4   Never underestimate a mother's influence on her son. (If you're feeling brave, watch "The Manchurian Candidate" right before your meeting.) She was the first and most important woman in his life, and their complex relationship, good or bad, has spanned decades. She's seen him through the chicken pox, the prom and his first major heartache. You are cutting in on a dance that's been going on for years.

5   A potential mother-in-law can be a lot of things. She can be your adversary, your ally, or your critic. Once in a while she might become your friend. She is never your own mother. Here are a few of the different guises she may take.

The Naysayer

6   This woman looks at the world through dark-gray glasses; she is negativity personified. She has frequent imagined illnesses and pains no one can ease. One of her favorite lines is "No one cares about me," closely followed by "He never comes to see me anymore."

7   The Naysayer sees the world as a bleak and dreary place, full of suffering and torment. She is convinced that human nature is rotten, and that young people today are selfish and immoral. Nothing, though, looks darker to her than her son's future with you.

8   You really don't have many options here; she will assign evil motives to your most innocent actions. No matter how hard you try to please her, she will find a way to get her digs in. "I really had no idea that Frank was dating such a talented girl. I don't know whether I'd spend so much money on painting lessons, though."

9   Grit your teeth and smile. You can probably pick up tips from your future husband.

The Baby-Crazed Fanatic

10   This woman's excitement at meeting you has nothing to do with you as an individual. She looks at you and sees fallopian tubes and a uterus. You are the answer to her prayers, the woman who will provide her with a soft little bundle of joy to croon sweet nothings to.

11   Within minutes of meeting you, she has informed you that most of her friends are grandparents already. "Do you come from a large family?" she asks eagerly, and coos with delight when you tell her that your younger sister already has three children.

12   You hate to burst her bubble; you hate to tell her that you really want to get your career off to a solid start before you even consider children. You honestly don't think you should be discussing the subject with her in the first place. But, before you can say anything, she puts her arm around your shoulder and says, "Well, I'm sure it won't be long before you have one, too."

"No One's Good Enough for My Son"

13   Similar to The Naysayer, but more upbeat. At least on one subject.

14   God made one perfect man, and it is her son. He has never done anything wrong in his life. He is handsome, talented and generous. His manners are beyond reproach, and he is so intelligent he scares her.

15   She has a tendency to rattle on and on about his accomplishments throughout the years, from the precocious age at which she removed his training wheels to the ease with which he graduated from college with honors.

16   This wonderful man, however, has dated only harpies and vipers, of which you are the latest. At the slightest prompting, she will tell you much more than you want to know about the terrible women who have tried to trap her little boy into matrimonial hell. Don't bother trying to impress her

with your sweet nature or good intentions. This woman would think Mother Teresa was a conniving shrew.

The Woman of the World

17   This mother-in-law has been everywhere, and she wants to make sure you know it. She's fond of saying things like, "And as you know, Paris is so lovely in the spring! You *have* been to Paris, haven't you, dear?" while you squirm on the couch and try to think of an impressive way to say that you've only been out of the Tri-State area four times in your life.

18   To her, you are a provincial little drip, and you will probably hinder her son's progress in life by making him settle down in some wretched suburb and take vacations to the Poconos.

19   There is only one way to deal with this woman. Lie. For every trip abroad, for every exotic excursion that she brags about, make up one of your own.

The Accomplished Mother-in-Law

20   It's impossible to compete with a woman who has more talents than Madonna has bras. She's a heart surgeon who also has a Ph.D. in romance poetry. She's a nationally ranked chess champion. In her spare time, she plays the violin in a string quartet, teaches blind children to ride horses and whips up impromptu four-star meals in her gourmet kitchen.

21   Just listening to her exhausts you. Your fiance warned you about her (he said, "Oh, Mother keeps herself busy"), but you never dreamed any single human being could cram so much into a lifetime.

22   On top of it all, she's polite and charming. And when she asks you, "And what do *you* do, dear?" you would rather curl up and die than admit you're a word processor who rents a lot of movies and takes three-hour naps on Sunday afternoon.

The Experienced Mother-in-Law

23   This mother has been through it before. You are not the first woman to sit in her house and joyously proclaim that you really and truly love her son and will do everything in your power to make him happy forever and ever.

24   Divorce has a strange effect on people, and it tends to make mothers either extremely suspicious or nostalgic, depending on her opinion of Wife No. 1.

25   If she hated Wife No. 1, you're in luck, because you are the sensible decision that her son made when he was old enough for it.

26   If she was fond of Wife No. 1, you're in trouble. You will be forever compared, unfairly, to a woman who's not there to speak for herself. Little

comments and asides ("Well, a lot of women these days can't cook. Of course, Freddy never could get Patrice out of the kitchen; she was always in there whipping up his favorites . . .") will forever remind you of who you're not.

The Pal

27   On the surface, this woman looks like a treat. She takes you warmly by the arm and insists that you call her Gladys. How sweet, you think. How friendly.

28   One day she wants to meet you for lunch. Next, she wants to go shopping for lingerie with you. Soon, she wants to double-date with you and her son. Her boyfriend has a tan and wears jogging shoes everywhere.

29   Before long, you start to feel as if you've inherited a younger sister. Things get bad when you get phone calls from her and she wants to talk about her sex life, or when she introduces you to the members of her jogging club as "my new best friend."

30   You will find yourself longing for the distance that your friends have from their mothers-in-law. You will find yourself plotting evil deeds that will make her despise you.

31   You find yourself saying "yes" when she asks you if you want to play tennis next weekend.

The Know-It-All

32   This woman knows more maxims than Aesop, and she won't keep any opinion to herself.

33   "All that will change when you get married," she says smugly when the two of you announce you're going out to dinner and a movie. "You won't have the money to fritter away."

34   When you get married and still fritter money away on going out, she predicts the end is near. "You won't be able to do that when you have kids."

35   You could try to shock her into silence by announcing that you aren't intending to have children, that you plan to go on throwing money away foolishly, living a life of decadence at expensive restaurants and nightclubs. However, she'll probably just nod and mumble about a fool and his money.

The Hot Tamale

36   Like The Pal, this woman sees you as a contemporary. Unlike The Pal, she sees you as competition.

37   This mother-in-law refuses to age, gracefully or not. She'll do whatever it takes to maintain her face and body; liposuction, face lifts and tummy tucks are as routine to her as a visit to the post office. She wears mini-skirts and too

much mascara. Her CD rack is filled with the B-52's and Paula Abdul, not Glenn Miller.

38   She coyly asks you if you want to borrow her Victoria's Secret catalog, then says that you probably won't find anything in it that's "your style."

39   She treats her son like a bit of an old fogey, and you find yourself feeling rather prudish around her. You may as well get used to this role reversal, unless you want to begin a long uphill battle to outdo a woman who's been practicing her young and silly act longer than you've been alive.

The Mother-in-Law Who Isn't

40   Maybe you're *not* getting married. Maybe you've decided, for whatever complicated reasons people decide these things today, that you're going to live together as man and wife without the benefit of official documents, bouquet-throwing and name-changing.

41   Do you still have a mother-in-law?

42   Well, yes. That is, she has the job without the title. Call her what you like (my lover's mother, my live-in-law, the mother of my significant other), she's still your mother-in-law, subject to all the complications that arise in legal unions.

43   You just can't call her Mom.

The Saint

44   For every hundred difficult mothers-in-law, there is one perfect one. She is as precious as she is rare.

45   She never insists that you call her "Mom-mom" or "Binky."

46   She never introduces you to her friends as "the one who finally snagged Junior."

47   She is friendly and warm without being overbearing; she doesn't plant slobbery kisses on your cheek when she hasn't seen you for a week.

48   You are comfortable talking to her about world events, shared friends and literature; neither of you feels the need to discuss your sex life or her friend's divorces.

49   She recognizes that however much she loves her son, he is a human being, complete with faults and virtues.

50   She accepts the fact that you have a career and interests of your own; she encourages and supports them.

51   She doesn't call you "that woman" when speaking to the other relatives.

52   She keeps her opinions on child-rearing to herself.

53   If you find yourself related by marriage to such a woman, cherish the connection as if she were royalty. She is.

54   So, there you have it. You may have spotted someone you know. You may be shaking your head wisely. But, before you get too carried away with yourself, remember one thing.

55   Someday, you might have a son. Someday, that son may fall in love with a woman he believes is *the one*. And someday, you may be stuck with a daughter-in-law you can't stand.

WHAT DID THE WRITER SAY AND WHAT DID YOU THINK?

1. Is there a thesis? If so, is it stated or implied?
2. Do any of the classifications overlap or repeat themselves?
3. Does the author show any sympathy for mothers-in-law? If so, where?
4. First published in a newspaper, this article provoked a number of angry letters. What would you guess the complaints were about?

HOW DID THE WRITER SAY IT?

1. Why is the introduction so much longer than usual?
2. How much of the humor is merely good-natured joking, and how much covers genuine irritation or resentment?
3. How does the description of "The Saint" help serve as a summary of the essay?
4. What stylistic features indicate this essay was first written for a newspaper?

WHAT ABOUT <u>YOUR</u> WRITING?

Charlotte Latvala begins "Mother-in-Law" with a charming two-paragraph rhapsody on romantic bliss, then devotes the rest of her essay to what pharmacists call unpleasant side effects. We'd like to suggest that the huge area of Romance, more specifically Romantic Highs and Lows, is one of those can't-miss general subjects like Family Life (see p. 218) or Nostalgia (see p. 56) that everyone has plenty to write about. Consider the hundreds—millions—of possibilities for a Narration paper represented merely by titles like "My First Date," "My Last Date," "My Worst Date," "My Best Date."

Stuck for a subject? Don't let anyone force unwanted or unworkable subjects on you, but think about the opportunities offered by Romantic Highs and Lows in all the rhetorical patterns, not just Narration.

Description? What about The Perfect Husband, Wife, In-Law, Wedding, honeymoon? What about "My Husband the Slob" or "My Wife the Scold"—with changes in relationships and character defects as necessary.

Examples? "Frogs I Have Kissed." "Lies My Mother Told Me." "It Won't Take Much to Win My Heart."

Process? Planning a wedding—probably limited to one specific topic like choosing a photographer or caterer. Planning a romantic getaway. How to fall out of love.

Comparison and Contrast? Past versus present and illusion versus reality themes always work well: a change in your ideas, a change in your expectations, a change in your character. "Where Did All The Magic Go?"

Cause and Effect? "I Was a Teenage Idiot." "He Said He Loved Me: Confessions of an Abused Spouse." "Love Required. Luck Helps." "Our Secret Ingredient."

Division and Classification? "Boys, Guys, Thugs, and Men." "The Three Kinds of Love Stories." "Styles in Relationships: No Size Fits All." "Approaches to Conflict: Ignoring, Confronting, or Solving."

Definition? Love versus Infatuation. Love versus Affection. "It Depends on What You Mean by 'Happy.'" "This is My, Uh, Boyfriend: There Must Be a Word." "What Does He Mean, I'm His 'Woman?'"

Argumentation? Gay marriages, pro or con. "Of Course Religion Matters." "What's Wrong with Arranged Marriages?" "'In Like' Is More Important Than 'In Love.'" "First, Let's Kill All the Songwriters."

If you tell us you're not in the mood to write a paper or that you're too busy, we may be sympathetic. Just don't tell us you have nothing to write about.

TAKE A LEFT TURN ONTO NOWHERE STREET

Anne Bernays

Anne Bernays is the author of seven novels, including *Professor Romeo* (1997) and the coauthor of *What If?: Writing Exercises for Fiction Writers* (1991). Fed up with the chaos created by what seem to be thousands of sets of bad directions, Bernays draws a deep breath and tries to make sense of it all.

Words to check:

impeccably (paragraph 2)	fraught (5)
sanguine (3)	ambiguity (8)
pixies (5)	verbatim (9)

1 It's a fair bet that if you have been at the mercy of homemade directions to "our place" more than once or twice, you have also gotten lost. When this happens, your first impulse is to blame your own stupidity. Forget that. It's their fault—that sweet old guy, that nice young couple who invited you for dinner or the weekend have given you the wrong directions. Just one error can keep you driving back and forth over the same stretch of alien turf for hours, switching among panic, frustration and fury.

2 Years ago, soon after my husband, Justin, and I were married, Justin's boss, the poet and anthologist Louis Untermeyer, and his wife, Bryna, asked us over for dinner. As we drove from New York City toward rural Connecticut, we ticked off, one by one, the course changes and landmarks indicated in the impeccably typed directions, which Bryna, a freelance editor, had sent. The only trouble was that she had neglected to tell us that the road sign on the crucial turnoff had been blown away during a recent storm.

3 We arrived at their house, steaming, more than an hour late, having backtracked for miles to find a telephone. It's hard to show up sanguine and all smiles after you've been calling each other blind and stupid for the last couple of hours.

4 Soon after we moved to Cambridge, Mass., we were invited to a party in nearby Winchester. Armed with a handdrawn map from our hostess, we drove for well over an hour before we stopped, my eyes brimming, under a bridge, hopelessly raking a flashlight beam over the map and snarling at each other. A police car drew up, and an officer stepped smartly out. "Where you folks headed?" I told him and handed him our map. He looked it over. "Holy moly," he said, "where'd you get this thing?"

5 Ever since that episode, we've tried to keep every set of directions sent to us, and now, several decades later, we have a collection of about three dozen. All but a few of these are faulty in one or more respects and all of them are proof that writing exact directions or producing a reliable map is no easy exercise. There are scores of ways in which you can lead people seriously astray, like those Olde English pixies who did it on purpose. Our collection—funny now, not so funny at the time—includes directions in assorted shapes and sizes; handwritten or typed narratives; free-form, all-too-creative maps with little stick figures, cars and houses; on colored paper and white; some photocopied, others dictated casually over the phone (probably the form most fraught with errors).

6   Occasionally the mistakes are huge such as instructing you to take a right turn when it should have been a left—and sometimes tiny, like saying six-tenths of a mile when it's really eight-tenths.

7   Breaking down the errors into categories helps to dramatize how tricky it is to compose a set of precise, clear directions that do what they're supposed to do, namely get you there in one psychic piece by the most straightforward route.

8   **Ambiguity.** By far the largest category, it includes directions studded with traps like "go west" and "cross the bridge," which could mean anything from a culvert to the Golden Gate. The "gray garage" you're looking for isn't gray at all; it's white, something you discover only after driving up and down the same stretch of road for half an hour, passing and ignoring a white garage. If you have a cell phone, you can call your hosts to find out where the heck you are, but only if they're within range. Usually, it seems, they're not.

9   Here is a verbatim example of near-fatal vagueness: "To get to Wachusett, take the Mass pike from Cambridge to 495 North (signs say Lowell, I think)." He thinks?

10   **Too Much Explicitness.** This is most often seen on maps that are drawn by hand. All too often the imp of creativity seems to have guided the fingers of the map maker, for more detail is given than most travelers need—markers both large and small that distract the anxiety-prone (that is, most people driving somewhere for the first time). Among these are the names and locations of streets you're not supposed to turn into; items like "grass island," as incidental to the route as the clouds above, or careful renderings of a "parking lot" "school gym" and something that looks like an upside-down lollipop.

11   **Night Blindness.** This category focuses on the assumption that you, the traveler, have night vision. Here are some of the landmarks we've been in-structed to look for even when our hosts knew we would be arriving after dark: "Catholic Cemetery," "big field," "statue of Charles Sumner," "library," "Methodist Church," and my favorite: "We're the pale green house."

12   **Out-of-Dateness.** The "blue" mailbox, for example, has been painted red since the directions were composed. The Sunoco station where you're sup-posed to turn was recently bought by Exxon.

13   **Just Plain Wrong.** As when we were told to take Exit 16 and our host was off by one digit; or when we were directed to bear right "after the boul-der" and finally discovered that the jog came first, the boulder second. We were very late for lunch.

14   **Crucial Omissions.** These are the vital markers your hosts have failed to include—for instance, arrows telling you which way to go on a hand-drawn

map; huge structures like gas tanks and cement factories; railroad crossings. For some reason, if the directions fail to account for the tracks you've just crossed, you automatically assume you've taken a wrong turn. And then there's the traveler's genuine nightmare: a fork in the road. It would be nice if you could follow Yogi Berra's advice: "When you come to a fork in the road, take it."

15   **Impossible to Follow.** "Go three-eighths of a mile." Likewise, complicated handwritten directions scrawled on three scraps of paper. Bad enough if you have a navigator with you, but what are you supposed to do if you're flying solo?

16   **Return-Trip Blues.** Sometimes it's impossible to turn the thing inside out for the return trip. Getting back home is often the riskiest leg of the journey, especially at night. I suggest asking your hosts if they have a spare room.

17   **Famous Last Words.** "If you have any trouble, just ask someone in the village." And "You can't miss it."

WHAT DID THE WRITER SAY AND WHAT DID YOU THINK?

1. In paragraph 5, the writer refers to "all-too-creative" maps, and in paragraph 10 she complains about "the imp of creativity." What does she have against creativity in written directions?
2. Where does the writer come closest to a direct thesis statement? State the thesis in your own words.
3. Are all the instructions as bad as the author thinks? Is the example in paragraph 9, for instance, really guilty of "near-fatal vagueness?"
4. Why is it impossible to follow the instruction to "go three-eighths of a mile?"
5. Chapter 1 of this book provides an example of bad instructions (p. 16) on "How to Get from Town to Camp Wilderness." Do these bad instructions fall into one or more of the categories in this essay or do they reveal categories of their own?

HOW DID THE WRITER SAY IT?

1. Why does the writer mention the Untermeyers by name in paragraph 2 but leave other creators of bad instructions anonymous? Is she merely showing off that she knows some famous people?
2. The names of each class generally communicate some helpful preliminary information. Are there any names that do not?
3. Explain the meaning of "Famous Last Words" (paragraph 17). Is this actually a separate category or just a different kind of concluding paragraph?

WHAT ABOUT <u>YOUR</u> WRITING?

Think of the possibilities of our interest being grabbed by a title like "Nine Kinds of Bad Directions" or "Common Errors of Direction Providers." Now consider Anne Bernays' title, "Take a Left onto Nowhere Street." It arouses our curiosity if for no other reason than our desire to find out what on earth the phrase means. The apparent nonsense of the wording may also make us anticipate a touch of humor, and we are motivated to read on.

A good title is worth fussing about. It usually helps identify your subject, as well as your attitude toward the subject. It enables the reader to become properly oriented even before looking at your opening sentence. A good title also stimulates curiosity: It makes the reader willing to bother with your opening sentence in the first place. A good title won't save a bad piece of writing, and a bad title won't destroy good writing, but good titles help, and writers shouldn't be shy about accepting all the help they can get.

Boring Title	Better Title
The Making of the Constitution	A More Perfect Union
Bad Roommates	Pest Control in the College Dorm
Great Vampire Movies	Fangs for the Memory
The New Father	Have a Baby, My Wife Just Had a Cigar
Problems of Medical Expenses	Your Money or Your Life

THE QUICK FIX SOCIETY
Janet Mendell Goldstein

Janet Mendell Goldstein was an educator for thirty years and now works as a freelance writer and textbook author. Her work has appeared in a variety of newspapers and magazines. This piece is from a series of articles about life in the modern age.

Words to check:

liposuction (paragraph 4)

1 My husband and I just got back from a week's vacation in West Virginia. Of course, we couldn't wait to get there, so we took the Pennsylvania Turnpike

and a couple of interstates. "Look at those gorgeous farms!" my husband exclaimed as pastoral scenery slid by us at 55 mph. "Did you see those cows?" But at 55 mph, it's difficult to see anything; the gorgeous farms look like moving green checkerboards, and the herd of cows is reduced to a sprinkling of dots in the rear-view mirror. For four hours, our only real amusement consisted of counting exit signs and wondering what it would feel like to hold still again. Getting there certainly didn't seem like half the fun; in fact, getting there wasn't any fun at all.

2   So, when it was time to return to our home outside of Philadelphia, I insisted that we take a different route. "Let's explore that countryside," I suggested. The two days it took us to make the return trip were studded with new experiences. We toured a Civil War battlefield and stood on the little hill that fifteen thousand Confederate soldiers had tried to take on another hot July afternoon, one hundred and twenty-five years ago, not knowing that half of them would perish in the vain attempt. We meandered through main streets of sleepy Pennsylvania Dutch towns, slowing to twenty miles an hour so as not to crowd the horses and buggies on their way to market. We admired toy trains and antique cars in county museums and saved 70 percent in factory outlets. We stuffed ourselves with spicy salads and homemade bread pudding in an "all-you-can-eat" farmhouse restaurant, then wandered outside to enjoy the sunshine and the herds of cows—no little dots this time—basking in it. And we returned home refreshed, reeducated, revitalized. This time, getting there had *been* the fun.

3   Why is it that the featureless turnpikes and interstates are the routes of choice for so many of us? Why doesn't everybody try slowing down and exploring the countryside? But more and more, the fast lane seems to be the only way for us to go. In fact, most Americans are constantly in a hurry—and not just to get from Point A to Point B. Our country has become a nation in search of the quick fix—in more ways than one.

4   **Now instead of later:** Once upon a time, Americans understood the principle of deferred gratification. We put a little of each paycheck away "for a rainy day." If we wanted a new sofa or a week at a lakeside cabin, we saved up for it, and the banks helped us out by providing special Christmas Club and Vacation Club accounts. If we lived in the right part of the country, we planted corn and beans and waited patiently for the harvest. If we wanted to be thinner, we simply ate less of our favorite foods and waited patiently for the scale to drop, a pound at a time. But today we aren't so patient. We take out loans instead of making deposits, or we use our VISA or Mastercard to get that furniture or vacation trip—relax now, pay later. We buy our food, like our clothing, ready-made and off the rack. And if we're in a hurry to lose weight, we try the latest miracle diet, guaranteed to shed ten pounds in ten days . . . unless we're rich enough to afford liposuction.

5   **Faster instead of slower:** Not only do we want it now; we don't even want to be kept waiting for it. This pervasive impatience, the "I hate-to-wait" syndrome, has infected every level of our lives. Instead of standing in line at the bank, we withdraw twenty dollars in as many seconds from an automatic teller machine. Then we take our fast money to a fast convenience store (why wait in line at the supermarket?), where we buy a frozen dinner all wrapped up and ready to be popped into the microwave . . . unless we don't care to wait even that long and pick up some fast food instead. And if our fast meal doesn't agree with us, we hurry to the medicine cabinet for—you guessed it—some fast relief. We like fast pictures, so we buy Polaroid cameras. We like fast entertainment, so we record our favorite TV show on the VCR so we can "zap" each commercial, and stop watching if nothing exciting happens in the opening thirty seconds. We like our information fast, too: messages flashed on a computer screen, documents faxed from your telephone to mine, current events in 90-second bursts on *Eyewitness News*, history reduced to "Bicentennial Minutes." Symbolically, the American eagle now flies for Express Mail. How dare anyone keep America waiting longer than overnight?

6   **Superficially instead of thoroughly:** What's more, we don't even want *all* of it. Once, we lingered over every word of a classic novel or the latest bestseller. Today, since faster is better, we read the condensed version or pop an audiocassette of the book into our car's tape player to listen to on the way to work. Or we buy the *Cliff's Notes*, especially if we are students, so we don't have to deal with the book at all. Once, we listened to every note of Beethoven's Fifth Symphony. Today, we don't have the time; instead, we can enjoy 26 seconds of that famous "da-da-da-DUM" theme—and 99 other musical excerpts almost as famous—on our "Greatest Moments of the Classics" CD. After all, why waste 45 minutes listening to the whole thing when someone else has saved us the trouble of picking out the best parts? Our magazine articles come to us pre-digested in *Reader's Digest*. Our news briefings, thanks to *USA Today*, are more brief than ever. Even our personal relationships have become compressed. Instead of devoting large segments of our days to our loved ones—after all, we *are* busy people—we substitute something called "quality time," which, more often than not, is no time at all. As we rush from book to music to news item to relationship, we do not realize that we are living our lives by the iceberg principle—paying attention only to the top and ignoring the 8/9 that lies just below the surface.

7   When did it all begin, this urge to do it now, to get it over with, to skim the surface of life? Why are we in such a hurry to save time? And what, pray tell, are we going to do with all the time we save—besides, of course, rushing out to save some more? The sad truth is that we don't know how to use the time we save, because all we're good at is *saving* time . . . not *spending* time.

8   Don't get me wrong. I'm not saying we should go back to growing our own vegetables or knitting our own sweaters or putting our paychecks into piggy banks. I'm not even advocating a mass movement to cut all our credit cards into little pieces. But I am saying that all of us need to think more seriously about putting the brakes on our "we-want-it-all-and-we-want-it-now" lifestyle before we speed completely out of control. Let's take the time to read every word of that story, hear every note of that music, savor even nuance of that countryside—or that other person. Let's rediscover life in the slow lane.

WHAT DID THE WRITER SAY AND WHAT DID YOU THINK?

1. This classification essay begins with two comparison-and-contrast paragraphs. What is being compared and contrasted?
2. Does the author have anything good to say about any of her three classes?
3. Does the author adequately distinguish between "now instead of later" and "faster instead of slower?" Are these classes too close to bother making any distinction between them?
4. Polaroid cameras (see paragraph 5) are far less popular than they once were. Are any of the other supporting details in this essay inaccurate or outdated? Are there enough such details to affect the validity of the author's main point?
5. Why is "spending time" more important than "saving time" (paragraph 7)?

HOW DID THE WRITER SAY IT?

1. Explain the phrase in paragraph 1: "Getting there certainly didn't seem like half the fun."
2. Explain the phrase in paragraph 8: "Let's discover life in the slow lane."
3. Explain the phrase in paragraph 6: "the iceberg principle."

WHAT ABOUT <u>YOUR</u> WRITING?

Janet Mendell Goldstein uses what can best be called *ironic quotation marks* in paragraph 4 when she writes, "We put a little of each paycheck away 'for a rainy day.'" She uses them again in paragraph 5: "... we record our favorite TV show on the VCR so we can 'zap' each commercial." The quotation marks indicate that in some way the writer is distancing herself from the word: She disapproves of it or is amused by it or feels generally that it is inappropriate.

Be cautious with ironic quotation marks. Some instructors may advise you to avoid them entirely. Too often writers use them as a kind of cheap visual aid instead of letting the careful choice and arrangement of words do the job more effectively. Goldstein at least puts the quotation marks around words that we can imagine other people actually saying. When writers put the quotation marks around their own words, the results are almost always crude sarcasm:

My high school "teacher" was a disgrace to the system.

Eleanor's "good friend" betrayed her.

Our family's "vacation" last summer was a catastrophe.

Closely related to this writing problem is the use of quotation marks around trite expressions and slang or other informal words and phrases:

I suspected the other team would get the "last laugh" after all.

He was a good looking young man, "tall, dark, and handsome."

The policeman continued to "hassle" us.

The fraternity party caused many people to get "smashed."

I don't dislike "veggies" nearly as much as I used to.

First, if you are forced to rely on a trite expression it seems bad policy to highlight your problem. Second, effective slang should sound natural, and if it does, there's no need to call special attention to it. Third, and most important, a writer can run the risk of coming through as an offensive snob: "I'm far too cultivated to employ language like this myself, but look how cute I can be."

By and large, quotation marks are best reserved for their more common functions:

Words and phrases pointed to as such

If I ever find out what the word "love" means, I won't tell you—I'll write a book.

He keeps confusing "there" and "their."

Note: Italics often substitute for quotation marks here.

Dialogue and short quotations

"Sit down and relax," she said.

Which Dickens novel begins with "It was the best of times, it was the worst of times"?

Titles of short works-stories, poems, magazine articles, songs, and so on

"Falling into Place" was written by Jaime O'Neill.

I love that old record of Judy Garland singing "Over the Rainbow."

THREE KINDS OF DISCIPLINE
John Holt

John Holt (1923–1985) was one of the important voices in modern American education. His work is much admired, even by many of those who disagree with his conclusions, for his ability to identify with children and sometimes to seem to enter their minds. Too sophisticated a writer and thinker to be associated consistently with any particular party line in education, Holt is viewed as one of the influences behind experiments with open classrooms in the 1960s and early 1970s. His books include *How Children Fail* (1964), *How Children Learn* (1967), *The Underachieving School* (1969), *What Do I Do Monday?* (1970), *Escape from Childhood* (1974), and *Never Too Late* (1978). This selection is an excerpt from Holt's influential *Freedom and Beyond* (1972).

Words to check:

impartial (paragraph 1)	impotent (3)	suppleness (4)
wheedled (1)	autocratic (4)	novice (4)

1 A child, in growing up, may meet and learn from three different kinds of disciplines. The first and most important is what we might call the Discipline of Nature or of Reality. When he is trying to do something real, if he does the wrong thing or doesn't do the right one, he doesn't get the result he wants. If he doesn't pile one block right on top of another, or tries to build on a slanting surface, his tower falls down. If he hits the wrong key, he hears the wrong note. If he doesn't hit the nail squarely on the head, it bends, and he has to pull it out and start with another. If he doesn't measure properly what he

is trying to build, it won't open, close, fit, stand up, fly, float, whistle, or do whatever he wants it to do. If he closes his eyes when he swings, he doesn't hit the ball. A child meets this kind of discipline every time he tries to *do* something, which is why it is so important in school to give children more chances to do things, instead of just reading or listening to someone talk (or pretending to). This discipline is a great teacher. The learner never has to wait long for his answer; it usually comes quickly, often instantly. Also it is clear, and very often points toward the needed correction; from what happened he can not only see that what he did was wrong, but also why, and what he needs to do instead. Finally, and most important, the giver of the answer, call it Nature, is impersonal, impartial, and indifferent. She does not give opinions, or make judgments; she cannot be wheedled, bullied, or fooled; she does not get angry or disappointed; she does not praise or blame; she does not remember past failures or hold grudges; with her one always gets a fresh start, this time is the one that counts.

2   The next discipline we might call the Discipline of Culture, of Society, of What People Really Do. Man is a social, a cultural animal. Children sense around them this culture, this network of agreements, customs, habits, and rules binding the adults together. They want to understand it and be a part of it. They watch very carefully what people around them are doing and want to do the same. They want to do right, unless they become convinced they can't do right. Thus children rarely misbehave seriously in church, but sit as quietly as they can. The example of all those grownups is contagious. Some mysterious ritual is going on, and children, who like rituals, want to be part of it. In the same way, the little children that I see at concerts or operas, though they may fidget a little, or perhaps take a nap now and then, rarely make any disturbance. With all those grownups sitting there, neither moving nor talking, it is the most natural thing in the world to imitate them. Children who live among adults who are habitually courteous to each other, and to them, will soon learn to be courteous. Children who live surrounded by people who speak a certain way will speak that way, however much we may try to tell them that speaking that way is bad or wrong.

3   The third discipline is the one most people mean when they speak of discipline—the Discipline of Superior Force, of sergeant to private, of "You do what I tell you or I'll make you wish you had." There is bound to be some of this in a child's life. Living as we do, surrounded by things that can hurt children, or that children can hurt, we cannot avoid it. We can't afford to let a small child find out from experience the danger of playing in a busy street, or of fooling with the pots on the top of a stove, or of eating up the pills in the medicine cabinet. So, along with other precautions, we say to him, "Don't

play in the street, or touch things on the stove, or go into the medicine cabinet, or I'll punish you." Between him and the danger too great for him to imagine we put a lesser danger, but one he can imagine and maybe therefore wants to avoid. He can have no idea of what it would be like to be hit by a car, but he can imagine being shouted at, or spanked, or sent to his room. He avoids these substitutes for the greater danger until he can understand it and avoid it for its own sake. But we ought to use this discipline only when it is necessary to protect the life, health, safety, or well-being of people or other living creatures, or to prevent destruction of things that people care about. We ought not to assume too long, as we usually do, that a child cannot understand the real nature of the danger from which we want to protect him. The sooner he avoids the danger, not to escape our punishment, but as a matter of good sense, the better. He can learn that faster than we think. In Mexico, for example, where people drive their cars with a good deal of spirit, I saw many children no older than five or four walking unattached on the streets. They understood about cars, they knew what to do. A child whose life is full of the threat and fear of punishment is locked into babyhood. There is no way for him to grow up, to learn to take responsibility for his life and acts. Most important of all, we should not assume that having to yield to the threat of our superior force is good for the child's character. It is never good for *anyone's* character. To bow to superior force makes us feel impotent and cowardly for not having had the strength or courage to resist. Worse, it makes us resentful and vengeful. We can hardly wait to make someone pay for our humiliation, yield to us as we were once made to yield. No, if we cannot always avoid using the Discipline of Superior Force, we should at least use it as seldom as we can.

4   There are places where all three disciplines overlap. Any very demanding human activity combines in it the disciplines of Superior Force, of Culture, and of Nature. The novice will be told, "Do it this way, never mind asking why, just do it that way, that is the way we always do it." But it probably *is* just the way they always do it, and usually for the very good reason that it is a way that has been found to work. Think, for example, of ballet training. The student in a class is told to do this exercise, or that; to stand so; to do this or that with his head, arms, shoulders, abdomen, hips, legs, feet. He is constantly corrected. There is no argument. But behind these seemingly autocratic demands by the teacher lie many decades of custom and tradition, and behind that, the necessities of dancing itself. You cannot make the moves of classical ballet unless over many years you have acquired, and renewed every day, the needed strength and suppleness in scores of muscles and joints. Nor can you do the difficult motions, making them look easy, unless you have learned

hundreds of easier ones first. Dance teachers may not always agree on all the details of teaching these strengths and skills. But no novice could learn them all by himself. You could not go for a night or two to watch the ballet and then, without any other knowledge at all, teach yourself how to do it. In the same way, you would be unlikely to learn any complicated and difficult human activity without drawing heavily on the experience of those who know it better. But the point is that the authority of these experts or teachers stems from, grows out of their greater competence and experience, the fact that what they do *works*, not the fact that they happen to be the teacher and as such have the power to kick a student out of the class. And the further point is that children are always and everywhere attracted to that competence, and ready and eager to submit themselves to a discipline that grows out of it. We hear constantly that children will never do anything unless compelled to by bribes or threats. But in their private lives, or in extracurricular activities in school, in sports, music, drama, art, running a newspaper, and so on, they often submit themselves willingly and wholeheartedly to very intense disciplines, simply because they want to learn to do a given thing well. Our Little-Napoleon football coaches, of whom we have too many and hear far too much, blind us to the fact that millions of children work hard every year getting better at sports and games without coaches barking and yelling at them.

WHAT DID THE WRITER SAY AND WHAT DID YOU THINK?

1. The author neatly defines and gives examples of three kinds of discipline. Where does he follow this book's advice to acknowledge the not-so-neat complications (see p. 227)? What is the complication?
2. What is the single principle of classification?
3. Is there a thesis? If so, is it ever stated?
4. Which kind of discipline does the author like most and which kind does he like least?
5. What are the dangers of "Discipline of Superior Force"? Why is it sometimes necessary?
6. Does the author paint too cheerful a picture of the "Discipline of Nature"? What happens with the child who bends the nail, gives up, and never learns how to use a hammer? How would the author reply to these questions?
7. A parent tells a child wearing a thin T-shirt to put on a coat before the child steps outside into bitter cold weather. The child refuses. What would the author's advice be?
8. Do you think the essay as a whole diminishes or increases the importance of a teacher? Explain.

HOW DID THE WRITER SAY IT?

1. Many English instructors would probably criticize Holt for his comma splices—a frequent punctuation error of many student writers (see pp. 212–214). Find at least two of the author's comma splices.
2. The description of Nature at the end of paragraph 1 presents an unstated contrast to someone or something else: "She does not give opinions or make judgments; she cannot be wheedled, bullied, or fooled; she does not get angry or disappointed; she does not praise or blame; she does not remember past failures or hold grudges; with her one always gets a fresh start, this time is the one that counts." What is Nature being contrasted to?
3. The author has least to say about the "Discipline of Society." Would more examples have been a good idea?
4. Do the concluding observations on football coaches strike you as an effective ending or the sudden raising of a trivial side issue?

WHAT ABOUT <u>YOUR</u> WRITING?

Critics make much, as they always have, about the sounds and "music" of poetry, but generally not enough is made of the sounds of prose. All readers have an inner ear that hears what they are reading, no matter how silent outwardly the act of reading may be. And the sounds can be good or bad, pleasant or unpleasant.

Apart from the rhymes and meter of poetry, the most common musical device is probably *alliteration:* the repetition of identical sounds at the beginning of words. (Once limited to consonant sounds only, alliteration in general usage now refers to vowel sounds as well.) Holt uses alliteration effectively when he writes in paragraph 1 that Nature is "impersonal, impartial, and indifferent." The repetition of sounds is pleasing, even downright catchy, in itself. Moreover, the repetition of sounds helps to reinforce thought: The three alliterative words are all related by being qualities of nature, and the identical sounds drive home that relationship.

A few moments' consideration can turn up a host of titles and famous phrases that show the appeal of alliteration:

"Little Boy Blue"	*The Great Gatsby*
East of Eden	calm, cool, and collected
in fine fettle	*The Brady Bunch*
Sighted sub, sank same	*All Things Bright and Beautiful*

The Pride and the Passion   "Love Me or Leave Me"

Boston Bruins   dry as dust

Philadelphia Phillies   through thick and thin

wit and wisdom   *The Doctor's Dilemma*

On a humble level, Chapter 1 of this book used alliteration to describe the importance to good writing of a thesis and support of a thesis: "The Persuasive Principle." The phrase seemed more vivid and easier to remember than "The Persuasive Idea" or "The Persuasive Slant."

Like most other good things, alliteration can be abused. Beware of pouring on too many identical sounds all at once. Remember, too, that alliteration is a special stylistic touch; if your reader expects it in every sentence, it loses its impact and distracts attention from your thought. Shakespeare parodied simple-minded overindulgence in alliteration in *A Midsummer Night's Dream* as some amateur playwrights came up with these lines for "he stabbed himself":

Whereat, with blade, with bloody blameful blade,
He bravely broach'd his boiling bloody breast.

Definition

One of the most frequent impediments to clear communication is the failure to define terms. Some conversations and writings aren't just impeded by that failure: They're made incomprehensible. In isolation, a catch phrase like *power to the people,* for example, can mean anything from revolution to better electric service. Far more often, failure to define or to agree on a definition can lead to hours—and years—of futile controversy, complete with name-calling and shaking fists. Think of UN debates on *aggression.* Think of the storms in American history over terms like *free speech, due process, states' rights,* and *quotas.*

A definition essay often includes a "dictionary definition" but goes far beyond it and is best thought of as providing an *extended definition.* It discusses the meaning of words and phrases to which even the best dictionaries can't do full justice.

Dictionary definitions work in two ways, both of them short, and one of them extremely formal. First, a dictionary can define by giving a direct synonym: *liberty* means *freedom; couch* means *sofa; plate* means *dish; cry* means *weep.* Second, a dictionary can, and for many terms must, use the techniques of a formal definition: A term is placed in the class it belongs to and then is differentiated from all the other members of the same class:

Term	Class	Differentiation
convertible	a car	with a top that can be raised and lowered
widow	a woman	whose husband has died
martini	a cocktail	made with gin or vodka and dry vermouth

Dictionary definitions, to repeat, are often incorporated into an extended definition, but no definition paper will discuss a term for which a dictionary definition alone would be sufficient. Some definition papers, in fact, may have as their central point the inadequacy or impossibility of good dictionary definitions for the term under consideration. (The skilled writer, however, will almost always avoid starting off with such tired phrases as "According to the dictionary" or "Webster says that.")

What terms are promising candidates for definition papers? Here are some suggestions:

Abstract concepts: love, morality, patriotism, apathy, equality

Controversial terms: suburban sprawl, the information explosion, the "glass ceiling," police brutality, racism, pro-choice, down-sizing

Common phrases and ideas: a good movie, the ideal vacation, the perfect job

A definition paper usually turns out to be an expression of opinion, a "What Such-and-Such Means to Me" paper. A good movie for one person will have to stimulate the mind; for another person it will have to give the mind a rest. The expression of an attitude toward the term is what gives life to a definition paper and makes it more interesting to read than a dictionary. In other words, a definition paper benefits from a thesis:

An ideal vacation can mean snoozing in the backyard just as much as seeing new sights.

Creative complaining is one of humanity's best hopes for progress.

Love is a severe mental illness curable only by time.

Definition papers follow no set pattern. Most turn out to be combinations of patterns that are studied separately in other chapters of this book. Which pattern or combination of patterns is used depends on which works best, and which works best depends on what's being defined and what the writer has to say about it.

A Definition Paper Can Compare and Contrast

A term can be made clearer and more interesting by distinguishing it from similar terms: a paper on socialism might distinguish it from communism; a paper on love might distinguish it from infatuation. Discussing opposites sometimes works well, too: a definition paper on a *liberal* might take the same set of circumstances and contrast a liberal's behavior to a conservative's. These negative techniques—showing what a term is not—often lead to successful papers.

A Definition Paper Can Classify

It may be both convenient and insightful to break some terms into separate classifications. Morality, for example, could be considered in two parts: passive morality—not doing evil; and active morality—doing good.

A Definition Paper Can Give Examples

A paper defining a good movie would naturally discuss specific examples of good movies that fit the definition. Without the examples the paper would probably be abstract and dull.

A Definition Paper Can Trace a Process

A writer engaged in defining *schizophrenia* might make the illness more understandable with a step-by-step analysis of its progress from the first signs of mental aberration to its full development.

A Definition Paper Can Study Cause-and-Effect Relationships

An advocate of women's liberation, in defining the term, could make the definition fuller and more persuasive by devoting some attention to the decades of polite and impolite discrimination that helped cause the birth, or rebirth, of the women's liberation movement.

A Definition Paper Can Use Narration

Narration is the telling of a story. A paper on *competition* could show the good and the bad sides of the term in action by telling the story of the author's friendly and unfriendly rivalry with a fellow student during high school days.

WRITING SUGGESTIONS FOR DEFINITION ESSAYS

Any of the terms below lend themselves to extended definitions. Remember that definition papers are not tied down to any one writing pattern. Use whatever approach works best. (See p. 256 for other subjects.)

1. Comfort food
2. A ham actor
3. Good sportsmanship
4. Conflict of interest
5. A good teacher
6. Fad
7. Atheism
8. An intellectual
9. Courtesy
10. Worship

11. A good marriage
12. Child abuse
13. Conscience
14. The ideal college
15. A good salesperson
16. Friendship
17. Courage
18. Jealousy
19. Obscenity
20. Humanity's best friend
21. Humanity's worst enemy
22. Fear
23. Road rage
24. Frustration
25. Writer's block

GROWING UP

Anonymous (student)

Thesis: Being tested for HIV taught me how to be a grown-up.

    I.   Grown-ups and fear
        A.   Still get scared
        B.   Face the fear

   II.   Grown-ups and responsibility
        A.   Temptation to ignore it
        B.   Responsibility to others

  III.   Grown-ups and reality
        A.   Temptation to deny it
        B.   Need to accept real world

Conclusion: Although being a grown-up is difficult, we can each work to become one.

Many, many years ago, I thought that a grown-up was someone who could drive a car. But when I finally was old enough to drive, I found out that I wasn't a grown-up yet. Then, I figured that a grown-up was a person who could vote. But when I cast my first vote, I realized that I still wasn't a grown-up. A little later, I decided that a grown-up was someone who went to college. But college wasn't what helped me to become a grown-up either.

It wasn't until I decided to get tested for HIV that I learned what really made someone a grown-up. I like to think, too, that as I learned what defined a grown-up, I also became one.

I had stopped by the free clinic where a friend of mine works, and while I was waiting for her, one of the other volunteers asked me if I wanted to be tested. My immediate reaction was, "Who, me?" As I thought about it for a while, though, I realized that the only reason not to be tested would be fear—fear of testing positive, fear of facing the facts. I took a deep breath, and I got tested. Grown-ups get scared, but they don't let fear keep them from doing what they need to do.

My test results, the clinic said, wouldn't come back for ten days. Those were ten very long days. I spent a lot of time thinking about what I would do if my results were positive. Who would I tell? Could I tell anyone? Was it really my problem if I had infected anyone? Would I have to change my life, or could I just pretend it wasn't true? I wrestled with those questions and many more for days, deciding that, however awful it might be, I would have to tell my "exes" if my test was positive, and that my life would have to change drastically. I owed that to anyone I had ever loved. Besides, however unpleasant it may be, a grown-up has a sense of responsibility to other people.

The day my results came back, I thought that I might try to avoid the whole problem by just not showing up to get my results. That way, I'd be no better or worse off than I had been before the test. I could just forget about it. I could go on as I had been going. When the time came, though, I knew that I had to go find out, that I couldn't ignore reality any longer. A grown-up has to learn to accept the real world.

The medical results of my test aren't important to anyone but myself and my "exes," but the mental results are important to anyone who has ever wondered what a grown-up is. I have discovered that grown-ups face fear, have a sense of responsibility, and learn to handle realities, even the grimmest ones. That's a lot to aim for, and no one can do all that all the time. Everyone, though, can do it sometimes. Whatever your age, once you find out what it means to be a grown-up, you can always work to be one.

THE REAL THING

Frankie Germany

Writers have been trying to define love since writing began. In "The Real Thing" Frankie Germany tries to do it with one simple, or seemingly simple, narrative.

Words to check:

surreptitiously (paragraph 8)　　　　poignant (8)
eavesdropped (8)

If I know what love is, it is because of you.
Herman Hesse

1 Cecile and I have been friends since college, for more than thirty years. Although we have never lived closer than 100 miles to each other, since we first met, our friendship has remained constant. We have seen each other through marriage, birth, divorce, the death of loved ones—all those times when you really need a friend.

2 In celebration of our friendship and our fiftieth birthday, Cecile and I took our first road trip together. We drove from my home in Texas to California and back. What a wonderful time we had!

3 The first day of our trip ended in Santa Fe, New Mexico. After the long drive, we were quite tired, so we decided to go to the restaurant near the hotel for dinner. We were seated in a rather quiet part of the dining room with only a few other patrons. We ordered our food and settled back to recount our day. As we talked, I glanced at the other people in the room. I noticed an attractive elderly couple sitting a short distance away from us. The gentleman was rather tall and athletic looking, with silver hair and a tanned complexion. The lady seated beside him was petite, well-dressed, and lovely. What caught my immediate attention was the look of adoration on the woman's face. She sat, chin resting gently on her hands, and stared into the face of the man as he talked. She reminded me of a teenager in love!

4 I called Cecile's attention to the couple. As we watched, he reached over to place a gentle kiss on her cheek. She smiled.

5 "Now that's what I call real love!" I said with a sigh. "I imagine they've been married for a long time. They look so in love!"

6 "Or maybe," remarked Cecile, "they haven't been together long. It could be they've just fallen in love."

7 "Well, whatever the case, it's obvious they care a great deal for each other. They are in love."

8 Cecile and I watched surreptitiously and unashamedly eavesdropped on their conversation. He was explaining to her about a new business investment he was considering and asking her opinion. She smiled and agreed with whatever he said. When the waitress came to take their order, he ordered for her, reminding her that the veal was her favorite. He caressed her hand as he talked, and she listened raptly to his every word. We were enthralled by the poignant scene we were witnessing.

9 Then the scene changed. A perplexed look came over the finely wrinkled but beautiful face. She looked at the man and said in a sweet voice, "Do I know you? What is this place? Where are we?"

10 "Now, sweetheart, you know me. I'm Ralph, your husband. And we're in Santa Fe. We are going to see our son in Missouri tomorrow. Don't you remember?"

11   "Oh, I'm not sure. I seem to have forgotten," she said quietly.

12   "That's okay, sweetheart. You'll be all right. Just eat your dinner, and we'll go and get some rest." He reached over and caressed her cheek. "You sure do look pretty tonight."

13   Tears coursed down our cheeks as Cecile and I looked at each other. "We were right," she said quietly. "It is the real thing. That is love."

WHAT DID THE WRITER SAY AND WHAT DID YOU THINK?

1. When the author and her friend first see an elderly couple in a restaurant, they correctly assume that the two people are "in love." What incorrect assumptions do they make?
2. The essay ends with the author and her friend arriving at a fuller definition of love—"the real thing." What are the new elements of the definition?
3. Express the thesis in your own words.

HOW DID THE WRITER SAY IT?

1. Is the author's definition of love ever specifically stated?
2. Is the one extended example in this essay enough to provide a useful definition? Would more examples have been desirable?

WHAT ABOUT <u>YOUR</u> WRITING?

Go easy on exclamation points. We like the term *comic-book punctuation* to describe the pouring on of artificial aids like exclamation points, question marks, italics, and capital letters to create emphasis. Writers guilty of these practices almost always deliver their messages too loudly and sometimes betray a lack of confidence in their command of words and their readers' intelligence.

Most instructors will agree that whatever the merits of "The Real Thing" as a whole, the author is too fond of exclamation points. The truth is that in paragraph 2 "What a wonderful time we had!" is not a particularly exciting sentence, and the exclamation point doesn't make the sentence more powerful. It only lets us know the author wishes it were more powerful. We feel the same about the exclamation points in paragraphs 3 and 5. Turn down the volume by getting rid of the exclamation points, and the sentences gain in dignity and thoughtfulness.

When words themselves haven't done the job adequately, the words need to be changed. The only way to fix a lame sentence is to fix the language, not toss in a pushy exclamation point. And two exclamation points are twice as bad, not twice as good. If your intended sarcasm in a sentence hasn't come through effectively with your words, a pushy little question mark isn't going to help, either.

Comic-Book Punctuation

I had never seen anyone with such an ego! Never!!

Art?? The movie was filth!

Professor Jones was a teacher (?) in Renaissance History.

Improved

Never had I seen anyone with such an ego.

The movie was not art. It was filth.

Professor Jones was a poor Renaissance History teacher.

Don't assume that punctuation has suddenly been banned. All the resources of the language, including punctuation, are at your disposal. When a character in a novel is choking to death, nobody will object to the exclamation point in "Aaargh!" In a textbook nobody will object to the italics in a sentence like "The first principle of good writing is the *persuasive principle*." The more flashy forms of punctuation, however, require extreme caution. It's a matter of taste.

MY WAY!
Margo Kaufman

Margo Kaufman has been a newspaper columnist and written essays for periodicals such as *Newsweek*, *Cosmopolitan*, and *The Village Voice*. A collection of her essays was published with the ingenious title *1-800-Am-I-Nuts* (1993). More recently, she has written *This Damn House: My Subcontract with America* (1997) and *Clara, the Early Years: The Story of the Pug Who Ruled My Life* (1998).

Words to check:

triceps (paragraph 1)   laissez-faire (16)
hyperventilating (15)

1   Is it my imagination, or is this the age of the control freak? I'm standing in front of the triceps machine at my gym. I've just set the weights, and I'm about to begin my exercise when a lightly muscled bully in turquoise

spandex interrupts her chest presses to bark at me. "I'm using that," she growls as she leaps up from her slant board, darts over to the triceps machine, and resets the weights.

2   I'm tempted to point out that, while she may have been planning to use the machine, she was, in fact, on the opposite side of the room. And that her muscles won't atrophy if she waits for me to finish. Instead, I go work on my biceps. Life's too short to fight over a Nautilus machine. Of course, *I'm* not a control freak.

3   Control freaks will fight over anything: a parking space, the room temperature, the last pair of marked-down Maude Frizon pumps, even whether you should barbecue with the top on or off the Weber kettle. Nothing is too insignificant. Everything has to be just so.

4   Just so *they* like it. "These people compulsively have to have their own way," says Los Angeles psychologist Gary Emery. "Their egos are based on being right," Emery says, "on proving they're the boss." (And it isn't enough for the control freak to win. Others have to lose.)

5   "Control freaks are overconcerned with the means, rather than the end," Emery says. "So it's more important that the string beans are the right kind than it is to just enjoy the meal."

6   "What do you mean just enjoy the meal?" scoffs my friend Marc. "There's a right way to do things and then there's everything else." It goes without saying that he, and only he, has access to that Big Right Way in the Sky. And that Marc lives alone.

7   "I really hate to be in any situation where my control over what I'm doing is compromised," he admits. "Like if somebody says, 'I'll handle the cooking and you can shuck the corn or slice the zucchini,' I tell them to do it without me."

8   A control freak's kitchen can be his or her castle. "Let me show you the right way to make rice," said my husband the first time I made the mistake of fixing dinner. By the time Duke had sharpened the knives, rechopped the vegetables into two-inch squares, and chided me for using the wrong size pan, I had decided to surrender all control of the stove. (For the record, this wasn't a big sacrifice. I don't like to cook.)

9   "It's easier in a marriage when you both don't care about the same things," says Milton Wolpin, a psychology professor at the University of Southern California. "Otherwise, everything would be a battle."

10   And every automobile would be a battleground. There's nothing worse than having two control freaks in the same car. "I prefer to drive," my friend Claire says. "But no sooner do I pull out of the driveway than Fred starts telling me what to do. He thinks that I'm an idiot behind the wheel and that I make a lot of stupid mistakes."

11   She doesn't think he drives any better. "I think he goes really, really fast, and I'm sure that someday he's going to kill us both," she says. "And I complain about it constantly. But it's still a little easier for me to take a back seat. I'd rather get to pick him apart than get picked on."

12   My friend Katie would withstand the abuse. "I like to control everything," she says. "From where we're going to eat to what we're going to eat to what movie we're going to see, what time we're going to see it, where we're going to see it, where we're going to park. Everything!"

13   But you can't control everything. So much of life is beyond our control. And to me, that's what makes it interesting. But not to Katie. "I don't like having my fate in someone else's hands," she says firmly. "If I take charge, I know that whatever it is will get done and it will get done well."

14   I shuffle my feet guiltily. Not too long ago I invited Katie and a bunch of friends out to dinner to celebrate my birthday. It was a control freak's nightmare. Not only did I pick the restaurant and arrange to pick up the check, but Duke also called in advance and ordered an elaborate Chinese banquet. I thought Katie was going to lose her mind.

15   "What did you order? I have to know," she cried, seizing a menu. "I'm a vegetarian. There are things I won't eat." Duke assured her that he had accounted for everyone's taste. Still, Katie didn't stop hyperventilating until the food arrived. "I was very pleasantly surprised," she confesses. "And I would trust Duke again."

16   "I'm sure there are areas where you're the control freak," says Professor Wolpin, "areas where you're more concerned about things than your husband." *Me?* The champion of laissez-faire? "You get very upset if you find something visible to the naked eye on the kitchen counter," Duke reminds me. "And you think you know much better than me what the right shirt for me to wear is."

17   But I'm just particular. I'm not a control freak.

18   "A control freak is just someone who cares about something more than you do," Wolpin says.

19   So what's wrong with being a control freak?

WHAT DID THE WRITER SAY AND WHAT DID YOU THINK?

1. The essay defines control freaks, but also expresses an attitude toward them. What is that attitude?
2. Almost all the essay consists of amusing examples of control freaks from the lives of the author and her friends. Are there any sections that try to go beyond mere entertainment?
3. What significant point is made in the last sentence?

HOW DID THE WRITER SAY IT?

1. Are there enough examples to make the definition clear?
2. Are the examples drawn from a broad enough range of experience to make the essay convincing?
3. What is gained by having so many direct quotations?

WHAT ABOUT YOUR WRITING?

Unfortunately, interviews have started to get a bad name. Many people understandably associate interviews with the more sordid side of television journalism. A microphone-wielding busybody asks a mother whose three children have just died in a fire if she feels sad. A scandalmonger, already sure of the identity of the good guys and bad guys, asks prepared—and loaded—questions of a surprised public figure whose possibly honest hesitations and uncertainties are made to appear shifty evasions.

Interviews need not be that way. In addition to getting some lively comments from friends whom she interviews about her subject, Margo Kaufman in "My Way!" interviews and quotes a Los Angeles psychologist and a professor at the University of Southern California to give some sense of serious research and thoughtfulness underlying an otherwise lightweight and even frivolous essay. The interviews add some welcome depth.

You are unlikely, outside of a journalism class, to be asked to write up an entire interview, but you can sometimes use interviews to add life and authenticity to more common writing assignments. Are you planning to sound off about food in the school cafeteria? Why not start with a few real quotes from people you've spoken to? Are you thinking about a paper that suggests that tastes in sports reveal a great deal about a person's character? Why rely on a few memories? Why not ask around? Some people will tell you they don't want to be bothered, but most will probably feel mildly flattered and be eager to cooperate. Remember that for a short paper you're usually looking only for interesting tidbits and a few good lines; you're not going to write a four-part report to the nation, and many interviews may take just a minute or two. Name names and quote directly whenever you can. A little material gathered from interviews can add a strong touch of fact to an otherwise purely personal essay.

SPANGLISH

Janice Castro, with Dan Cook and Cristina Garcia

While educators and politicians debate the merits of bilingual education, people in some parts of the country seem to be moving toward a form of bilingualism all on their own. "Spanglish" defines this amusing term and provides some light-hearted examples to make its case.

Words to check:

bemused (paragraph 1)   hybrids (6)
syntax (3)   gaffes (10)

1 In Manhattan a first-grader greets her visiting grandparents, happily exclaiming, "Come here, *siéntate!*" Her bemused grandfather, who does not speak Spanish, nevertheless knows she is asking him to sit down. A Miami personnel officer understands what a job applicant means when he says, "*Quiero un part time.*" Nor do drivers miss a beat reading a billboard alongside a Los Angeles street advertising CERVEZA—SIX PACK!

2   This free-form blend of Spanish and English, known as Spanglish, is common linguistic currency wherever concentrations of Hispanic Americans are found in the U.S. In Los Angeles, where 55% of the city's 3 million inhabitants speak Spanish, Spanglish is as much a part of daily life as sunglasses. Unlike the broken-English efforts of earlier immigrants from Europe, Asia and other regions, Spanglish has become a widely accepted conversational mode used casually—even playfully—by Spanish-speaking immigrants and native-born Americans alike.

3   Consisting of one part Hispanicized English, one part Americanized Spanish and more than a little fractured syntax, Spanglish is a bit like a Robin Williams comedy routine: a crackling line of cross-cultural patter straight from the melting pot. Often it enters Anglo homes and families through the children, who pick it up at school or at play with their young Hispanic contemporaries. In other cases, it comes from watching TV; many an Anglo child watching *Sesame Street* has learned *uno dos tres* almost as quickly as one two three.

4   Spanglish takes a variety of forms, from the Southern California Anglos who bid farewell with the utterly silly "*hasta la* bye-bye" to the Cuban-American drivers in Miami who *parquean* their *carros.* Some Spanglish sentences are mostly Spanish, with a quick detour for an English word or two. A Latino friend may cut short a conversation by glancing at his watch and excusing himself with the explanation that he must "*ir al* supermarket."

5   Many of the English words transplanted in this way are simply handier than their Spanish counterparts. No matter how distasteful the subject, for example, it is still easier to say "income tax" than *impuesto sobre la renta*. At the same time, many Spanish-speaking immigrants have adopted such terms as VCR, microwave and dishwasher for what they view as largely American phenomena. Still other English words convey a cultural context that is not implicit in the Spanish. A friend who invites you to a *lonche* most likely has in mind the brisk American custom of "doing lunch" rather than the languorous afternoon break traditionally implied by *almuerzo*.

6   Mainstream Americans exposed to similar hybrids of German, Chinese or Hindi might be mystified. But even Anglos who speak little or no Spanish are somewhat familiar with Spanglish. Living among them, for one thing, are 19 million Hispanics. In addition, more American high school and university students sign up for Spanish than for any other foreign language.

7   Only in the past ten years, though, has Spanglish begun to turn into a national slang. Its popularity has grown with the explosive increases in U.S. immigration from Latin American countries. English has increasingly collided with Spanish in retail stores, offices and classrooms, in pop music and on street corners. Anglos whose ancestors picked up such Spanish words as *rancho*, *bronco*, *tornado* and *incommunicado*, for instance, now freely use such Spanish words as *gracias*, *bueno*, *amigo* and *por favor*.

8   Among Latinos, Spanglish conversations often flow more easily from Spanish into several sentences of English and back.

9   Spanglish is a sort of code for Latinos: the speakers know Spanish, but their hybrid language reflects the American culture in which they live. Many lean to shorter, clipped phrases in place of the longer, more graceful expressions their parents used. Says Leonel de la Cuesta, an assistant professor of modern languages at Florida International University in Miami: "In the U.S., time is money, and that is showing up in Spanglish as an economy of language." Conversational examples: *taipiar* (type) and *winshi-wiper* (windshield wiper) replace *escribir a máquina* and *limpiaparabrisas*.

10   Major advertisers, eager to tap the estimated $134 billion in spending power wielded by Spanish-speaking Americans, have ventured into Spanglish to promote their products. In some cases, attempts to sprinkle Spanish through commercials have produced embarrassing gaffes. A Braniff airlines ad that sought to tell Spanish-speaking audiences they could settle back *en* (in) luxuriant *cuero* (leather) seats, for example, inadvertently said they could fly without clothes *(encuero)*. A fractured translation of the Miller Lite slogan told readers the beer was "Filling, and less delicious." Similar blunders are often made by Anglos trying to impress Spanish-speaking pals. But if Latinos

are amused by mangled Spanglish, they also recognize these goofs as a sort of friendly acceptance. As they might put it, *no problema*.

WHAT DID THE WRITER SAY AND WHAT DID YOU THINK?

1. How does Spanglish differ from the "broken English efforts of earlier immigrants"?
2. Do the authors seem to approve of and like Spanglish, or are they just providing an objective report?
3. What alleged advantage does some English terminology seem to have over the equivalent Spanish terms?

HOW DID THE WRITER SAY IT?

1. Are translations provided wherever necessary?
2. Are there enough examples? Do they cover a wide range of subjects?
3. Besides examples, what rhetorical pattern is used in this essay?

WHAT ABOUT **YOUR** WRITING?

One of the difficulties of translating is that the meaning of many words is determined by *connotation* as well as denotation, the bare dictionary meaning. Connotation involves implications, vibrations, what "Spanglish" in paragraph 5 calls the "cultural context" surrounding a word. "A friend who invites you to a *lonche* most likely has in mind the brisk American custom of 'doing lunch' rather than the languorous afternoon break traditionally implied by *almuerzo*." Try to translate an Americanism like *tailgate party* into a foreign language in anything less than a 500-word essay. The meaning of the term has little or nothing to do with dictionaries and everything to do with unspoken understandings about athletic events, friendships, huge parking lots, crisp Fall days, and the joys of junk food. (Try to translate junk food!)

Now ignore translations and think only about writing effective English. Isn't choosing the word with the right connotations one of the most important tests of a good writer? The main benefit of having a large vocabulary is not that it enables you to pick the fanciest word but that it gives you more choices when looking for the right word. Don't settle automatically for the first word that comes to your mind. Look for the word with the precise connotations that gets at the meaning you're thinking of. Why settle for *laugh* when what you really mean is *giggle* or *guffaw* or *snicker*? Why settle for *cry* when what you really mean is *bawl* or *blubber* or *weep*? Why settle for *unchanged* when *stubborn* or *unyielding* or *resolute* or *firm* come closer to what you want to communicate? Connotations determine the full meanings of many words, and skillful writers pick the words with the right connotations. The process sometimes takes a bit longer, but it's always worth it.

GROSS DOMESTIC NONSENSE
Wayne Muller

Wayne Muller is best known for his inspirational books on spirituality, among them *Legacy of the Heart: The Spiritual Advantages of a Painful Childhood* (1993), *How, Then, Shall We Live* (1997), and most recently, *Sabbath: Restoring the Sacred Rhythm of Rest* (1999). In "Gross Domestic Nonsense," published in the leading financial magazine *Forbes* he examines a much-used economic term.

Words to check:

festooned (paragraph 5)	insidiously (7)	perversity (12)
commemorative (5)	quantify (11)	celebratory (12)
depreciation (6)	skepticism (12)	

1 Every Tuesday and Friday my mother leaves her house and drives to the elementary school in her Florida community. She spends her morning helping first and second-graders—some of whom cannot even spell their names—learn to read.

2 In rural New Mexico, when winter comes, Max and his son David deliver firewood to their elderly neighbors. In northern California, my friend Dale donates his time to train volunteers to serve as compassionate helpers with people who are dying.

3 These people have one thing in common—besides their impulse to help out, that is. According to the standard economic measure of our national productivity, they are useless. The gross domestic product, or GDP, rises only when people produce, buy or sell goods and services. If no money changes hands, these volunteers officially contribute nothing of value.

4 Contrast this to the economic flurry that results when two troubled teenage boys in Littleton, Colo., blow up their school, murder a dozen of their fellow students and gun down a teacher for good measure. It makes for one very happy day as far as the GDP is concerned.

5 With every massacre, police and SWAT teams must work overtime; doctors, nurses and EMTs are summoned; television crews are flown in, housed and fed; news conferences held; bullet-shattered windows removed and replaced; coffins and burial plots hastily purchased; memorials held in settings

festooned with store-bought candles, flowers and commemorative plaques. Violence is a spectacular tonic for the GDP.

6   If you ask an economist what the "gross" in GDP stands for, he will tell you something about measuring output without deducting for business depreciation. If you ask me, it stands for the grotesque way in which a materialistic society measures its worth.

7   When we receive the report card of our economic health on the radio or television, what we will not be told—but what is insidiously embedded in the numbers—is that each tragedy contributed in some way to the well-being of our national economic strength.

8   Meanwhile, when parents stay home and care for their children, when people voluntarily tend to the sick, dying, or homeless, when neighbors volunteer to visit the elderly, or teach children to sing or read, or spend the morning in prayer, or meditate, or walk in the woods—these have no value. They diminish the gross domestic product by substituting unpaid labor and time for revenue-making activities.

9   What we desperately need is a broad, comprehensive indicator—Common Wealth Index, if you will. Ideally, the figure would somehow manage to calculate the true value of our common work, and measure more thoroughly the depth and breadth of our national well-being.

10   Thoughtful economists have been proposing a variety of alternative indicators to broaden the scope of the gross domestic product to honor and reflect the value of parks, schools, volunteerism, air and water quality, literacy, civility, even solitude and sunsets.

11   If we can count pork bellies, can we count generosity, honesty and love? No, this is not an easy task, and I do not expect the accountants who work for the Department of Commerce to succeed at it. But perhaps, if we focus our collective wisdom, we will find a way to quantify our true wealth.

12   Until then, I do expect that the rest of us will take the national income statistics with a certain skepticism. It is a horrific perversity if the measure of our national wealth performs a celebratory leap every time our children and loved ones are shot down.

WHAT DID THE WRITER SAY AND WHAT DID YOU THINK?

1. Gross domestic product is defined in a well-regarded current dictionary as "the total market value of all the goods and services produced by a nation during a specified period." In general, we assume that the nation is doing well when GDP is high, poorly when it is low. Why does the author want us to feel "a certain skepticism" about GDP?

2. Does the author have any specific suggestions for measuring the impact or value of good deeds?

3. Would the solution of all our society's problems result in economic catastrophe—unemployed social workers, prison guards, psychologists, military personnel, and so on?

HOW DID THE WRITER SAY IT?

1. What meanings of the word *gross* does the author explore in paragraph 6?
2. The author suggests what he calls a "Common Wealth Index" to measure our national well-being. Can you suggest a livelier term?

WHAT ABOUT **YOUR** WRITING?

In discussing the many economic benefits that can result from tragedy, Wayne Muller makes a topical reference to the school shootings in Littleton, Colorado, an event that had occurred only a few months before this essay was published. A topical reference is one pertaining to current events, personalities, problems, culture, and so on. Topicality presents some obvious opportunities for any writer—together with some not-so-obvious dangers.

Topical references, by their very nature, are specific references, and specific writing adds to the prospects for reader interest. Moreover, any writer may want to strike readers as being well informed and up-to-date. Muller's original readers, certainly, will have had vivid memories of the invasion of journalists, psychologists, and other ghouls to whom he refers. Topical references, too, may be more readily understood than more obscure references and allusions (see pp. 73–74). Your reference to a current hit song, a television show, a politician, a sports figure, a trial can enliven your writing and impress your audience.

While topicality, then, can help your writing from time to time, remember that it has its dangers. It can give a bogus contemporary feel that distracts a reader's attention from the real subject. It can date the essay and the ideas—sometime overnight. Let a few years go by and the horrendous problems of violence in our schools may be so much alleviated that Littleton seems like ancient history or so much intensified that Littleton, sad to say, seems more a mishap than a catastrophe. Topical references are tricky. Tastes in music change; television shows are cancelled; politicians retire or get defeated; athletes become newscasters. Today's recognition becomes tomorrow's puzzled stare. Today's fad becomes tomorrow's footnote. Don't be afraid of topical references, but do be careful.

THE HANDICAP OF DEFINITION
William Raspberry

A nationally syndicated columnist associated with the *Washington Post*, a professor at Duke University, and a Pulitzer Prize winning journalist, William Raspberry convincingly demonstrates that definitions do not merely take up space in dictionaries but affect our daily lives in countless crucial ways. As you read, note how important examples are for interest and clarity.

Words to check:

deprivation (paragraph 1)   quintessentially (9)
scrimping (5)   elocution (10)
academia (6)   prowess (13)

1   I know all about bad schools, mean politicians, economic deprivation and racism. Still, it occurs to me that one of the heaviest burdens black Americans—and black children in particular—have to bear is the handicap of definition: the question of what it means to be black.

2   Let me explain quickly what I mean. If a basketball fan says that the Boston Celtics' Larry Bird plays "black," the fan intends it—and Bird probably accepts it—as a compliment. Tell pop singer Tom Jones he moves "black" and he might grin in appreciation. Say to Teena Marie or The Average White Band that they sound "black" and they'll thank you.

3   But name one pursuit, aside from athletics, entertainment or sexual performance in which a white practitioner will feel complimented to be told he does it "black." Tell a white broadcaster he talks "black," and he'll sign up for diction lessons. Tell a white reporter he writes "black," and he'll take a writing course. Tell a white lawyer he reasons "black" and he might sue you for slander.

4   What we have here is a tragically limited definition of blackness, and it isn't only white people who buy it.

5   Think of all the ways black children can put one another down with charges of "whiteness." For many of these children, hard study and hard work are "white." Trying to please a teacher might be criticized as acting "white." Speaking correct English is "white." Scrimping today in the interest of tomorrow's goals is "white." Educational toys and games are "white."

6   An incredible array of habits and attitudes that are conducive to success in business, in academia, in the non-entertainment professions are likely to be thought of as somehow "white." Even economic success, unless it involves such "black" undertakings as numbers banking, is defined as "white."

7   And the results are devastating. I wouldn't deny that blacks often are better entertainers and athletes. My point is the harm that comes from too narrow a definition of what is black.

8   One reason black youngsters tend to do better at basketball, for instance, is that they assume they can learn to do it well, and so they practice constantly to prove themselves right.

9   Wouldn't it be wonderful if we would infect black children with the notion that excellence in math is "black" rather than white, or possibly Chinese? Wouldn't it be of enormous value if we could create the myth that morality, strong families, determination, courage and love of learning are traits brought by slaves from Mother Africa and therefore quintessentially black?

10   There is no doubt in my mind that most black youngsters could develop their mathematical reasoning, their elocution and their attitudes the way they develop their jump shots and their dance steps: by the combination of sustained, enthusiastic practice and the unquestioned belief that they can do it.

11   In one sense, what I am talking about is the importance of developing positive ethnic traditions. Maybe Jews have an innate talent for communication; maybe the Chinese are born with a gift for mathematical reasoning; maybe blacks are naturally blessed with athletic grace. I doubt it. What is at work, I suspect, is the assumption, inculcated early in their lives, that this is a thing our people do well.

12   Unfortunately, many of the things about which blacks make this assumption are things that do not contribute to their career success—except for that handful of the truly gifted who can make it as entertainers and athletes. And many of the things we concede to whites are the things that are essential to economic security.

13   So it is with a number of assumptions black youngsters make about what it is to be a "man": physical aggressiveness, sexual prowess, the refusal to submit to authority. The prisons are full of people who, by this perverted definition, are unmistakably men.

14   But the real problem is not so much that the things defined as "black" are negative. The problem is that the definition is much too narrow.

15   Somehow, we have to make our children understand that they are intelligent, competent people, capable of doing whatever they put their minds to and making it in the American mainstream, not just in a black subculture.

16   What we seem to be doing, instead, is raising up yet another generation of young blacks who will be failures—by definition.

WHAT DID THE WRITER SAY AND WHAT DID YOU THINK?

1. What qualities are commonly used to define "black," according to Raspberry? Are only white people guilty of using this definition?
2. What are the bad results of the acceptance of this definition?
3. How do some black children define "white," according to Raspberry?

4. Raspberry also criticizes the "assumptions black youngsters make about what it is to be a 'man.'" What problems are created by faulty definitions of "man"?
5. The essay ends on a pessimistic note. Is the pessimism unrelieved, or does the author see any hope?

HOW DID THE WRITER SAY IT?

1. Raspberry does not believe that bad definitions are the only problems black people face. Where does he make this clear?
2. Where is the thesis expressed most directly?

WHAT ABOUT <u>YOUR</u> WRITING?

Note how many words of qualification and caution are spread through the Raspberry essay. The author is dealing with difficult and controversial material, and he has no desire to pretend that he is God. He needs to demonstrate his awareness that he is often dealing with matters of speculation, not scientific and mathematical truths. He can't prove many of his points in any rigid way; he can only make them seem plausible. The persuasive power of the essay depends in part on whether Raspberry strikes the reader as reliable, a sensible person studying complex phenomena and trying to draw reasonable inferences from them. A by-no-means-complete list of qualifying words and phrases in "The Handicap of Definition" would include those in paragraphs 5 and 6: "many of these children"—not *most* or *all*; "might be criticized"—not *is criticized*; "likely to be thought of"—not *is always thought of.* Look at the use of *maybe* and *I suspect* in paragraph 11. Raspberry establishes a tone of reason; more, he establishes himself as a person of reason, a person with a fitting hesitation about insisting on the absolute truth of his own ideas. Words and phrases of caution and qualification can help any writer establish himself or herself as a trustworthy person.

Don't go overboard. Don't write *in my opinion* in every other sentence. Don't confuse being reasonable with being timid. Don't write cowardly nonsense like *I think that George Washington played an important part in the American Revolution* or *It seems to me that heroin is a dangerous drug.* Present the strongest case you can as strongly as you can. Raspberry goes all out in presenting his case, too, once he's laid the foundation. The foundations are important, however, and the wise writer will not neglect them.

Argumentation

In this chapter, argumentation does not refer to fighting or bickering. It refers to providing logical reasons in support of a particular point of view. In that sense, this whole book has been about argumentation. It has urged you from the start to form a thesis and devote your primary energies to proving or supporting it.

The readings in argumentation in this chapter have two outstanding characteristics. First, they employ no particular pattern of development consistently; a paragraph that describes may be followed by a paragraph that compares and contrasts and another that explores cause-and-effect relationships. To that extent, the readings here can be viewed simply as readings that refuse to fit neatly into one of the patterns dealt with in previous chapters. This mixture of patterns is a healthy antidote to excessive rigidity of thought; not all subjects lend themselves to only one pattern, and in such cases it's as absurd to write in only one pattern as it would be to play a round of golf with only one club.

The second characteristic of these readings in argumentation is that they rely, to a far greater extent than any others studied so far, on the techniques of formal logic. Formal logic generally combines two ways of thinking: induction and deduction.

Induction is the process of arriving at general conclusions by studying individual cases. All the cats we have seen or read about have whiskers. As far as we can determine, all the cats our friends and acquaintances have seen or read about also have whiskers. We therefore conclude that all cats have whiskers. We haven't come close to surveying all the cats in the world, and to reach our conclusion we must make an *inductive leap*. We work on the unproven assumption that what is true of some or many is true of all. Induction is often the only possible way to approach certain subjects, and it can be extremely convincing. Ultimately, however, the final step in the inductive process must be a leap, an intelligent guess, not proof in the strictest sense of the word.

Doctors use induction when, seeing a child with a fever and a particular kind of rash, they conclude that the child has chicken pox, since all the other children the doctors have known with those symptoms have turned out to have chicken pox. (The same symptoms could be those of an obscure tropical disease—just as some cats somewhere may have no whiskers—but the doctors are justified in making their inductive leap.) Customers in a supermarket use induction when they decide no longer to buy milk there. The three most recent times they bought milk it was sour, and by induction they conclude that milk supplies in that store are likely to be of poor quality. Readers use induction when, having been bored by three of a novelist's books, they conclude that the novelist is a boring writer.

Skillful induction is mostly a matter of seeing to it that conclusions about a group are drawn only from a study of well-chosen members of that group. Chapter 4 on examples discusses this issue in detail (pp. 100–101).

Deduction is the process of arriving at a conclusion by starting with a general premise or assumption instead of with a specific instance. The primary tool in deductive reasoning is the *syllogism*, a three-part argument consisting of two premises and a conclusion:

All Rembrandt paintings are great works of art.

The Night Watch is a Rembrandt painting.

Therefore, *The Night Watch* is a great work of art.

All doctors are quacks.

Smith is a doctor.

Therefore, Smith is a quack.

The syllogism is a tool for analyzing the validity of an argument. You'll rarely find a formal syllogism outside of textbooks on logic. Mostly, you'll find *enthymemes*, abbreviated syllogisms with one or more of the parts unstated:

The Night Watch is by Rembrandt, isn't it? And Rembrandt is a great painter, isn't he?

Look, Smith is a doctor. He must be a quack.

Translating such statements into a syllogism enables the logic to be examined more coolly and clearly than it otherwise could be. If both premises in a syllogism are true and the reasoning process from one part of the syllogism to the other is valid, the conclusions will be proven. No leap or intelligent guess will be required; the conclusion will be inescapable.

Few arguments worth going into, of course, are open-and-shut cases. The premises are often debatable, to mention just one possible source of difficulty. (*Are* all doctors quacks? Didn't Rembrandt ever have *any* off days?) Argumentation, therefore, usually combines deduction and induction. A deductive argument, for example, will often have to call upon induction to establish the soundness of its premises. A reader has been bored by three books a particular novelist has written and inductively arrives at a conclusion about that novelist's work. That inductive conclusion can now serve, in turn, as the first premise of a syllogism:

Books by Marcel Proust are likely to bore me.
Swann's Way is a book by Marcel Proust.
Therefore, *Swann's Way* is likely to bore me.

In addition to relying on formal logic, good argumentation, though it usually does not limit itself to one special rhetorical pattern, usually does require a special pattern of manners. The readers have not yet, in theory, made up their minds and need to be convinced not only that the writer's argument is logical but also that the writer is a reasonable, fair-minded person.

Go Easy on Universals–Qualify When Appropriate

Reasonable people can disagree. Logic beats chaos any day, but logic cannot create total uniformity of opinions. Be moderate with sweeping generalizations that use—or imply—terms like *all, every, always, never, nobody*. Qualifying terms like *usually, often, perhaps, it seems likely, probably, seldom, rarely, almost* can be helpful in establishing a climate of reason, a sense that the writer is fully aware of the complexities and ambiguities of human experience. Don't assume from these comments that you should not express strongly held views in a strong way or that obvious truths should be expressed with mealymouthed hypocrisy. Assume only that most writers are sometimes tempted to be carried away by enthusiasm for their own ideas into making gross overstatements—and the good writer successfully resists the temptation.

Give Consideration to Differing Opinions

After starting with a cool, impartial presentation of the issue and your way of dealing with it, present any opposition to your ideas fairly. Sometimes you may even wish to begin by outlining your opponents' point of view. Refute the opposition when you can. When you can't, concede that the opposition has a good point. Argumentation that shows awareness of only one viewpoint will rarely gain a reader's respect.

Be Cautious with Abuse and Ridicule

You may consider some of the opposition's arguments foolish or even dangerous. Moreover, one of the hazards built into any piece of argumentation is that it may commit itself so completely to the precision of logic that it reads as if it were written by a computer instead of by a human being. Though there's no law against introducing humor or even passion into argumentation, be careful that such elements do not sabotage the essential logical strengths of your paper. Be particularly careful that any irresistible abuse or ridicule is directed against the ideas of your opponents, not the opponents themselves.

Devote Most of Your Attention Toward Supporting Your View, Not Advocating It

You're trying to show that your opinion is logical. You're not trying, except in a minor way, to preach or to inspire. The introduction and conclusion will express your basic opinion. By and large, the rest of the paper will discuss your reasons for holding that opinion or for disagreeing with arguments against it.

Some Common Logical Fallacies

Very briefly, here are some of the most common logical fallacies. Good argumentation depends on sound logic, and it may be valuable to have a handy guide to possible pitfalls.

- *Hasty Generalization.* Not enough examples or untypical examples. (See pp. 100–101.)
- *Post Hoc, Ergo Propter Hoc.* "After this, therefore because of this." For further discussion, see page 194–195.

    I failed the test after I walked under the ladder; therefore I failed the test because I walked under the ladder.

- *Either/Or.* A writer presents a case as if there were only two alternatives and tries to force the reader to choose between them. Life usually offers more options than that:

    Either you're for me or against me.

    Either we abolish automobiles or we destroy our planet through pollution.

- *Non Sequitur.* "It does not follow"—often the result of omitting a necessary step in the thought process or of taking wild emotional flights in which no thought process ever existed:

  I despise Professor Jones; so I'm never going to read another book as long as I live.

  We all want to abolish war and poverty and racism. How could we possibly care who wins the football game?

- *Ignoring the Question.* Instead of dealing with the topic under discussion, the writer or speaker becomes unintentionally sidetracked or deliberately creates a diversion. The question can be ignored in a number of ways. Among them are:

  —*"Ad Hominem" Argument.* Arguing "to the man," attacking the person who raised the issue rather than dealing with the issue itself:

  How dare Senator Arnold advocate population control when she herself has six children?

  Senator Arnold's failure to practice what she preaches has nothing to do with the merits of population control.

  —*Setting Up a Straw Man.* Accusing one's opponents of saying something they never said or intended to say and then attacking them for saying it:

  You allege this movie has too much sex and violence, but people like you who want censorship are a menace to the basic constitutional rights of free American citizens.

  —*Question Begging.* Assuming the truth of a debatable point and basing the rest of the argument on that shaky assumption:

  What prison sentence shall be given those who have systematically concealed the truth about alien invasions of our planet?

  Before deciding on prison terms, the writer must first offer convincing evidence that there *have* been invasions and cover-ups.

  —*Shifting the Burden of Proof.* As in law, "He who asserts must prove." It is not logical argument to declare:

  I believe the government is run by secret foreign agents, and nobody can prove that I'm wrong.

- *Argument by Analogy.* An analogy is an extended comparison. It can be valuable in clarifying a difficult point or dramatizing an abstract idea. *It can never prove anything.* No matter how many suggestive similarities there may be, they can never be more than suggestive since there must also be differences.

—Analogy Used to Clarify or Dramatize.

> Finding a cure for cancer is much like finding a cure for inflation. The exact causes of the diseases are shrouded in mystery; medication carries the risk of unpredictable side effects, but without medication the illnesses grow beyond control; cures are increasingly difficult the longer they are delayed; and the experts always—but always—disagree.

—Invalid Argument by Analogy: Analogy Used to Prove.

> The Chairman has been unjustly criticized in this country for executing his political opponents in order to create a better society. Surely, one of the oldest truths is that you can't make an omelet without breaking a few eggs. It's too bad the beautiful shells have to be cracked open. There's a terrible mess for a little while. But the final result is well worth the effort, and only fools would waste tears over the sad fate of the poor little eggs. The Chairman has the right recipe for a greater tomorrow, and those who don't understand his techniques should stay out of the kitchen.

The second analogy assumes that a few similarities between breaking eggs and killing political opponents mean that the two actions are alike in all other respects. The writer thus attempts to prove that because one action is justified the other must be justified, too. Argument by analogy ignores all differences. Here, for example, nonhuman things are being compared to humans, nonliving things to living, breaking to killing, and so forth.

- **Faultily Constructed Syllogisms.**

    —Introduction of a New Term in the Conclusion. The two terms in the conclusion must have appeared previously in the premises. Note how the following syllogism introduces a new term in the conclusion and destroys all pretense at logic:

    All teachers are cruel.
    Mr. Jones is a teacher.
    Therefore, Mr. Jones should be fired.

    —Reasoning from Negative Premises. Two negative premises can never lead to any valid conclusion.

    No human being is free from prejudice.
    Fido is not a human being.
    Therefore . . .

    —Shift in Meaning of a Term. Some syllogisms are rendered invalid because a word has changed in meaning from one part of the syllogism to another:

Indian leaders live in India.

Sitting Bull is an Indian leader.

Therefore, Sitting Bull lives in India.

In the first premise *Indian leaders* referred to leaders of the nation in Asia. In the second premise, the same term shifted meaning and referred to a leader of Native Americans.

—*Improper Relationship between Terms.* A well-constructed syllogism establishes relationships that make a particular conclusion inevitable. The following syllogism does not:

Sexists refuse to hire women.

Jones refuses to hire women.

Therefore, Jones is a sexist.

The first premise does not establish that sexists are the *only* ones who refuse to hire women. Jones could theoretically be an ardent supporter of women's rights but be under strict orders—orders he despises—to hire only men. He could be the manager of a men's professional basketball team. Jones could also be the name of a six-week-old puppy. *All* syllogisms constructed with the same relationship between terms as this one will be logically invalid. Even if the conclusion is "true," it will be true by accident, not by logic. (Jones *could* be a sexist, after all.)

Politicians are corrupt.

Simmons is corrupt.

Therefore, Simmons is a politician.

Baptists are not Methodists.

She is not a Methodist.

Therefore, she is a Baptist.

WRITING SUGGESTIONS FOR ARGUMENTATION ESSAYS

Employing the techniques of formal argumentation, attack or defend one of the numbered statements below.

1. American drivers will never renounce their cars for mass transit systems.
2. The celibacy requirement for the Roman Catholic priesthood should be eliminated.
3. Most people get married (*or divorced*) for foolish reasons.
4. The world's worst bore is _____.
5. Parents who try to impose their values on young people are the only ones young people respect.

6. The *F* grade should be abolished.
7. The greatest baseball (*or other sport*) player of all time is _____ .
8. Elderly people should be required to take road tests before having their driving licenses renewed.
9. The greatest holiday of all is _____ .
10. Life is a constant process of discovering that older people have been idiots.
11. The worst show on television is _____ .
12. Required English courses should be abolished.
13. Students should have a voice in the hiring and firing of teachers.
14. Married couples should not be allowed to have more than two children.
15. Renting an apartment makes better financial sense than buying a house.
16. Cats make better pets than dogs.
17. The manufacture of cigarettes should be prohibited.
18. Automatic advancement to the next grade level must be eliminated from our schools.

SING IT WHEN IT COUNTS

Ben Ruggiero (student)

Thesis: "The Star-Spangled Banner" should not be sung before athletic events.

    I. No logical connection between patriotism and athletes.

    II. No logical connection between patriotism and audience.

    III. Refutation of "Part of the Spectacle" argument.
        A. National anthem is too important
        B. Other music makes more sense

Conclusion: We should restore dignity to the singing of the national anthem.

I'd like to have the singing of our national anthem saved for patriotic occasions and other serious ceremonies. I think it's stupid and offensive to sing it before athletic events.

    To prevent misunderstanding, let me state right away that I love and respect our national anthem. Some people complain that it's impossible to sing. Some say the words are old-fashioned and hard to understand. Some insist that it could easily be replaced by patriotic songs with better tunes. They may be right, or partly right, but what does that have to do with love? My parents are old-fashioned and hard to understand, too, but I have no intention of trading them in. My point is that I love and respect "The Star-Spangled Banner" so much—as I know millions of others do—that I want the travesty of singing it at so many unsuitable times to stop.

What is the possible connection between patriotic pride and two boxers trying to beat each other up? The question answers itself. The more a boxer thinks about "the rockets' red glare," the more likely he is to have his lights put out by his opponent. Why pretend otherwise? Do we seriously expect—or even want—two teams of competing millionaires on the gridiron or ballpark or basketball court or hockey rink to be thinking about an old war instead of a current game? I have nothing against the athletes. They're out there to play, not to show off their patriotism, however real it may be. If their minds are on higher things instead of on using their physical skills to win the game, they are playing under false pretenses.

Well, some people may suggest, perhaps the music is for the crowd rather than the players. But check out the crowd. How often have you seen anyone accept the invitation to "join in singing" our national anthem? The last time I looked, I doubt if one in a hundred even bothered to move his or her lips, much less actually sing. How many stand at anything even approaching attention? These members of the crowd are not expressing disrespect for their country, in my opinion. They just sense the complete absence of any connection between love of country and attending a ball game. They recognize a sham, a pointless ritual, when they see one—or hear one.

I suppose it's possible to argue that the playing of the national anthem isn't directly about patriotic feelings. It's part of the entertainment, part of the spectacle. I'd reply, first, that if that's true, it's exactly what's wrong. The last thing our national anthem should be is entertainment. It should be special, should compel attention and respect. Second, if you want entertaining music of some kind to add to the occasion, let's face the realities of the event. The event is not held to glorify America but to see if the team of one city, state, or region is better than another's. We already have plenty of good music for that. College fight songs work fine, for example. If spectacle and entertainment are what we want, when the Jets play the Chiefs in football we can have the band strike up with "The Sidewalks of New York" and "Everything's Up to Date in Kansas City." When the Atlanta Braves play the Chicago Cubs we can cheer to the strains of "Georgia on My Mind" and "My Kind of Town."

One serious exception to what I've been advocating occurs to me. I'll readily grant that playing the national anthem is appropriate when the service academies compete each other. Participants in those games are planning careers in which they will put their lives at risk for their country, and the music is much more than an empty formality to them.

I say let's restore some importance and dignity to the playing and singing of our national anthem. A presidential inauguration. Visits from foreign heads of state. Military parades. A veteran's funeral. People will stand at attention without being asked, and they'll sing the words, too, even if they get some of them wrong. Our national anthem should be saved for special occasions and be a source of pride, not a meaningless ritual.

THANKSGIVING'S NO TURKEY

Robert W. Gardner

Robert W. Gardner, a communications executive in Washington, DC, uses humor as well as logic to glorify one great American tradition and to denigrate another. The subject may be a matter of taste in more ways than one.

Words to check:

redemption (paragraph 2)   decamped (10)

1 I have never had to return a Thanksgiving gift. Of course not, you say, there are no Thanksgiving gifts. Exactly. That's just one reason I vastly prefer the coming celebration of turkey to its neighbor just down the calendar, Christmas.

2   Don't get me wrong. I love Christmas. The joy of anticipation in little children. The warmth of gathered families. The promise of redemption and salvation embodied in the religious celebration. I just can't stand what we've done to Christmas. The traffic at the malls. The chaos. The pressure. The endless advertising urging us to give, to spend, to buy happiness. The bills.

3   Thanksgiving is so easy. When was the last time you saw a neighbor standing in the snow trying to string Thanksgiving lights around his house? Do people shell out sixty-five bucks for a dead Thanksgiving tree for their family room? Do they sit hour after hour, addressing Thanksgiving cards they bought on sale back in May? Who, late on Thanksgiving Eve, will be driven to thoughts of suicide, murder or at least divorce upon reading the words "some assembly required"?

4   Thanksgiving is more like an old friend come to visit. There's a knock on the door, you greet each other warmly, and soon it seems you've never been apart. Here are the complete instructions for a Happy Thanksgiving: Roast a turkey, make way too much other food, and top it off with one of three or four approved desserts. You can watch a little football, or not. Take a walk. Loaf. Whatever. No one expects you to decorate the house, make a killer table centerpiece, invite the president's entire cabinet to your cocktail party, or stroll the neighborhood singing Thanksgiving carols.

5   At work, no one gets looped at the office Thanksgiving party or chases the secretaries into the storage rooms. Working couples don't have to wrestle with which party to attend (and which boss to offend) if their office wingdings are on the same day.

6   Christmas can come any day of the week, and does. Thanksgiving is always on Thursday. Most folks get Friday off. A four day weekend every year! No other holiday can make this offer.

7   Thanksgiving is budget-friendly. If you are invited out, bring the hosts a bottle of wine or a nice dessert. That's it. No gifts you can't afford. No endless worrying about what so-and-so got you last year or whether Grandma really wants another a) robe, b) toaster, or c) bottle of cologne.

8   There's the story one son told of giving his dad a bottle of Old Spice aftershave every year for 30-plus years, only to find half of them, unused, in a dresser drawer after his dad passed away. True story.

9   Why do you think retail chains have fiscal years that end Jan. 31? Because they do half or more of their annual sales in the days before Christmas. And who do you think buys all that stuff? You and me. Know anyone who went into debt counseling after a pre-Thanksgiving buying binge? Me neither.

10   Despite these clear advantages, Thanksgiving gets no respect. Oh sure, the kids bring home a picture they drew of the pilgrims or a one-eyed turkey. But everyone understands these are just warmups for the major Christmas art push about to follow. Thanksgiving was once the kick-off for the Christmas buying season, but even that distinction has decamped for a spot nearer to Halloween. The Thanksgiving parades can't hold a candle to the ones on Jan. 1. It's tough going for Turkey Day. So what should we do with Thanksgiving?

11   I think we should celebrate Thanksgiving as the last holiday that hasn't been taken away from us. No cute bunny. No speeches celebrating democracy. No collection of seven nearby presidential birthdays. No pressure to make this a "Thanksgiving to remember." Just four days off and one really good meal. And no kids waking you at 5 A.M. to see if some turkey's come down the chimney.

WHAT DID THE WRITER SAY AND WHAT DID YOU THINK?

1. Why are Thanksgiving and Christmas presented as rivals? Would it be as effective to write an essay on Thanksgiving versus the Fourth of July?
2. Does the author's argument rely primarily on induction or deduction? Explain.
3. Many of the author's reasons for preferring Thanksgiving to Christmas can be expressed in the sentence "Thanksgiving is so easy" (paragraph 3). Explain. Elsewhere (paragraph 11) Gardner refers to Thanksgiving as "the last holiday that hasn't been taken away from us." Explain.
4. Some readers may think that many of the author's observations about Christmas violate this book's warning to "be cautious with abuse and ridicule" (p. 278). Other readers may feel personally offended by the many apparent put-downs of Christmas. Where does the author take steps to soothe the feelings of such readers?

HOW DID THE WRITER SAY IT?

1. This book's discussion of argumentation essays noted that they "employ no particular pattern of development consistently" (p. 275). Still, "Thanksgiving's No Turkey" uses one pattern far more than any other. Which pattern?
2. How is the story in paragraph 8 about aftershave gifts relevant to the rest of the essay?
3. Explain the double meaning of "turkey" in the last sentence.

WHAT ABOUT YOUR WRITING?

Often, the most difficult part of writing an essay is trying to decide on a topic. An inexperienced writer can spend hours looking for a topic which engages his or her strongest beliefs and fiercest passions. Writers like Robert W. Gardner, however, know that sometimes the best essays come from taking a stand even when you don't really have one. Gardner, for example, probably realizes that the issue of Thanksgiving versus Christmas isn't a case of good versus evil, purity versus corruption, and the forces of light versus the forces of darkness. However, you certainly can't tell that from reading his essay.

Gardner has taken a firm stand on an issue just for the fun of it, just for the sake of producing an entertaining and original essay. He could just as easily have written an essay proving that Christmas was far better than Thanksgiving, or that cats are superior to dogs, that day is better than night, linguine better than macaroni, up better than down, or purple preferable to pink. None of these are terribly serious essay topics. None of them occupy the thoughts and emotions of the deepest thinkers. But they could all make interesting essays to write and to read.

While choosing to write an essay in support of something you don't really believe in and may not really care about might sound hypocritical, it is actually very good mental exercise. Debating teams, law students, and successful politicians know that it's good practice to try to structure logical and convincing arguments about seemingly outlandish topics. If you can learn to convince a reader that dark chocolate is superior to milk chocolate, you have learned the necessary techniques to convince them that the tax plan you are presenting is better than the one your opponent has suggested.

The next time you have a writing assignment, rather than spending hours trying to find a deep and important subject for your essay, why not see if you can convince your instructor that beagles are better than dachshunds, or that bowties look better than neckties? You might just find that you end up writing a livelier and more effective essay than when you take on weightier subjects.

WHAT'S WRONG WITH BLACK ENGLISH?

Rachel L. Jones

Rachel L. Jones wrote this essay for *Newsweek* magazine in 1982 when she was a student at Southern Illinois University. Ms. Jones has written for *The Chicago Reporter* and is now a feature writer for the *Detroit Free Press*. Her frequently anthologized essay is one of the important documents in the on-going debate over black English.

Words to check:

patois (paragraph 1)   doggedly (4)   rabid (5)

1   William Labov, a noted linguist, once said about the use of black English, "It is the goal of most black Americans to acquire full control of the standard language without giving up their own culture." He also suggested that there are certain advantages to having two ways to express one's feelings. I wonder if the good doctor might also consider the goals of those black Americans who have full control of standard English but who are every now and then troubled by that colorful, grammar-to-the-winds patois that is black English. Case in point—me.

2   I'm a 21-year-old black born to a family that would probably be considered lower-middle class—which in my mind is a polite way of describing a condition only slightly better than poverty. Let's just say we rarely if ever did the winter-vacation thing in the Caribbean. I've often had to defend my humble beginnings to a most unlikely group of people for an even less likely reason. Because of the way I talk, some of my black peers look at me sideways and ask, "Why do you talk like you're white?"

3   The first time it happened to me I was nine years old. Cornered in the school bathroom by the class bully and her sidekick, I was offered the opportunity to swallow a few of my teeth unless I satisfactorily explained why I always got good grades, why I talked "proper" or "white." I had no ready answer for her, save the fact that my mother had from the time I was old enough to talk stressed the importance of reading and learning, or that L. Frank Baum and Ray Bradbury were my closest companions. I read all my older brothers'

and sisters' literature textbooks more faithfully than they did, and even light-weights like the Bobbsey Twins and Trixie Belden were allowed into my bookish inner circle. I don't remember exactly what I told those girls, but I somehow talked my way out of a beating.

4   I was reminded once again of my "white pipes" problem while apartment hunting in Evanston, Illinois, last winter. I doggedly made out lists of available places and called all around. I would immediately be invited over—and immediately turned down. The thinly concealed looks of shock when the front door opened clued me in, along with the flustered instances of "just getting off the phone with the girl who was ahead of you and she wants the rooms." When I finally found a place to live, my roommate stirred up old memories when she remarked a few months later, "You know, I was surprised when I first saw you. You sounded white over the phone." Tell me another one, sister.

5   I should've asked her a question I've wanted an answer to for years: how does one "talk white"? The silly side of me pictures a rabid white foam spewing forth when I speak. I don't use Valley Girl jargon, so that's not what's meant in my case. Actually, I've pretty much deduced what people mean when they say that to me, and the implications are really frightening.

6   It means that I'm articulate and well-versed. It means that I can talk as freely about John Steinbeck as I can about Rick James. It means that "ain't" and "he be" are not staples of my vocabulary and are only used around family and friends. (It is almost Jekyll and Hyde-ish the way I can slip out of academic abstractions into a long, lean, double-negative-filled dialogue, but I've come to terms with that aspect of my personality.) As a child, I found it hard to believe that's what people meant by "talking proper"; that would've meant that good grades and standard English were equated with white skin, and that went against everything I'd ever been taught. Running into the same type of mentality as an adult has confirmed the depressing reality that for many blacks, standard English is not only unfamiliar, it is socially unacceptable.

7   James Baldwin once defended black English by saying it had added "vitality to the language," and even went so far as to label it a language in its own right, saying, "Language [i.e., black English] is a political instrument" and a "vivid and crucial key to identity." But did Malcolm X urge blacks to take power in this country "any way y'all can"? Did Martin Luther King Jr. say to blacks, "I has been to the mountaintop, and I done seed the Promised Land"? Toni Morrison, Alice Walker and James Baldwin did not achieve their eloquence, grace and stature by using only black English in their writing. Andrew Young, Tom Bradley and Barbara Jordan did not acquire political power by saying, "Y'all crazy if you ain't gon vote for me." They all have full command

of standard English, and I don't think that knowledge takes away from their blackness or commitment to black people.

8   I know from experience that it's important for black people, stripped of culture and heritage, to have something they can point to and say, "This is ours, we can comprehend it, *we* alone can speak it with a soulful flourish." I'd be lying if I said that the rhythms of my people caught up in "some serious rap" don't sound natural and right to me sometimes. But how heartwarming is it for those same brothers when they hit the pavement searching for employment? Studies have proven that the use of ethnic dialects decreases power in the marketplace. "I be" is acceptable on the corner, but not with the boss.

9   Am I letting capitalistic, European-oriented thinking fog the issue? Am I selling out blacks to an ideal of assimilating, being as much like white as possible? I have not formed a personal political ideology, but I do know this: it hurts me to hear black children use black English, knowing that they will be at yet another disadvantage in an educational system already full of stumbling blocks. It hurts me to sit in lecture halls and hear fellow black students complain that the professor "be tripping dem out using big words dey can't understand." And what hurts most is to be stripped of my own blackness simply because I know my way around the English language.

10   I would have to disagree with Labov in one respect. My goal is not so much to acquire full control of both standard and black English, but to one day see more black people less dependent on a dialect that excludes them from full participation in the world we live in. I don't think I talk white, I think I talk right.

WHAT DID THE WRITER SAY AND WHAT DID YOU THINK?

1. What is the thesis?
2. What specific problems has the author experienced because of her "white pipes"?
3. What problems does the author see black English causing for other blacks?
4. Does the author see any value to black English?

HOW DID THE WRITER SAY IT?

1. What is the significance of the story about searching for an apartment?
2. Why does the author quote James Baldwin directly instead of merely summarizing his statements?
3. Explain the rhyming last sentence.

WHAT ABOUT <u>YOUR</u> WRITING?

Aware that her support of standard English is likely to arouse hostility, Rachel L. Jones tries to turn the tables on her opponents by showing that they support standard English, too. If James Baldwin thinks black English is so fine, how come he is such a master of standard English and shows that mastery in everything he writes? Different readers will assess the validity of Jones's argument differently. As writing strategy, though, her approach can lead to interesting and effective papers.

Anticipate the strongest argument of your opponents, and try to turn it against them. If they contend that your stand against a new highway is holding back progress, show how they are holding back progress in mass transit systems, ecology, and so forth. If they maintain that grades in school are artificial and should be abolished, try to show that nothing is more artificial than an environment in which good work is not rewarded and bad work is not penalized. These approaches won't prove in themselves that your own position is correct, but they put your opponents on the defensive, and that's where you want them to be.

THE SMILEY-FACE APPROACH
Albert Shanker

Albert Shanker (1928–1997) was president of the American Federation of Teachers. The reading selection is from "Where We Stand," a long-running series of weekly commentaries printed as newspaper advertisements.

Words to check:

anomaly (paragraph 6)

1 The school board in Clark County, Nevada, has decided that its students deserve a new grading system. Now there will be no more hurt feelings—or damaged self-esteem—because somebody got a D or an F and no more swelled heads because of a straight-A report card. Here's how the system goes, according to the most recent issue of *The Quarterly Review of Doublespeak:*

> [S]tudents who earn D's or below will be characterized not as borderline passing or failing but as *emerging*. Those earning A's will no longer be commended for excellent work but will be told merely that they are *extending*,

and those in between will not be described as doing adequate or mediocre work but [that] they are *developing.*

2   The people who invented the traditional grading system undoubtedly thought it was a way of providing information. The Clark County innovation is more likely to produce headaches as those concerned try to figure out what the various "grades" mean. *Emerging* from what? (What if a student is not emerging but is still stuck?) And how is *emerging* different from *developing* or *extending?*

3   If you switched the grades around, would anybody notice? Probably not, and that is probably the point. Grades used to tell a ninth grader and his parents how successful the student was in mastering algebra. They also distinguished between levels of performance, showing who was doing well and who was not cutting it. The nearly indistinguishable present participles that the Clark County board plans to substitute for A's, B's, and the rest, imply that, if there is any difference, it's not important. The new "grades" are the educational equivalent of the familiar smiley face. Their message: "You are all terrific!"

4   What will students make of them? First graders were always smart enough to see that the Bluebird reading group was for kids who were having a tough time and the Cardinal group was for those who learned to read in the first two weeks, so Clark County students will probably be able to crack this code. But they'll get another message, too: If the difference between failing and outstanding work is not significant enough to be put in words that are plain and clear, why should they make a big effort to do well?

5   Parents who want only good news about their children will be big fans of the new system. But those who are used to discussing their children's grades with the kids will be in trouble. You can say to a child who has just gotten a C, "This shows you are not trying. You have to do better next time." (Or "That B in science is great; your hard work really paid off!") What can you say about *developing?* That it won't do?

6   Of course the Clark County board could solve these problems by collapsing the three grades into one (called *breathing*). And we could sit back and enjoy a laugh—if the foolishness in Clark County were an anomaly. Unfortunately, it isn't. And until we take it on—until we have schools, families, and communities sending consistent signals that achievement counts—all our "reforms" will fail.

7   For example, officials in many school districts have become uneasy with the practice of honoring the two top-ranking students in senior classes by naming them *valedictorian* and *salutatorian.* Some have stopped the practice altogether. Others, even more mysteriously, have decided that seniors should elect classmates to those honors. It's as though a basketball team decided that the high scorer for the year should be elected.

8   Officials in a large number of school districts have also gotten rid of class ranking—even though a majority of colleges say they would like this information for the admissions process. There are some good reasons for the change. For example, a student whose grades would put him in the top 10 percent in most schools might not make the top quarter or even the top half in a high-achieving school. However, problems like this could obviously be dealt with on a case-by-case basis. The real reason school officials insist on blurring the distinctions between students is that they think it is somehow unfair to acknowledge that some students have achieved more academically than others. (This is seldom a problem when it comes to sports.)

9   If this is our attitude towards academic achievement, we will never convince students that working hard in school is worthwhile. Fortunately, a countermovement is developing. One sign is the recent "education summit" where governors and business leaders endorsed high academic standards and agreed to cooperate in working for them. Another is President Clinton's proposal to recognize hard work and good grades by giving $1000 scholarships to the top 5 percent of high school graduates and a tax credit for a second year of college to students who get a B average the first year. But these initiatives are not enough. They will work only if we get rid of the smiley-face approach to academic achievement and attach real stakes to what students do in school when it comes to graduating from high school and getting a job or getting into college.

WHAT DID THE WRITER SAY AND WHAT DID YOU THINK?

1. Shanker recognizes and has some fun with the sillier aspects of the Clark County grading system, but he also thinks it does great harm. What is the harm?
2. The smiley-face approach in education does not apply to grades alone. What other areas are affected?
3. Does Shanker pay any attention to the reasoning of those who advocate the smiley-face approach?
4. Do you agree with Shanker that our schools value achievement in sports more than in academic areas?

HOW DID THE WRITER SAY IT?

1. Explain the comment, "If you switched the grades around, would anybody notice?"
2. Where does Shanker use ridicule? Is it justified? Excessive?
3. Which of the following best describes the conclusion: summary, prediction, call for action?

WHAT ABOUT <u>YOUR</u> WRITING?

Those experienced with the horrors of bureaucracies will be amused or angered—but not, unfortunately, surprised—by the language describing Clark County's new grading system, quoted in paragraph 1 of "The Smiley-Face Approach." The entire quoted passage is written in the *passive voice.*

Most English sentences use the *active voice.* It sounds natural. It's what readers expect. With the active voice, *the subject does the acting:*

Phillip went to the theater.

The pitcher throws a good curve ball.

I took the final examination.

In a sentence that uses the passive voice, the subject stands around "passively" and is *acted upon:*

The theater was gone to by Phillip.

A good curve ball is thrown by the pitcher.

The final examination was taken by me.

The passive voice can be awkward, pompous, wordy, and downright ugly. Sometimes it can even be sinister.

Take a close look at that passage describing the new grading system. The students are being *acted upon:* they "will be characterized"; they "will no longer be commended"; they "will be told"; they "will not be described." Who is responsible for these actions? Who do we complain to if we think the grading system is stupid or pernicious? The school board? The principal? The teachers? City Hall? Use of the passive voice makes these questions difficult or impossible to answer. Perhaps we are meant to sigh, shrug, and put the blame on the impersonal forces of Fate or Change or The Authorities. The passive voice, then, can sometimes involve moral issues even though it is most often a stylistic concern. Note the evasion of responsibility in the following sentences:

Funding was reduced for the hunger program.

The Accounts Receivable department has been determined to be 35% overstaffed.

Fred was deemed to be a disruptive influence.

In fairness, for some special situations the passive voice can be altogether acceptable. When the person or thing or group that does the acting is unknown or unimportant, the passive voice often sounds normal and natural—more so than the active voice in some cases—and there's no reason to avoid it. The passive sometimes works well, too, when the writer deliberately wants to sound formal and impersonal.

The flight was canceled because of mechanical difficulties.
In the Middle Ages, Aristotle was often referred to as "The Philosopher."
Payment must be received within ten days or legal steps will be taken.

Watch out for the passive voice, then. It shouldn't always be avoided, but most of the time the active voice works better—much better.

OLD FOLKS AT HOME
Bernard Sloan

Bernard Sloan's "Old Folks at Home" shows us that not every comment on controversial public issues needs to turn into a major research project. In this article Sloan draws heavily on personal knowledge and experience to present a forceful and disturbing argument for his point of view.

Words to check:

carp (paragraph 5)	demean (8)	callous (19)
tyranny (6)	cantankerous (18)	
mercenary (8)	infirmity (19)	

1 I once felt sorry for people in old-age homes. I accepted their portrayal on television specials as helpless innocents cast aside by their young, paying the price of growing old in America. I thought all these lonely old men and women were victims of the indifference and selfishness of the younger generation.

2 No more.

3 I have learned through personal experience why so many grandmothers and grandfathers end up in institutions for the aged, unwanted and unvisited. It isn't always their children who put them there. Sometimes they put themselves there.

4 These are the selfish, demanding elderly who are impossible to live with. Often they are people who were difficult to live with when they were younger,

but now they have age on their side. Their families, torn with pain and guilt, spend months or years struggling to do "the right thing." Finally, they give up.

5   I have been through it. I have friends who are going through it. Caring, concerned sons and daughters who try, God knows they try, but the harder they try the harder it gets. Their elderly parents who should know better carp and criticize and complain. Instead of compromising, they constantly test their children, forever setting up new challenges for them to meet, assuming the one-sided game can go on forever.

A Nightmare

6   It comes as a shock to them when the special privileges conferred by their age and relationship run out, and their son or daughter tolerates their tyranny no longer. "How can you do this to me?" the parent cries, bags packed.

7   It is not easy.

8   We have friends who spent a fortune remodeling their home to provide an apartment for the wife's aging mother. The daughter was determined to overcome their differences for the chance to be close to her mother, to give her mother the love of a family rather than the services of a mercenary. Instead, she provided herself and her family with a three-year nightmare, the old woman seizing every opportunity to demean her daughter's husband, criticize the children and turn every family argument into a screaming fight.

9   "She's tearing our family apart," the daughter cries. "I'm going to be the villain by casting her out, but she has to go, or it's the end of my marriage."

10   Our friend is now searching for a suitable home. In her desperation she will settle for the best home available, which will not necessarily be the best home.

11   Another friend not only brings her father-in-law cooked meals, she cleans his apartment every week. Not once has he thanked her. But he has managed to find fault with everything she does. How long will he be able to live by himself? Another year, perhaps. And then what? Who will he blame when he winds up in an institution? Not himself.

12   A business acquaintance makes solitary visits to his angry mother in her lonely apartment. His wife will no longer submit to the old woman's hostility. The old woman, an Italian Catholic, cannot forgive her son for marrying a French Catholic. Mixed marriages, she still proclaims regularly, don't work. Twenty-five years and three delightful children don't count.

13   Can't she read the handwriting on the wall? She is busy writing her own future.

14   When my mother became ill, I moved her from her Sun Belt apartment to our home so that she could spend her remaining time with her own family, her only grandchildren. Although she never approved of my wife (the wrong

religion again), we were positive she would relinquish her prejudices in exchange for love and care. No such luck. Instead of making an attempt to ad-
just to our household, my mother tried to manipulate the four of us to center
our lives around her.

15   My wife took her to the doctor regularly, supervised her medication,
bought and prepared special foods for her—all while working full time—yet
my mother found nothing right about anything she did. Our refrigerator
could be bulging, but my mother managed to crave the one thing missing. We
were made to feel guilty if we left her alone for an evening, and were maneu-
vered into quarrels if we stayed. After five months of this, we began to inves-
tigate "homes."

The Life of a Family

16   Even the most relentlessly cheerful were depressing. Amidst flowered
walls and piped-in music ("Heaven, I'm in Heaven") old people stared at television or gathered in activity rooms where they were kept busy with the arts
and crafts taught in the third grade. They were not bedridden, these people;
they required no nursing, no special care. Although unable to shop, cook and
take care of a home of their own, they were quite capable of participating in
the life of a family. Yet they were separated from their families.

17   How many of these people had driven their families to drive them out?
How many felt that reaching 60 or 70 or 80 entitled them to behave in a
manner that would never be tolerated in the young? As if the very fact of
being old excused them from the rules of common decency. As if the right to
be demanding and complaining was conferred upon them along with half
fares on buses and discount days at the market.

18   That cantankerous old man may be a laugh riot on the stage as he sends
comic characters scurrying at his every command, but he is hell to live with.
That feisty old lady may be hilarious when company comes, but she can drive
a family crazy. They are candidates for being "put away" as soon as the family
being destroyed gets up the courage.

19   I don't mean to suggest that there are not great numbers of old people
who must live in institutions because they are victims—victims of infirmity
and, yes, victims of callous, selfish children. But for our own sakes, and for our
children, it is pointless to ignore the fact that many of the elderly bear some
responsibility for their fate. After all, warm, loving, sharing people are a joy to
live with whatever their age.

WHAT DID THE WRITER SAY AND WHAT DID YOU THINK?

1. Where does the author first state the thesis? Express the thesis in your own
    words.

2. How many specific examples does the author use to support the thesis? Are there enough examples? Are they sufficiently varied?
3. Describe the nature of the elderly people with whom the author is concerned. What do they have in common in addition to some obvious character failings?

HOW DID THE WRITER SAY IT?

1. What argument against his position is the author trying to anticipate in paragraph 18?
2. The last paragraph has two purposes. One is to remind us of the thesis. What is the other purpose?

WHAT ABOUT YOUR WRITING?

To avoid monotony, the good writer varies sentence length. Long and short sentences are neither good nor bad in themselves. Variety is the key.

In the Sloan selection, notice how paragraph 1, beginning with a sentence of only nine words, is followed by two longish sentences of twenty-three and twenty words. Notice how those sentences are then followed by a two-word sentence. Again, paragraph 8, ending with a thirty-four word sentence, is followed by a sentence of a mere eight words.

Mathematical formulas are inapplicable, of course. There's no magic number of words at which a sentence ceases to be short and suddenly becomes long. There's no special point, for that matter, at which readers suddenly cease to be interested and become bored. Monotonous sentence length, however, contributes to boredom, and variety can often contribute to interest. So try to vary sentence length.

THE CASE FOR TORTURE

Michael Levin

Michael Levin is a Professor of Philosophy at the City College of New York and the Graduate Center, City University of New York. He is well known in Libertarian circles and has written much about social issues in the U.S., especially feminism, race, and crime. Some readers will be horrified when they read Levin's "The Case for Torture." Some readers will sense that they have always agreed with Levin but never realized they did. Few readers will be indifferent.

Words to check:

regime (paragraph 1)	extant (7)
arraign (3)	extort (10)
electrodes (4)	disingenuous (11)
irrevocably (7)	

1 It is generally assumed that torture is impermissible, a throwback to a more brutal age. Enlightened societies reject it outright, and regimes suspected of using it risk the wrath of the United States.

2 I believe this attitude is unwise. There are situations in which torture is not merely permissible but morally mandatory. Moreover, these situations are moving from the realm of imagination to fact.

3 Suppose a terrorist has hidden an atomic bomb on Manhattan Island which will detonate at noon on July 4 unless . . . (here follow the usual demands for money and release of his friends from jail). Suppose, further, that he is caught at 10 A.M. on the fateful day, but—preferring death to failure—won't disclose where the bomb is. What do we do? If we follow due process—wait for his lawyer, arraign him—millions of people will die. If the only way to save those lives is to subject the terrorist to the most excruciating possible pain, what grounds can there be for not doing so? I suggest there are none. In any case, I ask you to face the question with an open mind.

4 Torturing the terrorist is unconstitutional? Probably. But millions of lives surely outweigh constitutionality. Torture is barbaric? Mass murder is far more barbaric. Indeed, letting millions of innocents die in deference to one who flaunts his guilt is moral cowardice, an unwillingness to dirty one's hands. If you caught the terrorist, could you sleep nights knowing that millions died because you couldn't bring yourself to apply the electrodes?

5 Once you concede that torture is justified in extreme cases, you have admitted that the decision to use torture is a matter of balancing innocent lives against the means needed to save them. You must now face more realistic cases involving more modest numbers. Someone plants a bomb on a jumbo jet. He alone can disarm it, and his demands cannot be met (or if they can, we refuse to set a precedent by yielding to his threats). Surely we can, we must, do anything to the extortionist to save the passengers. How can we tell 300, or 100, or 10 people who never asked to be put in danger, "I'm sorry, you'll have to die in agony, we just couldn't bring ourselves to. . . ."

6 Here are the results of an informal poll about a third, hypothetical, case. Suppose a terrorist group kidnapped a newborn baby from a hospital. I asked four mothers if they would approve of torturing kidnappers if that were

necessary to get their own newborns back. All said yes, the most "liberal" adding that she would administer it herself.

7   I am not advocating torture as punishment. Punishment is addressed to deeds irrevocably past. Rather, I am advocating torture as an acceptable measure for preventing future evils. So understood, it is far less objectionable than many extant punishments. Opponents of the death penalty, for example, are forever insisting that executing a murderer will not bring back his victim (as if the purpose of capital punishment were supposed to be resurrection, not deterrence or retribution). But torture, in the cases described, is intended not to bring anyone back but to keep innocents from being dispatched. The most powerful argument against using torture as a punishment or to secure confessions is that such practices disregard the rights of the individual. Well, if the individual is all that important—and he is—it is correspondingly important to protect the rights of individuals threatened by terrorists. If life is so valuable that it must never be taken, the lives of the innocents must be saved even at the price of hurting the one who endangers them.

8   Better precedents for torture are assassination and preemptive attack. No Allied leader would have flinched at assassinating Hitler, had that been possible. (The Allies did assassinate Heydrich.) Americans would be angered to learn that Roosevelt could have had Hitler killed in 1943—thereby shortening the war and saving millions of lives—but refused on moral grounds. Similarly, if nation A learns that nation B is about to launch an unprovoked attack, A has a right to save itself by destroying B's military capability first. In the same way, if the police can by torture save those who would otherwise die at the hands of kidnappers or terrorists, they must.

9   There is an important difference between terrorists and their victims that should mute talk of the terrorists' "rights." The terrorist's victims are at risk unintentionally, not having asked to be endangered. But the terrorist knowingly initiated his actions. Unlike his victims, he volunteered for the risks of his deed. By threatening to kill for profit or idealism, he renounces civilized standards, and he can have no complaint if civilization tries to thwart him by whatever means necessary.

10   Just as torture is justified only to save lives (not extort confessions or recantations), it is justifiably administered only to those known to hold innocent lives in their hands. Ah, but how can the authorities ever be sure they have the right malefactor? Isn't there a danger of error and abuse? Won't We turn into Them?

11   Questions like these are disingenuous in a world in which terrorists proclaim themselves and perform for television. The name of their game is public recognition. After all, you can't very well intimidate a government into

releasing your freedom fighters unless you announce that it is your group that has seized its embassy. "Clear guilt" is difficult to define, but when 40 million people see a group of masked gunmen seize an airplane on the evening news, there is not much question about who the perpetrators are. There will be hard cases where the situation is murkier. Nonetheless, a line demarcating the legitimate use of torture can be drawn. Torture only the obviously guilty, and only for the sake of saving innocents, and the line between Us and Them will remain clear.

12   There is little danger that the Western democracies will lose their way if they choose to inflict pain as one way of preserving order. Paralysis in the face of evil is the greater danger. Some day soon a terrorist will threaten tens of thousands of lives, and torture will be the only way to save them. We had better start thinking about this.

WHAT DID THE WRITER SAY AND WHAT DID YOU THINK?

1. What is the thesis?
2. What examples support the thesis? Does it matter that the examples are hypothetical rather than factual?
3. Why does the author not advocate torture as punishment?
4. Why does the author believe that terrorists have no right to complain about torture?
5. How does the author respond to the argument that the use of torture will turn "Us into Them?"
6. Does the survey of four mothers in paragraph 6 provide logical support for the thesis?

HOW DID THE WRITER SAY IT?

1. Why are only three examples enough to support the author's highly controversial thesis? Would additional examples have strengthened the author's case?
2. What organizing principle determines the order in which the examples are presented?
3. What is the purpose of the quotation marks around *liberal* in paragraph 6?
4. The specific phrase "apply the electrodes" brings the horror of torture much more vividly to mind than would an abstract phrase like "inflict pain." Does the author's brutal honesty interfere with his chances of convincing the readers that his thesis is valid?

WHAT ABOUT YOUR WRITING?

Inseparable from Levin's presentation of his own point of view about torture is his attack on what he considers conventional attitudes. His scorn for those attitudes gives his thesis a dimension that it would not otherwise have had.

Getting started is a problem for many writers, and Levin here demonstrates one of the most effective ways of dealing with the problem: *Many people think such and such, but.* . . . Instead of opening with a direct and sometimes flat statement of your thesis, let your thesis emerge as a response to some other people's ignorance or superstition or sentimentality or general wrongheadedness. Your thesis will then exist in a dramatic context, not an intellectual vacuum, and will have built right into it the appeal of a lively argument.

Most people think such and such about torture, says Levin, *but.* . . . With a thesis that spanking small children is often the best method of handling certain difficulties, you might begin with a few satirical references to the belief that three-year-olds appreciate the fine points of logic and that the ideal family is a loosely organized debating society. With a thesis that country music is fun, you might begin by observing that respectable people traditionally are supposed to scorn country music as trivial and commercialized nonsense. Then, perhaps, you declare that you guess you're just not respectable, *but.* . . .

For other suggestions on getting started, consult pages 140–141.

A MODEST PROPOSAL

Jonathan Swift

Jonathan Swift (1667–1745) still has the power to inspire, to shock, and to offend. Active in politics, dean of St. Patrick's Cathedral (Church of England) in Dublin, Swift is the master of satire in English literature, as seen in *A Tale of A Tub* (1704), *The Battle of the Books* (1704), "An Argument Against Abolishing Christianity in England" (1708), *Gulliver's Travels* (1726), and, in the majesty of its full title, "A Modest Proposal for Preventing the Children of Poor People in Ireland from Being a Burden to Their Parents or Country, and for Making Them Beneficial to the Public" (1729). The fury, hatred, and cruelty in much of Swift's satire often make readers overlook his passionate and idealistic commitment to human welfare. Also too often overlooked is his spare and muscular prose style, especially remarkable in an age sometimes given to forced elegance.

"A Modest Proposal" is an attack on British oppression and exploitation of Ireland. As you read, distinguish between what is said and what is meant.

Words to check:

importuning	nutriment (7)	emulation (25)
(paragraph 1)	collateral (12)	brevity (26)
alms (1)	repine (13)	parsimony (28)
prodigious (2)	mandarins (17)	animosities (28)
dam (4)	desponding (18)	factions (28)
raiment (4)	tithes (20)	effectual (31)
proficiency (6)	curate (20)	sustenance (31)

1   It is a melancholy object to those who walk through this great town[1] or travel in the country, when they see the street, the roads, and cabin doors, crowded with beggars of the female sex, followed by three, four, or six children, all in rags, and importuning every passenger for alms. These mothers, instead of being able to work for their honest livelihood, are forced to employ all their time in strolling to beg sustenance for their helpless infants, who, as they grow up, either turn thieves for want of work or leave their dear native country, to fight for the Pretender in Spain, or sell themselves to the Barbadoes.[2]

2   I think it is agreed by all parties that this prodigious number of children in the arms, or on the backs, or at the heels of their mothers, and frequently of their fathers, is in the present deplorable state of the kingdom a very great additional grievance; and therefore whoever could find out a fair, cheap, and easy method of making these children sound and useful members of the common-wealth, would deserve so well of the public as to have his statue up for a preserver of the nation.

3   But my intention is very far from being confined to provide only for the children of professed beggars; it is of much greater extent, and shall take in the whole number of infants at a certain age, who are born of parents in effect as little able to support them, as those who demand our charity in the streets.

4   As to my own part, having turned my thoughts, for many years, upon this important subject, and maturely weighed the several schemes of other

---

[1] Dublin.

[2] The Pretender was James Francis Edward Stuart (1688–1766), son of the deposed Catholic king of England, James II. He claimed the British throne and was supported by most of Catholic Ireland. Many Irish tried to escape from their poverty by hiring themselves out as indentured servants in the Barbadoes and other West Indies islands.

projectors, I have always found them grossly mistaken in their computation. It is true, a child just dropt from its dam, may be supported by her milk for a solar year with little other nourishment, at most not above the value of two shillings, which the mother may certainly get, or the value in scraps, by her lawful occupation of begging; and it is exactly at one year old that I propose to provide for them in such a manner, as, instead of being a charge upon their parents, or the parish, or wanting food and raiment for the rest of their lives, they shall, on the contrary, contribute to the feeding and partly to the clothing of many thousands.

5   There is likewise another great advantage in my scheme, that it will prevent those voluntary abortions, and that horrid practice of women murdering their bastard children, alas! too frequent among us—sacrificing the poor innocent babes, I doubt,[3] more to avoid the expense than the shame—which would move tears and pity in the most savage and inhuman breast.

6   The number of souls in this kingdom being usually reckoned one million and a half, of these I calculate there may be about two hundred thousand couples whose wives are breeders; from which number I subtract thirty thousand couples, who are able to maintain their own children, although I apprehend there cannot be so many, under the present distresses of the kingdom; but this being granted, there will remain an hundred and seventy thousand breeders. I again subtract fifty thousand, for those women who miscarry, or whose children die by accident or disease within the year. There only remain an hundred and twenty thousand children of poor parents annually born: The question therefore is, How this number shall be reared, and provided for: which, as I have already said, under the present situation of affairs, is utterly impossible by all the methods hitherto proposed; for we can neither employ them in handicraft or agriculture; we neither build houses (I mean in the country) nor cultivate land: They can very seldom pick up a livelihood by stealing till they arrive at six years old, except where they are of towardly parts,[4] although, I confess, they learn the rudiments much earlier; during which time they can however be properly looked upon only as probationers; as I have been informed by a principal gentleman in the country of Cavan,[5] who protested to me, that he never knew above one or two instances under the age of six, even in a part of the kingdom so renowed for the quickest proficiency in that art.

7   I am assured by our merchants, that a boy or a girl before twelve years old, is no saleable commodity, and even when they come to this age, they will

---

[3] I think.

[4] Advanced talents.

[5] An especially poor district of Ireland.

not yield above three pounds, or three pounds and a half crown at most, on the exchange; which cannot turn to account either to the parents or kingdom, the charge of nutriment and rags having been at least four times that value.

8   I shall now therefore humbly propose my own thoughts, which I hope will not be liable to the least objection.

9   I have been assured by a very knowing American of my acquaintance in London, that a young healthy child well nursed is at a year old a most delicious nourishing and wholesome food, whether stewed, roasted, baked, or boiled; and I make no doubt that it will equally serve in a fricassee, or a ragout.

10   I do therefore humbly offer it to publick consideration, that of the hundred and twenty thousand children, already computed, twenty thousand may be reserved for breed, whereof only one fourth part to be males; which is more than we allow to sheep, black cattle, or swine; and my reason is that these children are seldom the fruits of marriage, a circumstance not much regarded by our savages; therefore one male will be sufficient to serve four females. That the remaining hundred thousand may, at a year old, be offered in the sale to the persons of quality and fortune through the kingdom; always advising the mother to let them suck plentifully in the last month, so as to render them plump and fat for a good table. A child will make two dishes at an entertainment for friends; and when the family dines alone, the fore or hind quarter will make a reasonable dish, and seasoned with a little pepper or salt will be very good boiled on the fourth day, especially in winter.

11   I have reckoned upon a medium that a child just born will weigh 12 pounds, and in a solar year, if tolerably nursed, increaseth to 28 pounds. I grant this food will be somewhat dear,[6] and therefore very proper for landlords, who, as they have already devoured most of the parents, seem to have the best title to the children.

12   Infant's flesh will be in season throughout the year, but more plentiful in March, and a little before and after; for we are told by a grave author, and eminent French physician,[7] that fish being a prolific diet, there are more children born in Roman Catholic countries about nine months after Lent than at any other season; therefore, reckoning a year after Lent, the markets will be more glutted than usual, because the number of popish infants is at least three to one in this kingdom: and therefore, it will have one other collateral advantage, by lessening the number of papists among us.

13   I have already computed the charge of nursing a beggar's child (in which list I reckon all cottagers, laborers, and four-fifths of the farmers) to be about

---

[6] Expensive.

[7] Francois Rabelais (c. 1494–1553) in *Gargantua and Pantagruel.*

two shillings per annum, rags included; and I believe no gentlemen would re-
pine to give ten shillings for the carcass of a good fat child, which, as I have
said, will make four dishes of excellent nutritive meat, when he hath only
some particular friend or his own family to dine with him. Thus the squire
will learn to be a good landlord, and grow popular among his tenants; the
mother will have eight shillings net profit, and be fit for work till she produces another child.

14   Those who are more thrifty (as I must confess the times require) may flay
the carcass, the skin of which artificially dressed will make admirable gloves
for ladies, and summer boots for fine gentlemen.

15   As to our city of Dublin, shambles[8] may be appointed for this purpose in
the most convenient parts of it, and butchers we may be assured will not be
wanting; although I rather recommend buying children alive and dressing
them hot from the knife, as we do roasting pigs.

16   A very worthy person, a true lover of his country, and whose virtues I
highly esteem, was lately pleased in discoursing on this matter to offer a refinement upon my scheme. He said that many gentlemen of this kingdom,
having of late destroyed their deer, he conceived that the want of venison
might be well supplied by the bodies of young lads and maidens, not exceed-
ing fourteen years of age nor under twelve; so great a number of both sexes in
every country being now ready to starve for want of work and service; and
there to be disposed of by their parents if alive, or otherwise by their nearest
relations. But with due deference to so excellent a friend, and so deserving a
patriot, I cannot be altogether in his sentiments; for as to the males, my
American acquaintance assured me from frequent experience, that their flesh
was generally tough and lean, like that of our schoolboys, by continual exercise, and their taste disagreeable, and to fatten them would not answer the
charge. Then as to the females, it would, I think with humble submission, be
a loss to the publick, because they soon would be breeders themselves: And
besides it is not improbable that some scrupulous people might be apt to
censure such a practice (although indeed very unjustly) as a little bordering
upon cruelty, which, I confess, hath always been with me the strongest objection against any project, how well soever intended.

17   But in order to justify my friend, he confessed, that this expedient was
put into his head by the famous Psalmanazar,[9] a native of the island Formosa,
who came from thence to London, about twenty years ago, and in conversation told my friend, that in his country when any young person happened to

---

[8] Slaughterhouses.

[9] George Psalmanazar (c. 1679–1763) was a Frenchman who pretended to be a Formosan and
wrote a popular, completely fictional account of the supposed customs of his native land.

be put to death, the executioner sold the carcass to persons of quality, as prime dainty, and that, in his time, the body of a plump girl of fifteen, who was crucified for an attempt to poison the Emperor, was sold to his Imperial Majesty's prime minister of state, and other great mandarins of the court, in joints from the gibbet, at four hundred crowns. Neither indeed can I deny, that if the same use were made of several plump young girls in this town, who, without one single groat to their fortunes, cannot stir abroad without a chair, and appear at a play-house and assemblies in foreign fineries which they never will pay for, the kingdom would not be the worse.

18   Some persons of a desponding spirit are in great concern about that vast number of poor people, who are aged, diseased, or maimed, and I have been desired to employ my thoughts what course may be taken, to ease the nation of so grievous an encumbrance. But I am not in the least pain upon that matter, because it is very well known, that they are every day dying, and rotting, by cold, and famine, and filth, and vermin, as fast as can be reasonably expected. And as to the young labourers, they are now in almost as hopeful a condition. They cannot get work, and consequently pine away for want of nourishment, to a degree, that if at any time they are accidentally hired to common labour, they have not strength to perform it, and thus the country and themselves are happily delivered from the evils to come.

19   I have too long digressed, and therefore shall return to my subject. I think the advantages by the proposal which I have made are obvious and many, as well as of the highest importance.

20   For *first*, as I have already observed, it would greatly lessen the number of papists, with whom we are yearly over-run, being the principal breeders of the nation, as well as our most dangerous enemies, and who stay at home on purpose with a design to deliver the kingdom to the Pretender, hoping to take their advantage by the absence of so many good Protestants, who have chosen rather to leave their country, than stay at home, and pay tithes against their conscience to an Episcopal curate.

21   Secondly, the poorer tenants will have something valuable of their own, which by law may be made liable to distress and help to pay their landlord's rent, their corn and cattle being already seized, and money a thing unknown.

22   Thirdly, whereas the maintenance of an hundred thousand children, from two years old and upward, cannot be computed at less than ten shillings apiece per annum, the nation's stock will be thereby increased fifty thousand pounds per annum, besides the profit of a new dish introduced to the tables of all gentlemen of fortune in the kingdom who have any refinement in taste. And the money will circulate among our selves, the goods being entirely of our own growth and manufacture.

23   Fourthly, the constant breeders, beside the gain of eight shillings sterling per annum by the sale of their children will be rid of the charge of maintaining them after the first year.

24   Fifthly, this food would likewise bring great custom[10] to taverns, where the vintners will certainly be so prudent as to procure the best receipts[11] for dressing it to perfection, and consequently have their houses frequented by all the fine gentlemen who justly value themselves upon their knowledge in good eating; and a skillful cook, who understands how to oblige his guests, will contrive to make it as expensive as they please.

25   Sixthly, this would be a great inducement to marriage, which all wise nations have either encouraged by rewards or enforced by laws and penalties. It would increase the care and the tenderness of mothers toward their children, when they were sure of a settlement for life to the poor babes, provided in some sort by the public, to their annual profit instead of expense. We should soon see an honest emulation among the married women, which of them could bring the fattest child to the market. Men would become as fond of their wives during the time of their pregnancy as they are now of their mares in foal, their cows in calf, their sows when they are ready to farrow; nor offer to beat or kick them (as is too frequent a practice) for fear of a miscarriage.

26   Many other advantages might be enumerated. For instance, the addition of some thousand carcasses in our exportation of barreled beef, the propagation of swine's flesh, and improvement in the art of making good bacon, so much wanted among us by the great destruction of pigs, too frequent at our table; which are no way comparable in taste or magnificence to a well-grown, fat, yearling child, which roasted whole will make a considerable figure at a lord mayor's feast or any other public entertainment. But this and many others I omit, being studious of[12] brevity.

27   Supposing that one thousand families in this city would be constant customers for infants' flesh, besides others who might have it at merry-meetings, particularly at weddings and christenings, I compute that Dublin would take off annually about twenty thousand carcasses; and the rest of the kingdom (where probably they will be sold somewhat cheaper) the remaining eighty thousand.

28   I can think of no one objection that will possibly be raised against this proposal, unless it should be urged that the number of people will be thereby much lessened in the kingdom. This I freely own, and 'twas indeed one principal design in offering it to the world. I desire the reader will observe that I

---

[10] Trade.

[11] Recipes.

[12] Concerned with.

calculate my remedy for this one individual kingdom of Ireland, and for no other that ever was, is, or, I think, ever can be upon earth. Therefore let no man talk to me of other expedients: of taxing our absentees at five shillings a pound: of using neither clothes, nor household furniture, except what is of our own growth and manufacture: of utterly rejecting the materials and instruments that promote foreign luxury: of curing the expensiveness of pride, vanity, idleness, and gaming in our women: of introducing a vein of parsimony, prudence and temperance: of learning to love our country, wherein we differ even from Laplanders, and the inhabitants of Topinamboo:[13] of quitting our animosities, and factions, nor act any longer like the Jews, who were murdering one another at the very moment their city was taken:[14] of being a little cautious not to sell our country and consciences for nothing: of teaching landlords to have at least one degree of mercy towards their tenants. Lastly, of putting a spirit of honesty, industry, and skill into our shop-keepers, who, if a resolution could now be taken to buy only our native goods, would immediately unite to cheat and exact[15] upon us in the price, the measure, and the goodness, nor could ever yet be brought to make one fair proposal of just dealing, though often and earnestly invited to it.

29   Therefore I repeat, let no man talk to me of these and the like expedients, till he hath at least some glimpse of hope, that there will ever be some hearty and sincere attempt to put them in practice.

30   But as to myself, having been wearied out for many years with offering vain, idle, visionary thoughts, and at length utterly despairing of success, I fortunately fell upon this proposal, which as it is wholly new, so it hath something solid and real, of no expense and little trouble, full in our own power, and whereby we can incur no danger in disobliging England. For this kind of commodity will not bear exportation, the flesh being of too tender a consistence, to admit a long continuance in salt, although perhaps I could name a country, which would be glad to eat up our whole nation without it.

31   After all, I am not so violently bent upon my own opinion, as to reject any offer, proposed by wise men, which shall be found equally innocent, cheap, easy, and effectual. But before something of that kind shall be advanced in contradiction to my scheme, and offering a better, I desire the author or authors, will be pleased maturely to consider two points. *First*, as things now stand, how they will be able to find food and raiment for a

---

[13] Jungle region of Brazil.

[14] Reference to the fall of Jerusalem, as described in the Bible.

[15] Impose.

hundred thousand useless mouths and backs. And *Secondly*, there being a round million of creatures in human figure throughout this kingdom, whose whole subsistence put into a common stock would leave them in debt two millions of pounds sterling, adding those who are beggars by profession, to the bulk of farmers, cottagers and labourers, with their wives and children, who are beggars in effect; I desire those politicians, who dislike my overture, and may perhaps be so bold to attempt an answer, that they will first ask the parents of these mortals, whether they would not at this day think it a great happiness to have been sold for food at a year old, in the manner I prescribe, and thereby have avoided such a perpetual scene of misfortunes as they have since gone through, by the oppression of landlords, the impossibility of paying rent without money or trade, the want of common sustenance, with neither house nor clothes to cover them from the inclemencies of the weather, and the most inevitable prospect of entailing the like or greater miseries upon their breed for ever.

32   I profess, in the sincerity of my heart, that I have not the least personal interest in endeavoring to promote this necessary work, having no other motive than the public good of my country, by advancing our trade, providing for infants, relieving the poor, and giving some pleasure to the rich. I have no children by which I can propose to get a single penny; the youngest being nine years old, and my wife past childbearing.

WHAT DID THE WRITER SAY AND WHAT DID YOU THINK?

1. "A Modest Proposal" is an ironic essay: The author deliberately writes what he does not mean. What is the real thesis? Is there more than one?
2. Is the essay only an attack on something? Does Swift ever present any serious proposals for improving conditions? If so, where?
3. What is the character of the "projector" of the proposal? Don't confuse him with Swift.
4. Are there any flaws in the logic? Could you refute the proposal by using logic? What assumptions about life and morality does the projector make before the logical argument begins?
5. What people or groups are singled out as special targets for Swift's attack?
6. Are the Irish presented completely as innocent victims, or are they also to blame?
7. Where does Swift's own sense of bitterness and rage come closest to emerging from beneath the cool irony?
8. Would it be possible to read this essay as a seriously intended proposal?

HOW DID THE WRITER SAY IT?

1. When does the reader start to realize that the essay is ironic? Before or after the actual proposal is made in paragraph 10?
2. Comment on the word choice in "a child just dropt from its dam" (paragraph 4), "two hundred thousand couples whose wives are breeders" (paragraph 6), "a boy or a girl before twelve years old, is no saleable commodity" (paragraph 7).
3. Comment on the word choice in "people might be apt to censure such a practice . . . as a little bordering on cruelty," (paragraph 16) and "they are every day dying, and rotting, by cold, and famine, and filth, and vermin, as fast as can be reasonably expected," (paragraph 18).
4. What is the purpose of the last paragraph?

WHAT ABOUT <u>YOUR</u> WRITING?

Verbal irony in its simplest form is saying the opposite, or near opposite, of what is meant. It can be seen at a primitive level when someone says, "Nice weather we're having," during a thunderstorm, and at the level of genius in "A Modest Proposal."

Nearly any subject can lend itself to the ironic approach, and you may want to consider trying your hand at an ironic paper. Successful irony has structured into it a strong element of humor and dramatic tension—tension between the surface statement and the underlying reality. With its special slant, it can also break through an audience's resistance toward reading another piece on a frequently discussed subject. It can often present familiar ideas in a fresh and exciting way.

A writer opposing capital punishment, for example, may be concerned about being perceived as a shallow idealist who thinks that all murderers are poor misunderstood victims of society. Using irony, the writer might be able to avoid the problem by pretending to be a bloodthirsty advocate of capital punishment, urging public executions, death by torture, and any other hideous ideas that come to mind. A writer supporting capital punishment, on the other hand, concerned about being perceived as an unfeeling brute, might pretend to be a simple-minded idealist, arguing ironically that if only society had provided more playgrounds and Boy Scout troops, the murderer would have become a priest or ecologist.

In writing an ironic essay, watch out for two pitfalls:

Don't Let the Reader Misunderstand

Exaggerate enough so that the reader knows what side you're really on.

Don't Lose the Ironic Tone

Don't let your true feelings enter directly. The worst enemy of an effective ironic paper is sincerity. Beware, in particular, of the last paragraph that introduces a "but seriously, folks," or "what I really mean to say" element. If the irony isn't clear long before that, the whole paper probably needs to be reworked.

Critics often distinguish between verbal irony and two other kinds. *Irony of fate* refers to events that turn out differently from a normal person's expectations. A man compulsively afraid of germs has his whole house sterilized, fills his medicine chest with every known drug, and dies before he's thirty by tripping over a discarded bottle of medicine and breaking his neck. Most short stories with surprise endings employ irony of fate. *Dramatic irony* occurs when a literary character says or does something without realizing its significance, but the audience or reader does realize it. The hero of a melodrama beats up some villains, turns to the audience, says "Virtue triumphs again," and does not see another villain sneaking up behind him with a club.

Sarcasm is verbal irony used in an extremely bitter and personal fashion: "You really have a big heart, don't you?"

What About the *Rest* of Your Writing?

Just because you've finished the class you bought this book for doesn't mean that you're finished with the lessons of this book. We're confident that the advice we've given you about the importance of the persuasive principle and other writing strategies and tactics will stand you in good stead every time you sit down to write. The persuasive principle doesn't cease to exist just because the semester or the quarter is finally over.

If you're about to move eagerly on to your next English class and begin seriously analyzing great literature, you're probably expecting to need the persuasive principle and all the other tools for writing that we've written about in the past ten chapters. After all, it's an English class. But even if you never take an English class again, don't forget what you've learned here. As we said in Chapter 1, every kind of writing benefits from having a thesis. Every kind of writing benefits from the persuasive principle. If your history professor asks for a description of the battle of Agincourt, don't just settle for turning in a collection of facts and figures. Remember the persuasive principle:

The French loss at the battle of Agincourt was the result of one major tactical error.

The English and French approaches to military tactics at the battle of Agincourt were decisively different.

Agincourt is a perfect example of how to lose a battle even when you have more troops, more armor, and more experienced tacticians than your opponent does.

The future usefulness of the lessons in this book doesn't stop with your academic life, either. The persuasive principle can help give life and unity to business and professional writing as well:

Both computer systems we are considering adopting have features that can help with our work, but one is clearly the better choice.

The abolishment of "Casual Fridays" in this office may not please everyone, but we're doing it to help maintain a professional environment, impress our clients, and eliminate some embarrassing mishaps.

The patient's accusations of malpractice are based on distortions, misunderstandings, and omissions.

And don't forget that we showed you throughout Chapter 1 and the rest of this book that the persuasive principle can enliven types of everyday writing as diverse as driving directions, personal ads, and thank you notes.

The class may be over, but your need for the persuasive principle isn't. It won't ever be.

Credits

"How Can I Make My House Look Good in a Hurry?" by Don Aslett. From HOW DO I CLEAN THE MOOSEHEAD AND 99 MORE TOUGH QUESTIONS ABOUT HOUSECLEANING. New American Library (division of Penguin Books), copyright © 1989, pp. 139–141.

"Hush Timmy—This is Like a Church" by Kurt Anderson from *Time*, 04/15/85. Copyright © 1985 Time Inc. Reprinted by permission.

"Take a Left onto Nowhere Street" by Anne Bernays. *New York Times*, 11/15/98, p. travel section 31. Copyright © 1998 by The New York Times Company. Reprinted by permission.

"12 Steps to Quit Smoking" by Robert Bezilla. Published by *The Cleveland Plain Dealer, The Spokane Review & Chronicle, Syracuse Herald-Journal* and *Palm Beach Newspapers.* Distributed by New York Times Syndication Sales Corporation. Copyright © 1994 by Robert Bezilla. Reprinted by permission of the author.

"That Lean and Hungry Look" by Suzanne Britt as appeared in *Newsweek*, 10/09/78. Reprinted by permission of the author.

"Spanglish Spoken Here" by Janice Castro, Dan Cook and Cristina Garcia from *Time*, 1988. Copyright © 1990 Time Inc. Reprinted by permission.

"The Prisoner's Dilemma" by Stephen Chapman. Copyright © 1980. Reprinted by permission of *The New Republic, Inc.*

"Only Daughter" by Sandra Cisneros. Copyright © 1990 by Sandra Cisneros. First published in GLAMOUR, November 1990. Reprinted by permission of Susan Bergholz Literary Services, New York. All rights reserved.

"Computer Games Anonymous" by Joanna Connors. Reprinted by permission of *The Cleveland Plain Dealer.*

From AEROBICS by Kenneth H. Cooper, M.D. Copyright © 1968 by Kenneth H. Cooper. Used by permission of Bantam Books, a division of Bantam Doubleday Dell Publishing Group, Inc.

"Lassie Never Chases Rabbits" by Kevin Cowherd in *The Cleveland Plain Dealer* 07/31/94, p. 4-c. Reprinted by permission.

"How to Speak to Animals" by Umberto Eco. From, HOW TO TRAVEL WITH A SALMON AND OTHER ESSAYS. Copyright Gruppo Editoriale Fabbi, Bompiani, Sonzogno, Estas.S.p.A., English translation copyright © 1994 by Harcourt.

"My Greatest Day in Baseball" from "The Boys of Summer" by Dick Feagler. In FEAGLER'S CLEVELAND by Dick Feagler, pp. 218–221. Reprinted with permission of Gray and Company, Publishers.

"Thanksgiving's No Turkey" by Robert W. Gardner from *The Wall Street Journal*, 11/20/95. Reprinted with permission of The Wall Street Journal. Copyright © 1995 Dow Jones and Company, Inc. All Rights Reserved.

"The Real Thing" by Frankie Germany. Reprinted by permission of the author, 1998. From A SECOND CHICKEN SOUP FOR THE WOMAN'S SOUL by Jack Canfield, et al. Pp. 128–130.

"The Quick Fix Society" by Janet Mendell Goldstein. Reprinted by permission of the author. Reprinted in THE MACMILLAN READER, 5th edition, © 1999, pp. 310–313.

"Foul Shots" by Rogelio R. Gomez from *The New York Times*, 10/13/91. Copyright © 1991 by The New York Times Company. Reprinted by permission.

"What Does it Mean to Be Creative" by S.I. Hayakawa. From THROUGH THE COMMUNICATION BARRIER, © 1979, Harper and Row. Reprinted by permission.

"Say Now, That Was Milo," by Cheryl Heckler-Feltz. Copyright © 1995, Cheryl Heckler-Feltz, Distributed by New York Times Special Features/Syndication Sales. Reprinted by permission.

Reprinted by permission of Holt Associates: FREEDOM AND BEYOND by John Holt. © Heineman, A division of Reed Elsevier Inc., Portsmouth,. NH, 1972).

"Salvation" from THE BIG SEA by Langston Hughes. Copyright © 1940© by Langston Hughes. Copyright renewed © 1968 by Arna Bontemps and George Houston Bass. Reprinted by permission of Hill and Wang, a division of Farrar, Straus, & Giroux, Inc.

"A Crime of Compassion" by Barbara Huttmann as appeared in NEWSWEEK, 08/08/83. Reprinted by permission of Barbara Huttmann.

"The Lottery" from THE LOTTERY AND OTHER STORIES by Shirley Jackson. Copyright © 1948, 1949 by Shirley Jackson, and copyright renewed © 1976, 1977 by Laurence Hyman, Barry Hyman, Mrs. Sarah Webster and Mrs. Joanne Schnurer. Reprinted by permission of Farrar, Straus, Giroux, Inc.

"My Way!" from 1-800-AM-I-NUTS by Margo Kaufman. Copyright © 1993 by Margo Kaufman. Reprinted by permission of Random House, Inc.

"Why We Crave Horror Movies" by Stephen King. Reprinted with Permission. © Stephen King. All rights reserved. Originally appeared in *Playboy*, 1982.

"Darkness at Noon" by Harold Krents from *New York Times*, 05/05/78. Copyright © 1978 by The New York Times Company. Reprinted by permission.

"Couple Lies" by Adair Lara as appeared in COSMOPOLITAN, September 1996. Reprinted by permission of the author.

From A SAND COUNTY ALMANAC by Aldo Leopold. Copyright © 1966 by Aldo Leopold. Used by permission of Oxford University Press, Inc.

"Corn Bread with Character" by Ronni Lundy. Reprinted by permission of the author.

"A Good PCA is Hard to Find" by Lorenzo W. Milam. Originally appeared as "A Good Man is Hard to Find." Copyright © 1999. Appeared in NEW MOBILITY, March 1999. Reprinted by permission.

"Winstead's Best Burgers" by Sarah Bryan Miller from *The Wall Street Journal*, 04/15/98. Reprinted with permission of *The Wall Street Journal*. Copyright © 1998 Dow Jones and Company, Inc. All Rights Reserved.

"Falling into Place" by Jaime O'Neill. *New York Times* Magazine. 08/15/93 in "About Men" feature. Copyright © 1993 by The New York Times Company. Reprinted by permission.

"The Spider and the Wasp" by Alexander Petrunkevitch from SCIENTIFIC AMERICAN, August 1952. Reprinted with permission. Copyright © 1952 by Scientific American, Inc. All rights reserved.

"I Am a Catholic" from LIVING OUT LOUD by Anna Quindlen. Copyright © 1987 by Anna Quindlen. Reprinted by permission of Random House, Inc.

"America: The Multinational Society" from WRITIN' IS FIGHTIN' by Ishmael Reed. Copyright © 1988 (Atheneum). Reprinted by permission.

"The Best Years of My Life" by Betty Rollin. Copyright © 1980 by Betty Rollin. Reprinted by permission of the William Morris Agency, Inc. on behalf of the author.

"Conversational Ballgames" from POLITE FICTION by Nancy Masterson Sakamoto.

"Where We Stand: The Smiley Face Approach" by Albert Shanker as appeared in *New York Times*, 06/16/96. Reprinted by permission of Albert Shanker.

"Old Folks at Home" by Bernard Sloan. From THE BEST FRIEND YOU'LL EVER HAVE, Crown Publishers © 1980. Reprinted by permission of the author.

"Fruitful Questions" by Jim Sollisch. Jim Sollisch is an advertising copywriter who also writes essays, novels, and does commentaries for National Public Radio. This essay appeared in *The Chicago Tribune* Magazine and is reprinted by permission of the author.

"How to Take a Job Interview" by Kirby W. Stanat from JOB HUNTING SECRETS AND TACTICS. Reprinted by permission of Kirby W. Stanat.

"Good Used Cars" by John Steinbeck. From THE GRAPES OF WRATH, © 1936, 1967, Viking Penguin. Used by permission of the publisher.

"A Cultural Divorce" by Elizabeth Wong as appeared in *Los Angeles Times*, 1989. Reprinted by permission of Elizabeth Wong.

From Chapter 1, "The Transaction" in ON WRITING WELL, 5th Edition by William K. Zinsser. Copyright © 1976, 1980, 1985, 1988, 1994 by William K. Zinsser. Reprinted by permission of the author.

Index